1st Workshop on Meta Learning and Its Applications to Natural Language Processing (MetaNLP 2021)

Held online due to COVID-19

Bangkok, Thailand
5 August 2021

ISBN: 978-1-7138-3380-2

Printed from e-media with permission by:

Curran Associates, Inc.
57 Morehouse Lane
Red Hook, NY 12571

Some format issues inherent in the e-media version may also appear in this print version.

Association for Computational Linguistics
209 N. Eighth Street
Stroudsburg, Pennsylvania 18360

Phone: 1-570-476-8006
Fax: 1-570-476-0860

acl@aclweb.org

Additional copies of this publication are available from:

Curran Associates, Inc.
57 Morehouse Lane
Red Hook, NY 12571 USA
Phone: 845-758-0400
Fax: 845-758-2633
Email: curran@proceedings.com
Web: www.proceedings.com

MetaNLP 2021

The 1st Workshop on Meta Learning and Its Applications to Natural Language Processing

Proceedings of the Workshop

August 5, 2021
Bangkok, Thailand (online)

Welcome to the ACL 2021 Workshop on **Meta Learning and Its Applications to Natural Language Processing (MetaNLP)**.

Deep learning based natural language processing (NLP) has become the mainstream of research in recent years and significantly outperforms conventional methods. However, deep learning models are notorious for being data and computation hungry. These downsides limit such models' application from deployment to different domains, languages, countries, or styles, since collecting in-genre data and model training from scratch are costly. The long-tail nature of human language makes challenges even more significant.

Meta-learning, or 'Learning to Learn', aims to learn better learning algorithms, including better parameter initialization, optimization strategy, network architecture, distance metrics, and beyond. Meta-learning has been shown to allow faster fine-tuning, converge to better performance, and achieve outstanding results for few-shot learning in many applications. Meta-learning is one of the most important new techniques in machine learning in recent years, but the method is mainly investigated with applications in computer vision. It is believed that meta-learning has excellent potential to be applied in NLP, and some works have been proposed with notable achievements in several relevant problems, e.g., relation extraction, machine translation, and dialogue generation and state tracking. However, it does not catch the same level of attention as in the image processing community.

The goal of this workshop is to bring concentrated discussions on meta-learning for the field of NLP via several invited talks, oral and poster sessions with high-quality papers, and a panel of leading researchers from industry and academia. Alongside research work on new meta-learning methods, data, applications, and results, this workshop will call for novel work on understanding, analyzing, and comparing different meta-learning approaches for NLP.

We hope you will enjoy MetaNLP 2021 at ACL and contribute to the future success of our community!

MetaNLP 2021 Organizers: Hung-Yi Lee, Mitra Mohtarami, Shang-Wen Li, Di Jin, Mandy Korpusik, Shuyan Dong, Ngoc Thang Vu, Dilek Hakkani-Tur

Organizers:

Hung-Yi Lee, National Taiwan University

Mitra Mohtarami, Massachusetts Institute of Technology

Shang-Wen Li, Amazon

Di Jin, Amazon

Mandy Korpusik, Loyola Marymount University

Shuyan Dong, Amazon

Ngoc Thang Vu, University of Stuttgart

Dilek Hakkani-Tur, Amazon

Program Committee:

Trapit Bansal, Yangbin Chen, Yutian Chen, Samuel Coope, Jennifer Drexler, Tianyu Gao, Yutai Hou, Kuan Po Huang, Sathish Indurthi, Ankit Jain, Ping Jian, Tom Ko, Cheng-I Lai, Zhaojiang Lin, Yijia Liu, Colin Lockard, Hongyin Luo, Meryem M'hamdi, Andrea Madotto, Fei Mi, Mehrad Moradshahi, Hoang Long Nguyen, Mohammad Salameh, Hsuan Su, Jian Sun, Chenglong Wang, Yuan-Kuei Wu, Yu Zhang

Invited Speaker:

Andreas Vlachos, University of Cambridge

Chelsea Finn, StanfordUniversity

Eric Xing, Carnegie Mellon University

Heng Ji, University of Illinois Urbana-Champaign

Zhou Yu, Columbia University

Table of Contents

Conference Program

Thursday, August 05, 2021 [UTC+0]

10:00–10:15 Opening Remarks

10:15–11:00 *Invited talk: Meta-Learning for Few-Shot Learning in NLP*
Andreas Vlachos

11:00–12:00 Oral Presentations

Don't Miss the Labels: Label-semantic Augmented Meta-Learner for Few-Shot Text Classification (ACL findings)
Qiaoyang Luo

Learning to Bridge Metric Spaces: Few-shot Joint Learning of Intent Detection and Slot Filling (ACL findings)
Yutai Ho

Meta-Reinforcement Learning for Mastering Multiple Skills and Generalizing across Environments in Text-based Games
Zhenjie Zhao, Mingfei Sun and Xiaojuan Ma

12:00–13:00 Oral Presentations

Few-Shot Event Detection with Prototypical Amortized Conditional Random Field (ACL findings)
Xin Cong

Meta-Learning for Improving Rare Word Recognition in end-to-end ASR (ICASSP 2021 cross submission)
Florian Lux and Ngoc Thang Vu

Minimax and Neyman–Pearson Meta-Learning for Outlier Languages (ACL findings)
Edoardo Maria Ponti

13:00–13:15 Break

13:15–14:00 *Invited talk: Meta-Learning for Dialog Systems*
Yu Zhou

14:00–14:45 *Invited talk: TBA*
Eric Xing

14:45–15:00 Break

15:00–16:00 Oral Presentations

Soft Layer Selection with Meta-Learning for Zero-Shot Cross-Lingual Transfer
Weijia Xu, Batool Haider, Jason Krone and Saab Mansour

Zero-Shot Compositional Concept Learning
GUANGYUE XU, Parisa Kordjamshidi and Joyce Chai

Few Shot Dialogue State Tracking using Meta-learning (EACL 2021 cross submission)
Saket Dingliwal, Shuyang Gao, Sanchit Agarwal, Chien-Wei Lin, Tagyoung Chung and Dilek Hakkani-Tur

16:00–17:00 Poster Session

Meta-learning for Task-oriented Household Text Games (extended abstract)
Zhenjie Zhao and Xiaojuan Ma

Multi-Pair Text Style Transfer for Unbalanced Data via Task-Adaptive Meta-Learning
Xing Han and Jessica Lundin

Patching Errors in Pre-trained Language Models (extended abstract)
Eric Mitchell, Spencer Braun, Charles Lin, Chelsea Finn and Christopher Manning

On the cross-lingual transferability of multilingual prototypical models across NLU tasks
Oralie Cattan, Sophie Rosset and Christophe Servan

Meta-Learning for Few-Shot Named Entity Recognition
Cyprien de Lichy, Hadrien Glaude and William Campbell

Multi-accent Speech Separation with One Shot Learning
Kuan Po Huang, Yuan-Kuei Wu and Hung-yi Lee

Semi-supervised Meta-learning for Cross-domain Few-shot Intent Classification
Yue Li and Jiong Zhang

Meta-learning for Classifying Previously Unseen Data Source into Previously Unseen Emotional Categories
Gaël Guibon, Matthieu Labeau, Hélène Flamein, Luce Lefeuvre and Chloé Clavel

Meta-learning for downstream aware and agnostic pretraining (extended abstract)
Hongyin Luo, Shuyan Dong, Yung-Sung Chuang and Shang-Wen Li

17:00–17:15 **Break**

17:15–18:00 *Invited talk: Few-Shot Learning to Give Feedback in the Real World*
Chelsea Finn

18:00–18:45 *Invited talk: Learning from Annotation Guideline: A Case Study on Event Extraction*
Heng Ji

18:45–19:00 **Closing Remarks**

Meta-Reinforcement Learning for Mastering Multiple Skills and Generalizing across Environments in Text-based Games

Zhenjie Zhao
Nanjing University of Information Science and Technology
zzhaoao@nuist.edu.cn

Mingfei Sun
University of Oxford
mingfei.sun@cs.ox.ac.uk

Xiaojuan Ma
The Hong Kong University of Scinece and Technology
mxj@cse.ust.hk

Abstract

Text-based games can be used to develop task-oriented text agents for accomplishing tasks with high-level language instructions, which has potential applications in domains such as human-robot interaction. Given a text instruction, reinforcement learning is commonly used to train agents to complete the intended task owing to its convenience of learning policies automatically. However, because of the large space of combinatorial text actions, learning a policy network that generates an action word by word with reinforcement learning is challenging. Recent research works show that imitation learning provides an effective way of training a generation-based policy network. However, trained agents with imitation learning are hard to master a wide spectrum of task types or skills, and it is also difficult for them to generalize to new environments. In this paper, we propose a meta-reinforcement learning based method to train text agents through learning-to-explore. In particular, the text agent first explores the environment to gather task-specific information and then adapts the execution policy for solving the task with this information. On the publicly available testbed ALFWorld, we conducted a comparison study with imitation learning and show the superiority of our method.

1 Introduction

A text-based game, such as Zork (Infocom, 1980), is a text-based simulation environment that a player uses text commands to interact with. For example, given the current text description of a game environment, users need to change the environmental state by inputting a text action, and the environment returns a text description of the next environmental state. Users have to take text actions to change the environmental state iteratively until an expected final state is achieved (Côté et al., 2018). Solving text-based games requires non-trivial natural language understanding/generalization and sequential decision making. Developing agents that can play text-based games automatically is promising for enabling task-oriented, language-based human-robot interaction (HRI) experience (Scheutz et al., 2011). Supposing that a text agent can reason a given command and generate a sequence of text actions for accomplishing the task, we can then use text as a proxy and connect text inputs and outputs of the agent with multi-modal signals, such as vision and physical actions, to allow a physical robot operate in the physical space (Shridhar et al., 2021).

Given a text instruction or goal, reinforcement learning (RL) (Sutton and Barto, 2018) is commonly used to train agents to finish the intended task automatically. In general, there are two approaches to train a policy network to obtain the corresponding text action: generation-based methods that generate a text action word by word and choice-based methods that select the optimal action from a list of candidates (Côté et al., 2018). The list of action candidates in a choice-based method may be limited by pre-defined rules and hard to generalize to a new environment. In contrast, generation-based methods can generate more possibilities and potentially have a better generalization ability. Therefore, to allow a text agent to fully explore in an environment and obtain best performance, a generation-based method is needed (Yao et al., 2020). However, the combinatorial action space precludes reinforcement learning from working well on a generation-based policy network. Recent research shows that imitation learning (Ross et al., 2011) provides an effective way to train a generation-based policy network using demonstrations or dense reinforcement signals (Shridhar et al., 2021). However, it is still difficult for the trained policy to master multiple task types or skills and generalize across environments (Shridhar et al.,

Proceedings of the 1st Workshop on Meta Learning and Its Applications to Natural Language Processing (MetaNLP 2021), pages 1–10
Bangkok, Thailand (online), August 5, 2021.

2021). For example, an agent trained on the task type of *slicing an apple* cannot work on a task of *pouring water*. Such lack of the ability to generalize precludes the agent from working on a real interaction scenario. To achieve real-world HRI experience with text agents, two requirements should be fulfilled: 1) a trained agent should master multiple skills simultaneously and work on any task type that it has seen during training; 2) a trained agent should also generalize to unseen environments.

Meta-reinforcement learning (meta-RL) is a commonly used technique to train an agent that generalizes across multiple tasks through summarizing experience over those tasks. The underlying idea of meta-RL is to incorporate meta-learning into reinforcement learning training, such that the trained agent, *e.g.*, text-based agents, could master multiple skills and generalize across different environments (Finn et al., 2017; Liu et al., 2020). In this paper, we propose a meta-RL based method to train text agents through learning-to-explore. In particular, a text agent first explores an environment to gather task-specific information. It then updates the agent's policy towards solving the task with this task-specific information for better generalization performance. On a publicly available testbed, ALFWorld (Shridhar et al., 2021), we conducted experiments on all its six task types (*i.e.*, *pick & place*, *examine in light*, *clean & place*, *heat & place*, *cool & place*, and *pick two & place*), where for each task type, there is a set of unique environments sampled from the distribution defined by their task type (see Section 5.1 for statistics). Results suggest that our method generally masters multiple skills and enables better generalization performance on new environments compared to ALFWorld (Shridhar et al., 2021). We provide further analysis and discussion to show the importance of task diversity for meta-RL. The contributions of this paper are:

- From the perspective of human-robot interaction, we identify the generalization problem of training an agent to master multiple skills and generalize on new environments. We propose to use meta-RL methods to achieve it.

- We design an efficient learning-to-explore approach which enables a generation-based agent to master multiple skills and generalize across a wide spectrum of environments.

2 Related Work

2.1 Language-based Human-Robot Interaction

Enabling a robot to accomplish tasks with language goals is a long-term study of human-robot interaction (Scheutz et al., 2011), where the core problem is to ground language goals with multi-modal signals and generate an action sequence for the robot to accomplish the task. Because of the characteristic of sequential decision making, reinforcement learning (Sutton and Barto, 2018) is commonly used. Previous research works using reinforcement learning have studied the problem on simplified block worlds (Janner et al., 2018; Bisk et al., 2018), which could be far from being realistic. The recent interests on embodied artificial intelligence (embodied AI) have contributed to several realistic simulation environments, such as Gibson (Xia et al., 2018), Habitat (Savva et al., 2019), RoboTHOR (Deitke et al., 2020), and ALFRED (Shridhar et al., 2020). However, because of physical constraints in a real environment, gap between a simulation environment and a real world still exists (Deitke et al., 2020; Shridhar et al., 2021). Researchers have also explored the idea of finding a mapping between vision signals of a real robot and language signals directly (Blukis et al., 2020), but this mapping requires detailed annotated data and it is usually expensive to obtain physical interaction data. An alternative method of deploying an agent on a real robot is to train the agent on abstract text space, such as TextWorld (Côté et al., 2018), and then connect text with multi-modal signals of the robot (Shridhar et al., 2021). For example, by connecting text with the simulated environment ALFRED (Shridhar et al., 2020), researchers have shown that the trained text agent has better generalization ability than training an embodied agent end-to-end directly (Shridhar et al., 2021). However, how to make a text agent generalize across different tasks so that one robot can work on tasks of different types and in unseen environments is still a challenging problem, which is the focus of this paper.

2.2 Text-based Games

The success of deep reinforcement learning (RL) on Atari games (Mnih et al., 2015) inspires the use of RL on text-based games. There are a variety of ways to use deep reinforcement learning on text-based games. For example, using the deep Q-learning (DQN) framework, Narasimhan et al. (2015) leverage the Long Short-Term Memory (LSTM) as the policy network to predict action for each state. In (He et al., 2016), researchers propose the deep reinforcement relevance network (DRRN), which encodes states and actions separately and then calculates Q-values by integrating the information of the two channels. However, the compositional and combinatorial properties of natural language lead to large state and action spaces, which makes solving text-based games with deep reinforcement learning very challenging. To deal with this problem, in fiction-style text games, Adhikari et al. (2020) use a graph-aided transformer (GATA) to capture game dynamics so that it can plan well and select text actions more effectively. Ammanabrolu and Riedl (2019) learn a knowledge graph during the exploration of an agent, and use it to prune the action space. Furthermore, Murugesan et al. (2021) show that incorporating common sense knowledge also helps reduce the action space and allows an agent to choose an action more effectively. Recently, Yao et al. (2020) show that given a text state, a fine-tuned language model GPT can generate a corresponding text action set, which significantly reduces the action space and also improves the performance. Previous research works mainly focus on learning an agent to solve one text game effectively. However, in reality, we usually hope an agent can learn a wide spectrum of tasks and generalize well to unseen environments. In (Adolphs and Hofmann, 2020), in terms of environments and task descriptions, researchers show that an actor-critic framework with action space pruning can learn an agent to generalize to unseen games that belongs to the same family when training. In this paper, with meta-reinforcement learning, we investigate if an agent can master multiple task types and generalize to unseen environments.

2.3 Meta-reinforcement Learning

Meta-learning is a machine learning paradigm that tries to leverage common knowledge among tasks to generalize to new data (Thrun and Pratt, 1998; Vilalta and Drissi, 2002). Meta-reinforcement learning, in particular, augments Markov decision processes with particular task labels, and tries to use shared experience of interacting with different tasks to adapt to a new task efficiently (Liu et al., 2020). In general, there are three ways of conducting meta-reinforcement learning: memory-based methods, optimization-based methods, and learning-to-explore. For memory-based methods, researchers have proposed RL^2 (Duan et al., 2016), which uses a recurrent neural network (RNN) to encode a "fast" RL algorithm, and the RNN module is trained with another "slow" RL algorithm. Memory-based methods are usually hard to optimize and suffer from the sample efficiency problem (Duan et al., 2016). For optimization-based methods, in (Finn et al., 2017), researchers propose a model-agnostic meta-reinforcement learning algorithm that uses a nested optimization procedure to obtain maximal rewards with limited number of sample trajectories. Optimization-based methods usually require on-policy reinforcement learning algorithms and are hard to use value-based methods (Finn et al., 2017), which also leads to the sample efficiency problem. Learning-to-explore is a newly proposed meta-reinforcement learning approach that can potentially leverage any reinforcement learning method with good optimization properties by decoupling an episode into two stages: exploration and execution (Rakelly et al., 2019; Liu et al., 2020). The exploration stage is used to recognize task-specific information, which could be useful for the execution stage for fast and efficient adaptation.

For embodied AI, using meta-reinforcement learning, researchers have explored to improve generalization ability of an agent to unseen environments (Wortsman et al., 2019). However, as aforementioned, deploying such an agent on a real robot is still a challenging problem owing to the domain gap between a simulation environment and a physical environment. In this paper, we instead try to use the learning-to-explore method of meta-reinforcement learning to increase the generalization ability of a text agent so that it can master multiple skills and work on new environments, which can potentially facilitate real-world human-robot interaction applications.

3 Problem Formulation

3.1 Text-based Game Preliminary

Given a language goal g, playing a text-based game can be modeled as a partially observable Markov decision process (POMDP) $(S, P, A, \Omega, O, R, \gamma)$ (Côté et al., 2018), where S is the set of environmental states, P is the set of transition probabilities, A is the set of actions, Ω is the set of observations, O is the set of observation probabilities, R is the reward function, and γ is the discount factor. If we input an action a_t to the environment, it will transition from the current state s_t to a new state s_{t+1} with probability $P(s_{t+1}|s_t, a_t)$, output an observation o_{t+1} based on the new state with probability $O(o_{t+1}|s_{t+1})$, and get a reward $R(g, a_t, s_t)$ depending on the goal g, the current action a_t, and the current state s_t. Given the initial environment state s_0 and a goal g, we want to learn a policy $\pi(a|o, g)$ that can generate an action sequence $(a_0, a_1, \ldots, a_T)$ to accomplish the task and obtain maximal discounted reward $\sum_{t=0}^{T} \gamma^t R(g, a_t, s_t)$. In text-based games, o and a refer to text sentences.

3.2 Learning-to-Explore in Text-based Games

In meta-reinforcement learning, we consider a family of POMDPs $\{(S_\mu, A_\mu, \Omega_\mu, \gamma, O_\mu, R, P_\mu)\}$ indexed by μ, where $\mu \in \mathcal{M}$ denotes a task and $\mathcal{M}$ denotes the family of POMDPs or tasks. Here, we consider that the reward function is independent of tasks and can be applied for all POMDPs. The tasks in the family have task-dependent set of states S_μ, actions A_μ, observations Ω_μ, observation probabilities O_μ, and dynamics P_μ. Following the setting in (Liu et al., 2020), given a goal g, a task-based meta-reinforcement learning problem consists of sampling a task $\mu \sim p(\mu)$ and running a trial, where a trial contains an exploration episode, followed by several execution episodes. We also call a goal as a task type or a skill because it usually constrains how an agent solves a task μ. We call a POMDP without the reward function as an environment, contextualized with the task specifier μ, since it defines a game environment that an agent can interact with. A task denoted by μ then contains a task type, an environment, and a reward function. Given a set of training tasks $\mathcal{M}_{train}$, we want to train a policy $\pi(a|o, g)$ that can generalize well across a set of testing tasks $\mathcal{M}_{test}$. For training, we first fit a task-specific feature vector z'_μ using the exploration episode, and then use it to adapt to the task quickly during execution. The task-specific adaptation helps the policy π to recognize which task type it works on and generalize well on a new unseen environment.

4 Method

We use neural networks to map observations to actions. Given the general setting of meta-reinforcement learning through learning-to-explore, our method contains three modules: an execution

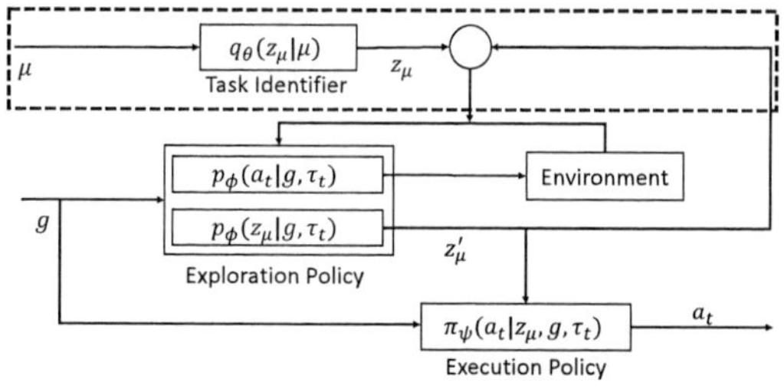

Figure 1: Overview of our method, where g is the language goal, μ denotes a task index, z_μ and z'_μ are hidden feature vectors of a task, and a_t is the generated text action. The dotted line box is only used during training. For simplicity, we did not draw the inputs of roll-out trajectories.

policy neural network π_ψ, a task identifier neural network q_θ, and an exploration policy neural network p_ϕ, where ψ, θ, and ϕ denote parameters of the three neural networks, respectively. As shown in Figure 1, an exploration policy p_ϕ is trained to generate a task-specific feature vector z'_μ, which is then input to an execution policy π_ψ for generating actions. During training, a task identifier is used to generate supervised signals z_μ of z'_μ, and is not used during testing. Because of z'_μ, π_ψ can adapt quickly and generalize well in a new task.

The π_ψ, q_θ and p_ϕ are all encoder-decoder architectures. For π_ψ, it takes a goal g and a K-step roll-out trajectory $\tau_t = (o_0, a_{t-K}, o_{t-K+1}, \ldots, a_{t-1}, o_t)$ from time $t-K+1$ to time t as inputs, and outputs the current action a_t, where o_0 is obtained by executing the "look" action at the beginning. o_0 is used because it is the only observation that lists the different areas of the room. q_θ takes a task index μ as an input and outputs the task-specific feature z_μ, which is only used during training. p_ϕ takes a goal and a K-step roll-out trajectory $\tau_t = (o_0, a_{t-K}, o_{t-K+1}, \ldots, a_{t-1}, o_t)$ as inputs and outputs an estimated task-specific feature z'_μ.

Our goal is to make an execution policy $\pi(a_t|g, \tau_t)$ generalizable across tasks. If we train π using imitation learning, it is critical to have enough training samples of $\{(g, \tau_t, a_t)\}$ following some distributions to have good generalization performance. But because of the combinatorial complexity of τ_t, it is hard to obtain enough data of a_t. Learning from conditional variational auto-encoder (CVAE) (Sohn et al., 2015), we factorize π with a task-specific hidden variable z and use z to facilitate the generation of a_t, namely,

$$\pi(a_t|g,\tau_t) = \int_{z \in Z} p(z|g,\tau_t)\pi(a_t|z,g,\tau_t)dz, \tag{1}$$

where $Z \sim \mathcal{N}(z_\mu, \sigma^2 I)$ is assumed to follow a Gaussian distribution, the aforementioned task-specific feature vector z_μ is the mean vector and σ^2 is the variance. During testing, we can then generate actions by first generating a task-specific hidden variable z with $p(z|g,\tau_t)$ and then generating the action with $\pi(a_t|z,g,\tau_t)$. Because z encodes task-specific features, it helps π generate more proper actions for the current task μ.

Optimizing (1) amounts to maximise evidence lower bound (ELBO) (Sohn et al., 2015):

$$\begin{aligned} \mathrm{ELBO}(a_t,g,\tau_t) = \mathbb{E}_{q(z|a_t,g,\tau_t)}[\log \pi(a_t|z,g,\tau_t)] \\ - \mathrm{KL}(q(z|a_t,g,\tau_t))||p(z|g,\tau_t)), \end{aligned} \tag{2}$$

where $q(z|a_t,g,\tau_t))$ is the approximate posterior probability of z and $p(z|g,\tau_t)$ is the prior probability of z. To implement (2), we use the execution policy network $\pi_\psi(a_t|z_\mu,\tau_t)$, the task identifier $q_\theta(z_\mu|\mu)$, and the exploration policy network $p_\phi(z'_\mu|g,\tau_t)$ to approximate the execution policy, the posterior, and the prior, respectively, and assume that both $q_\theta(z_\mu|\mu)$ and $p_\phi(z'_\mu|g,\tau_t)$ are Gaussian. It is easy to show that the new objective is:

$$\mathbb{E}_{q_\theta(z_\mu|a_t,g,\tau_t)}[\log \pi_\psi(a_t|z_\mu,g,\tau_t)] - \frac{||z_\mu - z'_\mu||_2^2}{2\sigma^2}, \tag{3}$$

where we assume σ^2 is the same for both the posterior and prior. In the following, we introduce the details of the execution policy network, the task identifier, and the exploration policy network.

4.1 Execution Policy

The architecture of the execution policy network is similar to the policy network in (Shridhar et al., 2021). In particular, a QANet (Yu et al., 2018) is used to first encode g, τ_t as a recurrent hidden state h_t and then decode h_t to get a_t. Different from (Shridhar et al., 2021), during encoding, we concatenate the initial encoding h_{RNN} and z_μ as an input to obtain h_t, namely,

$$\begin{aligned} h_{RNN} &= \mathrm{Encode}(g,\tau_t), \\ h_t &= \mathrm{GRU}(\mathrm{ReLU}(\mathbf{W}(h_{RNN} \oplus z_\mu) + \mathbf{b}), h_{t-1}), \end{aligned}$$

where $\oplus$ denotes the concatenation operation, $\mathbf{W} \in R^{d_e \times 2d_e}$ is a weight matrix, $\mathbf{b} \in R^{d_e}$ is a bias vector, $h_{RNN} \in R^{d_e}$, $h_t \in R^{d_h}$, d_e is the dimension of z_μ, d_h is the dimension of h_t, GRU denotes a gated recurrent unit, and ReLU denotes a ReLU activation function. Compared to selecting text actions from a set of valid actions, generating text actions word by word is more likely to explore multiple possibilities for performing actions to achieve higher rewards (Yao et al., 2020). However, Shridhar et al. (2021) show that when trained from a sparse reinforcement learning signal in ALFWorld, generation-based methods are hard to get good performance. Because it is relatively easy to get demonstrations from a text-based game, similar to (Shridhar et al., 2021), the imitation learning method DAgger (Ross et al., 2011) is used to train a generation-based execution policy π_ψ. In this case, optimizing the execution policy network is to optimize the first term of (3).

4.2 Task Identifier

We use a task identifier $q_\theta(z_\mu|\mu)$ to approximate the approximate posterior $q(z|a_t,g,\tau_t)$. The task identifier is used to generate task-specific features during training. We implement it as a simple two-layer fully connected network as:

$$z_\mu = \mathrm{ReLU}(\mathbf{W}_2\mathrm{ReLU}(\mathbf{W}_1\mathbf{e}(\mu) + \mathbf{b}_1) + \mathbf{b}_2),$$

where $\mathbf{e}(\mu)$ is the one-hot encoding of the task index μ, $\mathbf{W}_2 \in R^{d_e \times d_e}$, $\mathbf{W}_1 \in R^{d_e \times N}$, $\mathbf{b_1}, \mathbf{b_2} \in R^{d_e}$, d_e is the dimension of the task embedding z_μ, N is the number of training game environments.

4.3 Exploration Policy

We use an exploration policy network $p_\phi(z'_\mu|g,\tau_t)$ to approximate the prior $p(z|g,\tau_t)$. The exploration policy needs to explore the environment to gather task-specific trajectory within T^{exp}. Because we train the model end-to-end, it will optimize the agent to explore the environment in this fixed number of steps, which also saves time. The architecture is similar to the execution policy network. An encoder takes g, τ_t as inputs and generates a hidden state h_t, and the hidden state is then used to obtain z'_μ via a fully connected layer:

$$z'_\mu = \mathrm{ReLU}(\mathbf{W}h_t + \mathbf{b}),$$

where $\mathbf{W} \in R^{d_e \times d_h}$, $\mathbf{b} \in R^{d_e}$.

Algorithm 1: The training procedure

```
Input: training tasks $\mathcal{M}_{train}$
Output: execution policies $\pi_\psi$, exploration policy $p_\phi$

initialize hyper-parameters $M_{step}, B, T^{exp}, T^{exec}$
initialize $\pi_\psi$, $p_\phi$, and $q_\phi$

$i \leftarrow 0$
while True do
    if $i > M_{step}$ then
        break
    end

    randomly sample $B$ games $\mathcal{M}_B$ from $\mathcal{M}_{train}$

    // Evaluate the task identifier
    calculate $z_\mu$ with $q_\phi$

    // Exploration
    execute "look" and get $o_0$
    for t=1:$T^{exp}$ do
        $a_t \leftarrow p_\phi(a_t|g, \tau_t)$
        compose $\tau_t$ by adding $a_t$ and $o_t$
        evaluate $\mathcal{M}_B$ with $a_t$ and get $o_{t+1}$
        $z'_\mu \leftarrow p_\phi(z'_\mu|g, \tau_t)$
        calculate (4) and update
    end

    // Execution
    execute "look" and get $o_0$
    for t=1:$T^{exec}$ do
        $a_t \leftarrow \pi_\psi(a_t|z_\mu, g, \tau_t)$
        compose $\tau_t$ by adding $a_t$ and $o_t$
        get demonstrations from $\mathcal{M}_B$
        calculate likelihood of $a_t$ using
          demonstrations and update
        if done then
            break
        end
    end

    $i \leftarrow i + B$
end
```

For the exploration policy, in addition to obtain z'_μ, we also decode h_t to get an exploration action a_t: $p_\phi(a_t|g, \tau_t)$. In other words, we adopt a multi-task learning method to train the exploration network. In this way, the exploration policy also learns how to solve the problem, which could help the learning of z'_μ. We optimize the following multi-task objective:

$$\mathcal{L} = \mathcal{L}_\mu + \mathcal{L}_{dqn}, \tag{4}$$

where $\mathcal{L}_\mu$ is the task embedding loss and $\mathcal{L}_{dqn}$ is the DQN loss. In particular, $\mathcal{L}_\mu$ is the second term in (3), except that we do not consider the coefficient $1/2\sigma^2$. For the DQN loss $\mathcal{L}_{dqn}$, we use the deep Q-learning (DQN) method to train the exploration policy. Unlike the execution policy network, we do not use demonstrations here because we want the policy network to *explore* the environment more. DQN is an off-policy method that can leverage replay buffer to deal with the sample efficiency problem. Here, we use DQN for its simplicity, but it is possible to use other more sophisticated off-policy methods. Because it is generally difficult to train a generation-based text agent with only the sparse rewards provided by the environment, we adopt the choice-based method to train the text agent. We empirically turn the reward function to be dense by adding the second term in Eq(3) to the reward function: $R_{new} = 0.5 \times R_{old} + 0.5 \times ||z_\mu - z'_\mu||_2^2$ to encourage per-step optimization, where R_{old} is the reward provided by the environment.

The training procedure of the proposed method, as presented in Algorithm 1, runs as follows: first, we randomly samples a batch of tasks $\mathcal{M}_B$ from $\mathcal{M}_{train}$; second, with task indices, we evaluates q_θ to obtain the task-specific features z_μ; third, the exploration agent explores $\mathcal{M}_B$ by taking actions with p_ϕ, and updates p_ϕ according to Eq(4) through a DQN learning. z'_μ is also obtained by p_ϕ during exploring; fourth, the execution agent takes actions with π_ψ and we update the likelihood (the first term in Eq(3)) with demonstrations of the training data. The end-to-end training runs iteratively up to a maximal step M_{step}. In Algorithm 1, B denotes the sampling size of tasks, T^{exp} is the step number of exploration, and T^{exec} is the step number of execution.

5 Experiments

To demonstrate the generalization ability of our meta-reinforcement learning algorithm across tasks, we conducted a set of experiments with the ALFWorld platform (Shridhar et al., 2021). Text environments of ALFWorld are aligned with 3D simulated environments from ALFRED (Shridhar et al., 2020), which makes ALFWorld a good proxy for our human-robot interaction scenario.

5.1 Dataset

The ALFWorld dataset (Shridhar et al., 2021) contains six task types, including *pick & place, examine in light, clean & place, heat & place, cool & place, and pick two & place.* While all the task types require some basic common sub-tasks such as finding an object, picking it up, and placing it to a particular place; some task types require more complex interactions with certain objects (*e.g.*, heating an object with a heat source). Each task type contains a set of training environments, and two sets of test environments. The first test set (**seen**) contains environments that are different, but sampled from the same game distributions as the training set (*e.g.*, same rooms but with different scene layouts). The second test set (**unseen**) contains environments that do not appear in the training set (*i.e.*, unseen rooms with different receptacles and scene layouts). The statistics of the dataset is shown in Table 1. The task types *pick & place* and *pick two & place* have more training environments than others. Our generalization goal is to train a text agent on the training set of all tasks simultaneously, and during testing, given any task type, the agent can have good performance on both seen and unseen environments, *i.e.*, the agent masters all the six task types and generalizes well on both seen and unseen environments.

task type	train	seen	unseen
pick & place	790	35	24
examine in light	308	13	18
clean & place	650	27	31
heat & place	459	16	23
cool & place	533	25	21
pick two & place	813	24	17
all tasks	3553	140	134

Table 1: The statistics of the ALFWorld dataset.

5.2 Baseline and Implementation Details

We compare our method (denoted as Ours) with the state-of-the-art generation-based agent (denoted as ALFWorld). Transfer learning is another way to improve the generalization ability of an agent, but it usually considers transferring knowledge from a source task to a target task without the setting of multiple tasks (Zhuang et al., 2021). We leave it as a future direction to investigate. We adopt the implementation of ALFWorld from the original paper (Shridhar et al., 2021) and use their pretrained model for conducting all comparison experiments. For the hyper-parameters in Algorithm 1, T^{exp} is set as 10 empirically, $M_{step} = 500,000$ (50K), $B = 10$, $T^{exec} = 50$ are kept as the default values of ALFWorld. The trajectory length K is set as 3 empirically. Following ALFWorld (Shridhar et al., 2021), we use beam search with width 10 for decoding. We ran all experiments on a server with Intel(R) Xeon(R) Silver 4216 CPU @ 2.10GHz, 32G Memory, Nvidia GPU 2080Ti, Ubuntu 16.04.

5.3 Evaluation Metric

We use success rate as the evaluation metric for our experiment. In particular, for $|\mathcal{M}_{test}|$ text games being evaluated, if an agent can finish S tasks, then the success rate of the agent is $sr = \frac{S}{|\mathcal{M}_{test}|}$. Similar to (Shridhar et al., 2021), we evaluate three times on the testing data and report averaged scores.

	ALFWorld		Ours	
task type	**seen**	**unseen**	**seen**	**unseen**
pick & place	46.7	34.7	**51.4**	**50.0**
examine in light	25.7	**22.2**	**38.5**	**22.2**
clean & place	44.4	39.8	**48.1**	**54.8**
heat & place	**58.3**	44.9	50.0	**56.5**
cool & place	38.7	47.6	**44.0**	**76.2**
pick two & place	**23.6**	**27.4**	12.5	23.5
all tasks	39.3	37.6	**41.4**	**49.3**

Table 2: Experiment results of the generalization ability on each individual task type and the union of them.

5.4 Results and Analysis

We show the performance of our model on both seen and unseen test sets in Table 2, compared with numbers computed using the code and model checkpoint provided by ALFWorld (Shridhar et al., 2021). We observe that in most experiment settings, our method outperforms ALFWorld. This is especially obvious in the unseen setting, where the testing environments contain unseen rooms with different receptacles and scene layouts, our method outperforms ALFWorld by a significant margin. This suggests that the task-specific features generated by our agent indeed enable the agent learning from a wide spectrum of task types. The larger performance gap between our method and ALFWorld on the unseen test set (*e.g.*, 49.3 *vs* 37.6 when testing on the union of all task types) further advocates that the task-specific features generated by our method are useful when tackling with completely unfamiliar environments.

On the other hand, we observe that our method's performance on the *pick two & place* tasks are lower than ALFWorld. As mentioned in (Shridhar et al., 2021), the *pick two & place* task type is unique and is considerably more difficult compared to other tasks, in the sense that it is the only task type which requires an agent to grasp and operate more than one object. Intuitively, this aligns with the common sense that a person who has learned to ride all kinds of bicycles can easily ride a new bicycle, but does not necessarily know how to drive a car. We suspect that the decrease in performance may be caused by the agent being overfitting to the majority of training data in which only single object is picked up. Namely, the current developed method could work better on scenarios where a text-based game has the same difficulty level. In other words, the current developed method can only work on scenarios where a text-based game has the same difficulty level as the majority of training games, and it is still hard to generalize to tasks with a higher difficulty level. As a future direction, we plan to investigate the explainability of why an end-to-end trained agent works on certain tasks through counterfactuals (Pearl and Mackenzie, 2018), and improve our method to specifically tackle such problems where a certain dimension of task representations is significantly different from and unbalanced in the majority of training data.

Finally, compared to a dedicated model trained specifically on one task type (Table 2 left in (Shridhar et al., 2021)), the performance of our method is generally $10\% \sim 20\%$ behind, and there is still a lot of room for improvement to achieve human-level intelligence. However, our method shows that learning task-specific features through meta-reinforcement learning help an agent generalize across a wide spectrum of task types, which is vital towards real-world applications of human-robot interaction.

5.5 Discussion

To investigate whether different task types help improve performance of each other, we experimented with a setting where an agent is trained on the six task types separately with our method. The results are shown in Table 3. Compared to the setting where the agent is trained on the union of all task types (Table 2), the performance shows a significant drop in most of the task types. This trend is especially clear in the *pick two & place* tasks. When trained solely on this type of tasks, our agent produces a zero success rate. This suggests that for a meta-reinforcement learning based method like ours, it is essential to have a diverse set of task types as well as a large enough training dataset.

task type	seen	unseen
pick & place	57.1	25.0
examine in light	23.1	11.1
clean & place	51.9	58.1
heat & place	31.3	30.4
cool & place	12.0	9.5
pick two & place	0.0	0.0

Table 3: Testing results of training a separate agent on each of the six task types.

6 Conclusion

We study the generalization issue of text-based games, and develop a meta-reinforcement learning method with a learning-to-explore approach. In particular, we first use an exploration policy network to learn a task-specific feature vector, and use this feature vector to help another execution policy network adapt to a new task. To train the exploration and execution policy network, we use a task identifier to embed a task index, and maximize the likelihood of the execution policy network end-to-end. To demonstrate the generalization ability of our method, we conducted a set of experiments on the publicly available testbed ALFWorld. In general, we find that our method has better generalization performance on a wide spectrum of task types and environments. We leave the investigation of explanability, the unbalance problem of task types, and the training speed as the future research directions.

Acknowledgments

The authors thank Mohit Shridhar for clarifying the experiment section in ALFWorld, Xingdi (Eric) Yuan and Marc-Alexandre Côté for their insightful discussions and editing of the initial version of this paper, as well as constructive suggestions from all anonymous reviewers. Zhenjie Zhao is supported by the Startup Foundation for Introducing Talent of NUIST. This work is also supported by the Hong Kong General Research Fund (GRF) with grant No. 16204420.

References

Ashutosh Adhikari, Xingdi Yuan, Marc-Alexandre Côté, Mikuláš Zelinka, Marc-Antoine Rondeau, Romain Laroche, Pascal Poupart, Jian Tang, Adam Trischler, and Will Hamilton. 2020. Learning dynamic belief graphs to generalize on text-based games. In *Advances in Neural Information Processing Systems*, volume 33, pages 3045–3057. Curran Associates, Inc.

Leonard Adolphs and Thomas Hofmann. 2020. LeDeepChef deep reinforcement learning agent for families of text-based games. *Proceedings of the AAAI Conference on Artificial Intelligence*, 34(05):7342–7349.

Prithviraj Ammanabrolu and Mark Riedl. 2019. Playing text-adventure games with graph-based deep reinforcement learning. In *Proceedings of the 2019 Conference of the North American Chapter of the Association for Computational Linguistics: Human*

Language Technologies, Volume 1 (Long and Short Papers), pages 3557–3565, Minneapolis, Minnesota. Association for Computational Linguistics.

Yonatan Bisk, K. Shih, Yejin Choi, and Daniel Marcu. 2018. Learning interpretable spatial operations in a rich 3D blocks world. In *Proceedings of the AAAI Conference on Artificial Intelligence (AAAI)*.

Valts Blukis, Ross A. Knepper, and Yoav Artzi. 2020. Few-shot object grounding and mapping for natural language robot instruction following. In *Proceedings of the Conference on Robot Learning*.

Marc-Alexandre Côté, Ákos Kádár, Xingdi Yuan, Ben Kybartas, Tavian Barnes, Emery Fine, J. Moore, Matthew J. Hausknecht, Layla El Asri, Mahmoud Adada, Wendy Tay, and Adam Trischler. 2018. Textworld: A learning environment for text-based games. In *Computer Games Workshop at ICML/IJCAI 2018*.

Matt Deitke, Winson Han, Alvaro Herrasti, Aniruddha Kembhavi, Eric Kolve, Roozbeh Mottaghi, Jordi Salvador, Dustin Schwenk, Eli VanderBilt, Matthew Wallingford, Luca Weihs, Mark Yatskar, and Ali Farhadi. 2020. RoboTHOR: An open simulation-to-real embodied AI platform. In *Proceedings of the IEEE/CVF Conference on Computer Vision and Pattern Recognition (CVPR)*.

Yan Duan, John Schulman, Xi Chen, Peter L Bartlett, Ilya Sutskever, and Pieter Abbeel. 2016. RL^2: Fast reinforcement learning via slow reinforcement learning. *arXiv:1611.02779*.

Chelsea Finn, Pieter Abbeel, and Sergey Levine. 2017. Model-agnostic meta-learning for fast adaptation of deep networks. In *Proceedings of the 34th International Conference on Machine Learning*, volume 70 of *Proceedings of Machine Learning Research*, pages 1126–1135. PMLR.

Ji He, Jianshu Chen, Xiaodong He, Jianfeng Gao, Lihong Li, Li Deng, and Mari Ostendorf. 2016. Deep reinforcement learning with a natural language action space. In *Proceedings of the 54th Annual Meeting of the Association for Computational Linguistics*, pages 1621–1630, Berlin, Germany. Association for Computational Linguistics.

Infocom. 1980. Zork I. http://ifdb.tads.org/viewgame?id=0dbnusxunq7fw5ro.

Michael Janner, Karthik Narasimhan, and Regina Barzilay. 2018. Representation learning for grounded spatial reasoning. *Transactions of the Association for Computational Linguistics*, 6:49–61.

Evan Zheran Liu, Aditi Raghunathan, Percy Liang, and Chelsea Finn. 2020. Explore then execute: Adapting without rewards via factorized meta-reinforcement learning. *arXiv:2008.02790*.

Volodymyr Mnih, Koray Kavukcuoglu, David Silver, Andrei A. Rusu, Joel Veness, Marc G. Bellemare, Alex Graves, Martin Riedmiller, Andreas K. Fidjeland, Georg Ostrovski, Stig Petersen, Charles Beattie, Amir Sadik, Ioannis Antonoglou, Helen King, Dharshan Kumaran, Daan Wierstra, Shane Legg, and Demis Hassabis. 2015. Human-level control through deep reinforcement learning. *Nature*, 518(7540):529–533.

Keerthiram Murugesan, Mattia Atzeni, Pavan Kapanipathi, Pushkar Shukla, Sadhana Kumaravel, Gerald Tesauro, Kartik Talamadupula, Mrinmaya Sachan, and Murray Campbell. 2021. Text-based RL agents with commonsense knowledge: New challenges, environments and baselines. *Proceedings of the AAAI Conference on Artificial Intelligence*, 35(10):9018–9027.

Karthik Narasimhan, Tejas Kulkarni, and Regina Barzilay. 2015. Language understanding for text-based games using deep reinforcement learning. In *Proceedings of the 2015 Conference on Empirical Methods in Natural Language Processing*, pages 1–11, Lisbon, Portugal. Association for Computational Linguistics.

Judea Pearl and Dana Mackenzie. 2018. *The book of why*. Basic Books, New York.

Kate Rakelly, Aurick Zhou, Chelsea Finn, Sergey Levine, and Deirdre Quillen. 2019. Efficient off-policy meta-reinforcement learning via probabilistic context variables. In *Proceedings of the 36th International Conference on Machine Learning*, volume 97 of *Proceedings of Machine Learning Research*, pages 5331–5340. PMLR.

Stephane Ross, Geoffrey Gordon, and Drew Bagnell. 2011. A reduction of imitation learning and structured prediction to no-regret online learning. In *Proceedings of the Fourteenth International Conference on Artificial Intelligence and Statistics*, volume 15 of *Proceedings of Machine Learning Research*, pages 627–635, Fort Lauderdale, FL, USA. PMLR.

Manolis Savva, Abhishek Kadian, Oleksandr Maksymets, Yili Zhao, Erik Wijmans, Bhavana Jain, Julian Straub, Jia Liu, Vladlen Koltun, Jitendra Malik, Devi Parikh, and Dhruv Batra. 2019. Habitat: A platform for embodied AI research. In *2019 IEEE/CVF International Conference on Computer Vision (ICCV)*, pages 9338–9346.

Matthias Scheutz, Rehj Cantrell, and Paul Schermerhorn. 2011. Toward humanlike task-based dialogue processing for human robot interaction. *AI Magazine*, 32(4):77–84.

Mohit Shridhar, Jesse Thomason, Daniel Gordon, Yonatan Bisk, Winson Han, Roozbeh Mottaghi, Luke Zettlemoyer, and Dieter Fox. 2020. ALFRED: A benchmark for interpreting grounded instructions for everyday tasks. In *Proceedings of the IEEE/CVF Conference on Computer Vision and Pattern Recognition (CVPR)*, pages 10740–10749.

Mohit Shridhar, Xingdi Yuan, Marc-Alexandre Côté, Yonatan Bisk, Adam Trischler, and Matthew Hausknecht. 2021. ALFWorld: Aligning Text and Embodied Environments for Interactive Learning. In *Proceedings of the International Conference on Learning Representations (ICLR)*.

Kihyuk Sohn, Honglak Lee, and Xinchen Yan. 2015. Learning structured output representation using deep conditional generative models. In *Advances in Neural Information Processing Systems*, volume 28. Curran Associates, Inc.

Richard S Sutton and Andrew G Barto. 2018. *Reinforcement learning: An introduction.* MIT press.

Sebastian Thrun and Lorien Pratt, editors. 1998. *Learning to learn.* Kluwer Academic Publishers.

Ricardo Vilalta and Youssef Drissi. 2002. A perspective view and survey of meta-learning. *Artificial Intelligence Review*, 18(2):77–95.

Mitchell Wortsman, Kiana Ehsani, Mohammad Rastegari, Ali Farhadi, and Roozbeh Mottaghi. 2019. Learning to learn how to learn: Self-adaptive visual navigation using meta-learning. In *Proceedings of the IEEE/CVF Conference on Computer Vision and Pattern Recognition (CVPR)*, pages 6750–6759.

Fei Xia, Amir R. Zamir, Zhiyang He, Alexander Sax, Jitendra Malik, and Silvio Savarese. 2018. Gibson env: Real-world perception for embodied agents. In *Proceedings of the IEEE Conference on Computer Vision and Pattern Recognition (CVPR)*, pages 9068–9079.

Shunyu Yao, Rohan Rao, Matthew Hausknecht, and Karthik Narasimhan. 2020. Keep CALM and explore: Language models for action generation in text-based games. In *Proceedings of the 2020 Conference on Empirical Methods in Natural Language Processing (EMNLP)*, pages 8736–8754, Online. Association for Computational Linguistics.

Adams Wei Yu, David Dohan, Quoc Le, Thang Luong, Rui Zhao, and Kai Chen. 2018. Fast and accurate reading comprehension by combining self-attention and convolution. In *International Conference on Learning Representations*.

Fuzhen Zhuang, Zhiyuan Qi, Keyu Duan, Dongbo Xi, Yongchun Zhu, Hengshu Zhu, Hui Xiong, and Qing He. 2021. A comprehensive survey on transfer learning. *Proceedings of the IEEE*, 109(1):43–76.

Soft Layer Selection with Meta-Learning for Zero-Shot Cross-Lingual Transfer

Weijia Xu*† Batool Haider‡ Jason Krone‡ Saab Mansour‡
†Department of Computer Science, University of Maryland
‡Amazon AI
weijia@cs.umd.edu, {bhaider, kronej, saabm}@amazon.com

Abstract

Multilingual pre-trained contextual embedding models (Devlin et al., 2019) have achieved impressive performance on zero-shot cross-lingual transfer tasks. Finding the most effective strategy to fine-tune these models on high-resource languages so that it transfers well to the zero-shot languages is a non-trivial task. In this paper, we propose a novel meta-optimizer to soft-select which layers of the pre-trained model to freeze during fine-tuning. We train the meta-optimizer by simulating the zero-shot transfer scenario. Results on cross-lingual natural language inference show that our approach improves over the simple fine-tuning baseline and X-MAML (Nooralahzadeh et al., 2020).

1 Introduction

Despite the impressive performance of neural models on a wide variety of NLP tasks, these models are extremely data hungry – training them requires a large amount of annotated data. As collecting such amounts of data for every language of interest is extremely expensive, cross-lingual transfer that aims to transfer the task knowledge from high-resource (*source*) languages for which annotated data are more readily available to low resource (*target*) languages becomes a promising direction. Cross-lingual transfer approaches using cross-lingual resources such as machine translation (MT) systems (Wan, 2009; Conneau et al., 2018) or bilingual dictionaries (Prettenhofer and Stein, 2010) have effectively reduced the amount of annotated data required to obtain reasonable performance on the target language. However, such cross-lingual resources are often limited for low-resource languages.

Recent advances in cross-lingual contextual embedding models have reduced the need for cross-lingual supervision (Devlin et al., 2019; Lample and Conneau, 2019). Wu and Dredze (2019) show that multilingual BERT (mBERT) (Devlin et al., 2019), a contextual embedding model pre-trained on the concatenated Wikipedia data from 104 languages without cross-lingual alignment, does surprisingly well on zero-shot cross-lingual transfer tasks, where they fine-tune the model on the annotated data from the source languages and evaluate on the target language. Wu and Dredze (2019) propose to freeze the bottom layers of mBERT during fine-tuning to improve the cross-lingual performance over the simple fine-tune-all-parameters strategy, as different layers of mBERT captures different linguistic information (Jawahar et al., 2019).

Selecting which layers to freeze for a downstream task is a non-trivial problem. In this paper, we propose a novel meta-learning algorithm for soft layer selection. Our meta-learning algorithm learns layer-wise update rate by simulating the zero-shot transfer scenario – at each round, we randomly split the source languages into a held-out language and the rest as training languages, fine-tune the model on the training languages, and update the meta-parameters based on the model performance on the held-out language. We build the meta-optimizer on top of a standard optimizer and learnable update rates, so that it generalizes well to large numbers of updates. Our method uses much less meta-parameters than the X-MAML approach (Nooralahzadeh et al., 2020) adapted from model-agnostic meta-learning (MAML) (Finn et al., 2017) to zero-shot cross-lingual transfer.

Experiments on zero-shot cross-lingual natural language inference show that our approach outperforms both the simple fine-tuning baseline and the X-MAML algorithm and that our approach brings larger gains when transferring from multiple source languages. Ablation study shows that both

*Work done while interning at Amazon AI.

Proceedings of the 1st Workshop on Meta Learning and Its Applications to Natural Language Processing (MetaNLP 2021), pages 11–18
Bangkok, Thailand (online), August 5, 2021.

the layer-wise update rate and cross-lingual meta-training are key to the success of our approach.

2 Meta-Learning for Zero-Shot Cross-lingual Transfer

The idea of transfer learning is to improve the performance on the target task $\mathcal{T}^0$ by learning from a set of related source tasks $\{\mathcal{T}^1, \mathcal{T}^2, ..., \mathcal{T}^K\}$. In the context of cross-lingual transfer, we treat different languages as separate tasks, and our goal is to transfer the task knowledge from the source languages to the target language. In contrast to the transfer learning case where the inputs of the source and target tasks are from the same language, in cross-lingual transfer learning we need to handle inputs from different languages with different vocabularies and syntactic structures. To handle the issue, we use the pre-trained multilingual BERT (Devlin et al., 2019), a language model encoder trained on the concatenation of monolingual corpora from 104 languages.

The most widely used approach to zero-shot cross-lingual transfer using multilingual BERT is to fine-tune the BERT model θ on the source language tasks $\mathcal{T}^{1...K}$ with training objective $\mathcal{L}$

$$\boldsymbol{\theta}^* = \text{Learn}(\mathcal{L}, \mathcal{T}^1, ..., \mathcal{T}^K; \boldsymbol{\theta})$$

and then evaluate the fine-tuned model $\boldsymbol{\theta}^*$ on the target language task $\mathcal{T}^0$. The gap between training and testing can lead to sub-optimal performance on the target language.

To address the issue, we propose to train a meta-optimizer f_ϕ for fine-tuning so that the fine-tuned model generalizes better to unseen languages. We train the meta-optimizer by

$$\phi^* = \text{Learn}(\mathcal{L}, \mathcal{T}^k; \text{MetaLearn}(\mathcal{L}, \mathcal{T}^{1...K} \backslash \mathcal{T}^k; \phi))$$

where $\mathcal{T}^k$ is a "surprise" language randomly selected from the source language tasks $\mathcal{T}^{1...K}$.

2.1 Meta-Optimizer

Our meta-optimizer consists of a standard optimizer as the base optimizer and a set of meta-parameters to control the layer-wise update rates. An update step is formulated as:

$$\begin{aligned} \boldsymbol{\theta}^t &= \boldsymbol{\theta}^{t-1} - \boldsymbol{\lambda} \odot \Delta\boldsymbol{\theta}^t \\ \Delta\boldsymbol{\theta}^t &= f_{opt}(\boldsymbol{g}^1, ..., \boldsymbol{g}^t) \end{aligned} \tag{1}$$

where $\boldsymbol{\theta}^t$ represent the parameters of the learner model at time step t, and $\Delta\boldsymbol{\theta}^t$ is the update vector produced by the base optimizer f_{opt} given the

Algorithm 1: Meta-Training

Input: Training data $\{\mathcal{D}_1, ..., \mathcal{D}_K\}$ in the source languages, learner model M with parameters $\boldsymbol{\theta}$, and meta-optimizer with base optimizer f_{opt} and meta-parameters ϕ.

Output: Meta-optimizer with parameters ϕ.

$s \leftarrow 1$
Randomly initialize ϕ^0.
repeat N **times**
  $t \leftarrow 1$
  Initialize $\boldsymbol{\theta}^0$ with mBERT and random values for the classification layer.
  Randomly select a test language k to form the test data $\mathcal{D}_{test} = \mathcal{D}_k$.
  $\mathcal{D}_{train} \leftarrow \{\mathcal{D}_1, ..., \mathcal{D}_K\} \setminus \mathcal{D}_{test}$
  repeat L **times**
    $\boldsymbol{X}^t, \boldsymbol{Y}^t \leftarrow$ random batch from $\mathcal{D}_{train}$
    $\mathcal{L}^t \leftarrow \mathcal{L}(M(\boldsymbol{X}^t; \boldsymbol{\theta}^{t-1}), \boldsymbol{Y}^t)$
    $\boldsymbol{g}^{1...t} \leftarrow [\boldsymbol{g}^{1...t-1}, \nabla_{\boldsymbol{\theta}^{t-1}} \mathcal{L}^t]$
    $\Delta\boldsymbol{\theta}^t \leftarrow f_{opt}(\boldsymbol{g}^1, ..., \boldsymbol{g}^t)$
    $\boldsymbol{\theta}^t \leftarrow \boldsymbol{\theta}^{t-1} - \sigma(\phi^{s-1}) \odot \Delta\boldsymbol{\theta}_t$
    $t \leftarrow t + 1$
  end
  $\boldsymbol{X}, \boldsymbol{Y} \leftarrow \mathcal{D}_{test}$
  $\mathcal{L}_{test} \leftarrow \mathcal{L}(M(\boldsymbol{X}; \boldsymbol{\theta}^t), \boldsymbol{Y})$
  $\phi^s \leftarrow \text{Update}(\phi^{s-1}, \nabla_{\phi^{s-1}} \mathcal{L}_{test})$
  $s \leftarrow s + 1$
end

gradients $\{\boldsymbol{g}^i = \nabla_{\boldsymbol{\theta}^{i-1}} \mathcal{L}^i\}_{i=1}^t$ at the current and previous steps. The function f_{opt} is defined by the optimization algorithm and its hyper-parameters. For example, a typical gradient descent algorithm uses $f_{opt} = \alpha \boldsymbol{g}^t$ where α represents the learning rate. A standard optimization algorithm will update the model parameters by:

$$\boldsymbol{\theta}^t = \boldsymbol{\theta}^{t-1} - f_{opt}(\boldsymbol{g}^1, ..., \boldsymbol{g}^t) \tag{2}$$

Our meta-optimizer is different in that we perform gated update using parametric update rates $\boldsymbol{\lambda}$, which is computed by $\boldsymbol{\lambda} = \sigma(\phi)$, where ϕ represents the meta-parameters of the meta-optimizer f_ϕ. The sigmoid function ensures that the update rates are within the range $[0, 1]$. Different from Andrychowicz et al. (2016) in which the optimizer parameters are shared across all coordi-

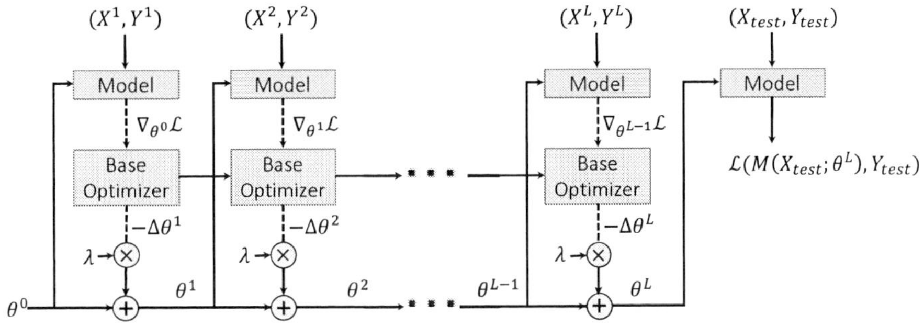

Figure 1: Computational graph for the forward pass of the meta-optimizer. Each batch $(\boldsymbol{X}^t, \boldsymbol{Y}^t)$ is from the training data $\mathcal{D}_{train}$, and $(\boldsymbol{X}_{test}, \boldsymbol{Y}_{test})$ denotes the entire test set. The meta-learner is comprised of a base optimizer that takes the history and current step gradients as inputs and suggests an update $\Delta\theta^t$, and the meta parameters that control the layer-wise update rates $\boldsymbol{\lambda}$ for the learner model $\boldsymbol{\theta}$. The dashed arrows indicate that we do not back-propagate the gradients through that step when updating the meta-parameters.

nates of the model, our meta-optimizer learns different update rates for different model layers. This is based on the findings that different layers of the BERT encoder capture different linguistic information, with syntactic features in middle layers and semantic information in higher layers (Jawahar et al., 2019). And thus, different layers may generalize differently across languages.

Figure 1 illustrates the computational graph for the forward pass when training the meta-optimizer. Note that as the losses $\mathcal{L}^t$ and gradients $\nabla_{\theta^{t-1}}\mathcal{L}^t$ are dependent on the parameters of the meta-optimizer, computing the gradients along the dashed edges would normally require taking second derivatives, which is computationally expensive. Following Andrychowicz et al. (2016), we drop the gradients along the dashed edges and only compute gradients along the solid edges.

2.2 Meta-Training

A good meta-optimizer will, given the training data in the source languages and the training objective, suggest an update rule for the learner model so that it performs well on the target language. Thus, we would like the training condition to match that of the test time. However, in zero-shot transfer we assume no access to the target language data, so we need to simulate the test scenario using only the training data on the source languages.

As shown in Algorithm 1, at each episode in the outer loop, we randomly choose a test language k to construct the test data $\mathcal{D}_{test} = \mathcal{D}_k$ and use the remaining data as the training data $\mathcal{D}_{train}$. Then, we re-initialize the parameters of the learner model and start the training simulation. At each training step, we first use the base optimizer f_{opt} to compute the update vector $\Delta\boldsymbol{\theta}^t$ based on the current and history gradients $\boldsymbol{g}^{1...t}$. We then perform the gated update using the meta-optimizer ϕ^{s-1} with Eq. (1). The resulting model $\boldsymbol{\theta}^t$ can be viewed as the output of a forward pass of the meta-optimizer. After every L iterations of model update, we compute the gradient of the loss on the test data $\mathcal{D}_{test}$ with respect to the old meta parameters ϕ^{s-1} and make an update to the meta parameters. Our meta-learning algorithm is different from X-MAML (Nooralahzadeh et al., 2020) in that 1) X-MAML is designed mainly for few-shot transfer while our algorithm is designated for zero-shot transfer, and 2) our algorithm uses much less meta-parameters than X-MAML as it only requires training the update rate for each layer while in X-MAML we meta-learn the initial parameters of the entire model.

3 Experiments

We evaluate our meta-learning approach on natural language inference. Natural Language Inference (NLI) can be cast into a sequence pair classification problem where, given a premise and a hypothesis sentence, the model needs to predict whether the premise entails the hypothesis, contradicts it, or neither (neutral). We use the Multi-Genre Natural Language Inference Corpus (Williams et al., 2018), which consists of 433k English sentence pairs labeled with textual entailment information, and the XNLI dataset (Conneau

	fr	es	de	ar	ur	bg	sw	th	tr	vi	zh	ru	el	hi	avg
Devlin et al. (2019)	–	74.30	70.50	62.10	58.35	–	–	–	–	–	63.80	–	–	–	–
Wu and Dredze (2019)	74.60	74.90	72.00	66.10	58.60	69.80	49.40	55.70	62.00	71.90	70.40	69.80	67.90	61.20	66.02
Nooralahzadeh et al. (2020)	74.42	75.07	71.83	66.05	61.51	69.45	49.76	55.39	61.20	71.82	71.11	70.19	67.95	62.20	66.28
Aux. language	el	el	el	el	el	el	el	el	el	el	ur	ur	ur	ur	
Fine-tuning baseline	75.42	75.77	72.57	67.22	61.08	70.23	**51.70**	**51.03**	**64.26**	71.61	**72.52**	69.97	69.16	55.40	66.28
Meta-Optimizer	**75.78**	**75.87**	**73.15**	**67.34**	**62.00**	**70.47**	51.22	50.54	63.96	**72.06**	72.32	**70.20**	**69.34**	**55.88**	**66.44**
Aux. language: el + ur															
Fine-tuning baseline	74.87	75.78	72.27	66.96	62.73	70.16	50.21	48.20	63.86	71.61	71.97	70.24	69.64	56.04	66.04
Meta-Optimizer	**75.53**	**75.93**	**72.68**	**67.04**	**63.33**	**70.88**	**51.51**	**49.89**	**64.33**	**72.06**	**72.36**	**70.32**	**70.38**	**56.29**	**66.61**

Table 1: Accuracy of our approach compared with baselines on the XNLI dataset (averaged over five runs). We compare our approach (*Meta-Optimizer*) with our fine-tuning baseline with one or two auxiliary languages, the fine-tuning results in Devlin et al. (2019), the highest scores (with a selected subset of layers fixed during fine-tuning) in Wu and Dredze (2019), the best zero-shot results using X-MAML (Nooralahzadeh et al., 2020) with one auxiliary language. We boldface the highest scores within each auxiliary language setting.

et al., 2018), which has 2.5k development and 5k test sentence pairs in 15 languages including English (en), French (fr), Spanish (es), German (de), Greek (el), Bulgarian (bg), Russian (ru), Turkish (tr), Arabic (ar), Vietnamese (vi), Thai (th), Chinese (zh), Hindi (hi), Swahili (sw), and Urdu (ur). We use this dataset to evaluate the effectiveness of our meta-learning algorithm when transferring from English and one or more low-resource auxiliary languages to the target language.

3.1 Model and Training Configurations

Our model is based on the multilingual BERT (mBERT) (Devlin et al., 2019) implemented in GluonNLP (Guo et al., 2020). As in previous work (Devlin et al., 2019; Wu and Dredze, 2019), we tokenize the input sentences using WordPiece, concatenate them, feed the sequence to BERT, and use the hidden representation of the first token ($[CLS]$) for classification. The final output is computed by applying a linear projection and a softmax layer to the hidden representation. We use a dropout rate of 0.1 on the final encoder layer and fix the embedding layer during fine-tuning. Following Nooralahzadeh et al. (2020), we fine-tune mBERT by 1) fine-tune mBERT on the English data for one epoch to get initial model parameters, and 2) continue fine-tuning the model on the other source languages for two epochs. We compare using the standard optimizer (fine-tuning baseline) and our meta-optimizer for Step 2. We use Adam optimizer (Kingma and Ba, 2015) with a learning rate of 2×10^{-5}, $\beta_1 = 0.9$, and $\beta_2 = 0.999$ as the standard optimizer and base optimizer in our meta-optimizer. To train our meta-optimizer, we use Adam with a learning rate of 0.05 for $N = 10$ epochs with $L = 15$ training batches per iteration (Algorithm 1). Different from Nooralahzadeh et al. (2020) who select the auxiliary languages for each target language that lead to the best transfer results, we simulate a more realistic scenario where only a limited set of auxiliary languages is available. We choose two distant auxiliary languages – Greek (Hellenic branch of the Indo-European language family) and Urdu (Indo-Aryan branch of the Indo-European language family) – and evaluate the transfer performance on the other languages.

3.2 Main Results

As shown in Table 1, we compare our meta-learning approach with the fine-tuning baseline and the zero-shot transfer results reported in prior work that uses mBERT. Our approach outperforms the fine-tuning methods in Devlin et al. (2019) by 1.6–8.5%. Compared with the best fine-tuning method in Wu and Dredze (2019) which freezes a selected subset of mBERT layers during fine-tuning, our approach achieves +0.4% higher accuracy on average. We compare our approach with a strong fine-tuning baseline which achieves competitive accuracy scores to the best X-MAML results (Nooralahzadeh et al., 2020) using a single auxiliary language, even though we limit our choice of the auxiliary language to Greek and Urdu, while Nooralahzadeh et al. (2020) select the best auxiliary language among all languages except for the target one. Overall, our approach outperforms the strong fine-tuning

	fr	es	de	ar	ur	bg	sw	th	tr	vi	zh	ru	el	hi	avg
Meta-Optim	**75.53**	**75.93**	**72.68**	**67.04**	**63.33**	**70.88**	**51.51**	**49.89**	**64.33**	**72.06**	**72.36**	**70.32**	**70.38**	**56.29**	**66.61**
No layer-wise update	73.45	73.90	70.73	65.19	60.31	69.10	50.87	46.47	62.74	70.42	70.24	68.85	68.17	53.50	64.57
No cross-lingual meta-train	73.66	74.84	71.54	66.15	61.16	69.33	50.89	48.43	63.16	71.57	70.53	69.14	67.93	55.07	65.24

Table 2: Ablation results on the XNLI dataset using Greek and Urdu as the auxiliary languages (averaged over five runs). Results show that ablating the layer-wise update rate or cross-lingual meta-training degrades accuracy on all target languages.

baseline on 10 out of 14 languages and by +0.2% accuracy on average.

Our approach brings larger gains when using two auxiliary languages – it outperforms the fine-tuning baseline on all languages and improves the average accuracy by +0.6%. This suggests that our meta-learning approach is more effective when transferring from multiple source languages.[1]

3.3 Ablation Study

Our approach is different from Andrychowicz et al. (2016) in that 1) it adopts layer-wise update rates while the meta-parameters are shared across all model parameters in Andrychowicz et al. (2016), and 2) it trains the meta-parameters in a cross-lingual setting while Andrychowicz et al. (2016) is designated to few-shot learning. We conduct ablation experiments on XNLI using Greek and Urdu as the auxiliary languages to understand how they contribute to the model performance.

Impact of Layer-Wise Update Rate We compare our approach with its variant that replaces the layer-wise update rate with one update rate for all layers. Table 2 shows that our approach significantly outperforms this variant on all target languages with an average margin of 2.0%. This suggests that layer-wise update rate contributes greatly to the effectiveness of our approach.

Impact of Cross-Lingual Meta-Training We measure the impact of cross-lingual meta-training by replacing the cross-lingual meta-training in our approach with a joint training of the layer-wise update rate and model parameters. As shown in Table 2, ablating the cross-lingual meta-training degrades accuracy significantly on all target languages by 1.4% on average, which shows that our cross-lingual meta-training strategy is beneficial.

[1]Using two auxiliary languages improves over one auxiliary language the most on lower-resource languages in mBERT pre-training (such as Turkish and Hindi), but does not bring gains or even hurts on high-resource languages (such as French and German). This is consistent with the findings in prior work that the choice of the auxiliary languages is crucial in cross-lingual transfer (Lin et al., 2019). We leave further investigation on its impact on our meta-learning approach for future work.

4 Related Work

4.1 Cross-lingual Transfer Learning

The idea of cross-lingual transfer is to use the annotated data in the source languages to improve the task performance on the target language with minimal or even zero target labeled data (aka zero-shot). There is a large body of work on using external cross-lingual resources such as bilingual word dictionaries (Prettenhofer and Stein, 2010; Schuster et al., 2019b; Liu et al., 2020a), MT systems (Wan, 2009), or parallel corpora (Eriguchi et al., 2018; Yu et al., 2018; Singla et al., 2018; Conneau et al., 2018) to bridge the gap between the source and target languages. Recent advances in unsupervised cross-lingual representations have paved the road for transfer learning without cross-lingual resources (Yang et al., 2017; Chen et al., 2018; Schuster et al., 2019a). Our work builds on Mulcaire et al. (2019); Lample and Conneau (2019); Pires et al. (2019) who show that language models trained on monolingual text from multiple languages provide powerful multilingual representations that generalize across languages. Recent work has shown that more advanced techniques such as freezing the model's bottom layers (Wu and Dredze, 2019) or continual learning (Liu et al., 2020b) can further boost the cross-lingual performance on downstream tasks. In this paper, we explore meta-learning to softly select the layers to freeze during fine-tuning.

4.2 Meta Learning

A typical meta-learning algorithm consists of two loops of training: 1) an *inner loop* where the learner model is trained, and 2) an *outer loop* where, given a meta-objective, we optimize a set of meta-parameters which controls aspects of the learning process in the inner loop. The goal is to find the optimal meta-parameters such that the inner loop performs well on the meta-objective. Existing meta-learning approaches differ in the choice of meta-parameters to be optimized and the meta-objective. Depending on the choice of meta-parameters, existing work can be divided into four categories: (a) neural architecture search (Stanley and Miikkulainen, 2002; Zoph and Le, 2016; Baker et al., 2016; Real et al., 2017; Zoph et al., 2018); (b) metric-based (Koch et al., 2015; Vinyals et al., 2016); (c) model-agnostic (MAML) (Finn et al., 2017; Ravi and Larochelle, 2016); (d) model-based (learning update rules) (Schmidhuber, 1987; Hochreiter et al., 2001; Maclaurin et al., 2015; Li and Malik, 2017).

In this paper, we focus on model-based meta-learning for zero-shot cross-lingual transfer. Early work introduces a type of networks that can update their own weights (Schmidhuber, 1987, 1992, 1993). More recently, Andrychowicz et al. (2016) propose to model gradient-based update rules using an RNN and optimize it with gradient descent. However, as Wichrowska et al. (2017) point out, the RNN-based meta-optimizers fail to make progress when run for large numbers of steps. They address the issue by incorporating features motivated by the standard optimizers into the meta-optimizer. We instead base our meta-optimizer on a standard optmizer like Adam so that it generalizes better to large-scale training.

Meta-learning has been previously applied to few-shot cross-lingual named entity recognition (Wu et al., 2019), low-resource machine translation (Gu et al., 2018), and improving cross-domain generalization for semantic parsing (Wang et al., 2021). For zero-shot cross-lingual transfer, Nooralahzadeh et al. (2020) introduce an optimization-based meta-learning algorithm called X-MAML which meta-learns the initial model parameters on supervised data from low-resource languages. By contrast, our meta-learning algorithm requires much less meta-parameters and is thus simpler than X-MAML. Bansal et al. (2020) show that MAML combined with meta-learning for learning rates improves few-shot learning. Different from their approach which learns layer-wise learning rates only for task-specific layers specified as a hyper-parameter as part of the MAML algorithm, our approach learns layer-wise learning rates for all layers, and we show the effectiveness of our approach without being used with MAML on zero-shot cross-lingual transfer.

5 Conclusion

We propose a novel meta-optimizer that learns to soft-select which layers to freeze when fine-tuning a pretrained language model (mBERT) for zero-shot cross-lingual transfer. Our meta-optimizer learns the update rate for each layer by simulating the zero-shot transfer scenario where the model fine-tuned on the source languages is tested on an unseen language. Experiments show that our approach outperforms the simple fine-tuning baseline and the X-MAML algorithm on cross-lingual natural language inference.

References

Marcin Andrychowicz, Misha Denil, Sergio Gómez, Matthew W Hoffman, David Pfau, Tom Schaul, Brendan Shillingford, and Nando de Freitas. 2016. Learning to learn by gradient descent by gradient descent. In *Advances in Neural Information Processing Systems*, pages 3981–3989. Curran Associates, Inc.

Bowen Baker, Otkrist Gupta, Nikhil Naik, and Ramesh Raskar. 2016. Designing neural network architectures using reinforcement learning. *arXiv preprint arXiv:1611.02167*.

Trapit Bansal, Rishikesh Jha, and Andrew McCallum. 2020. Learning to few-shot learn across diverse natural language classification tasks. In *Proceedings of the 28th International Conference on Computational Linguistics*, pages 5108–5123, Barcelona, Spain (Online). International Committee on Computational Linguistics.

Xilun Chen, Yu Sun, Ben Athiwaratkun, Claire Cardie, and Kilian Weinberger. 2018. Adversarial deep averaging networks for cross-lingual sentiment classification. *Transactions of the Association for Computational Linguistics*, 6:557–570.

Alexis Conneau, Ruty Rinott, Guillaume Lample, Adina Williams, Samuel Bowman, Holger Schwenk, and Veselin Stoyanov. 2018. XNLI: Evaluating cross-lingual sentence representations. In *Proceedings of the 2018 Conference on Empirical Methods in Natural Language Processing*, pages 2475–2485, Brussels, Belgium. Association for Computational Linguistics.

Jacob Devlin, Ming-Wei Chang, Kenton Lee, and Kristina Toutanova. 2019. BERT: Pre-training of deep bidirectional transformers for language understanding. In *Proceedings of the 2019 Conference of the North American Chapter of the Association for Computational Linguistics: Human Language*

Technologies, Volume 1 (Long and Short Papers), pages 4171–4186, Minneapolis, Minnesota. Association for Computational Linguistics.

Akiko Eriguchi, Melvin Johnson, Orhan Firat, Hideto Kazawa, and Wolfgang Macherey. 2018. Zero-shot cross-lingual classification using multilingual neural machine translation. *CoRR*, abs/1809.04686.

Chelsea Finn, Pieter Abbeel, and Sergey Levine. 2017. Model-agnostic meta-learning for fast adaptation of deep networks. In *Proceedings of the 34th International Conference on Machine Learning-Volume 70*, pages 1126–1135. JMLR. org.

Jiatao Gu, Yong Wang, Yun Chen, Victor O. K. Li, and Kyunghyun Cho. 2018. Meta-learning for low-resource neural machine translation. In *Proceedings of the 2018 Conference on Empirical Methods in Natural Language Processing*, pages 3622–3631, Brussels, Belgium. Association for Computational Linguistics.

Jian Guo, He He, Tong He, Leonard Lausen, Mu Li, Haibin Lin, Xingjian Shi, Chenguang Wang, Junyuan Xie, Sheng Zha, Aston Zhang, Hang Zhang, Zhi Zhang, Zhongyue Zhang, Shuai Zheng, and Yi Zhu. 2020. Gluoncv and gluonnlp: Deep learning in computer vision and natural language processing. *Journal of Machine Learning Research*, 21(23):1–7.

Sepp Hochreiter, A Steven Younger, and Peter R Conwell. 2001. Learning to learn using gradient descent. In *International Conference on Artificial Neural Networks*, pages 87–94. Springer.

Ganesh Jawahar, Benoît Sagot, and Djamé Seddah. 2019. What does BERT learn about the structure of language? In *Proceedings of the 57th Annual Meeting of the Association for Computational Linguistics*, pages 3651–3657. Association for Computational Linguistics.

Diederick P Kingma and Jimmy Ba. 2015. Adam: A method for stochastic optimization. In *International Conference on Learning Representations (ICLR)*.

Gregory Koch, Richard Zemel, and Ruslan Salakhutdinov. 2015. Siamese neural networks for one-shot image recognition. In *ICML deep learning workshop*, volume 2. Lille.

Guillaume Lample and Alexis Conneau. 2019. Cross-lingual language model pretraining. *Advances in Neural Information Processing Systems (NeurIPS)*.

Ke Li and Jitendra Malik. 2017. Learning to optimize. In *International Conference on Learning Representations*.

Yu-Hsiang Lin, Chian-Yu Chen, Jean Lee, Zirui Li, Yuyan Zhang, Mengzhou Xia, Shruti Rijhwani, Junxian He, Zhisong Zhang, Xuezhe Ma, Antonios Anastasopoulos, Patrick Littell, and Graham Neubig. 2019. Choosing transfer languages for cross-lingual learning. In *Proceedings of the 57th Annual Meeting of the Association for Computational Linguistics*, pages 3125–3135, Florence, Italy. Association for Computational Linguistics.

Zihan Liu, Genta Indra Winata, Zhaojiang Lin, Peng Xu, and Pascale Fung. 2020a. Attention-informed mixed-language training for zero-shot cross-lingual task-oriented dialogue systems. *Proceedings of the AAAI Conference on Artificial Intelligence*, 34(05):8433–8440.

Zihan Liu, Genta Indra Winata, Andrea Madotto, and Pascale Fung. 2020b. Exploring fine-tuning techniques for pre-trained cross-lingual models via continual learning.

Dougal Maclaurin, David Duvenaud, and Ryan Adams. 2015. Gradient-based hyperparameter optimization through reversible learning. In *International Conference on Machine Learning*, pages 2113–2122.

Phoebe Mulcaire, Jungo Kasai, and Noah A. Smith. 2019. Polyglot contextual representations improve crosslingual transfer. In *Proceedings of the 2019 Conference of the North American Chapter of the Association for Computational Linguistics: Human Language Technologies, Volume 1 (Long and Short Papers)*, pages 3912–3918. Association for Computational Linguistics.

Farhad Nooralahzadeh, Giannis Bekoulis, Johannes Bjerva, and Isabelle Augenstein. 2020. Zero-shot cross-lingual transfer with meta learning. In *Proceedings of the 2020 Conference on Empirical Methods in Natural Language Processing (EMNLP)*, pages 4547–4562, Online. Association for Computational Linguistics.

Telmo Pires, Eva Schlinger, and Dan Garrette. 2019. How multilingual is multilingual bert? *CoRR*, abs/1906.01502.

Peter Prettenhofer and Benno Stein. 2010. Cross-language text classification using structural correspondence learning. In *Proceedings of the 48th Annual Meeting of the Association for Computational Linguistics*, pages 1118–1127. Association for Computational Linguistics.

Sachin Ravi and Hugo Larochelle. 2016. Optimization as a model for few-shot learning. In *International Conference on Learning Representations*.

Esteban Real, Sherry Moore, Andrew Selle, Saurabh Saxena, Yutaka Leon Suematsu, Jie Tan, Quoc V Le, and Alexey Kurakin. 2017. Large-scale evolution of image classifiers. In *Proceedings of the 34th International Conference on Machine Learning-Volume 70*, pages 2902–2911. JMLR. org.

Jürgen Schmidhuber. 1987. *Evolutionary principles in self-referential learning, or on learning how to learn: the meta-meta-... hook*. Ph.D. thesis, Technische Universität München.

Jürgen Schmidhuber. 1992. Learning to control fast-weight memories: An alternative to dynamic recurrent networks. *Neural Computation*, 4(1):131–139.

Jürgen Schmidhuber. 1993. A neural network that embeds its own meta-levels. In *IEEE International Conference on Neural Networks*, pages 407–412. IEEE.

Sebastian Schuster, Sonal Gupta, Rushin Shah, and Mike Lewis. 2019a. Cross-lingual transfer learning for multilingual task oriented dialog. In *Proceedings of the 2019 Conference of the North American Chapter of the Association for Computational Linguistics: Human Language Technologies, Volume 1 (Long and Short Papers)*, pages 3795–3805. Association for Computational Linguistics.

Tal Schuster, Ori Ram, Regina Barzilay, and Amir Globerson. 2019b. Cross-lingual alignment of contextual word embeddings, with applications to zero-shot dependency parsing. In *Proceedings of the 2019 Conference of the North American Chapter of the Association for Computational Linguistics: Human Language Technologies, Volume 1 (Long and Short Papers)*, pages 1599–1613. Association for Computational Linguistics.

Karan Singla, Dogan Can, and Shrikanth Narayanan. 2018. A multi-task approach to learning multilingual representations. In *Proceedings of the 56th Annual Meeting of the Association for Computational Linguistics (Volume 2: Short Papers)*, pages 214–220. Association for Computational Linguistics.

Kenneth O Stanley and Risto Miikkulainen. 2002. Evolving neural networks through augmenting topologies. *Evolutionary computation*, 10(2):99–127.

Oriol Vinyals, Charles Blundell, Timothy Lillicrap, Daan Wierstra, et al. 2016. Matching networks for one shot learning. In *Advances in neural information processing systems*, pages 3630–3638.

Xiaojun Wan. 2009. Co-training for cross-lingual sentiment classification. In *Proceedings of the Joint Conference of the 47th Annual Meeting of the ACL and the 4th International Joint Conference on Natural Language Processing of the AFNLP*, pages 235–243. Association for Computational Linguistics.

Bailin Wang, Mirella Lapata, and Ivan Titov. 2021. Meta-learning for domain generalization in semantic parsing. In *Proceedings of the 2021 Conference of the North American Chapter of the Association for Computational Linguistics: Human Language Technologies*, pages 366–379, Online. Association for Computational Linguistics.

Olga Wichrowska, Niru Maheswaranathan, Matthew W Hoffman, Sergio Gómez Colmenarejo, Misha Denil, Nando Freitas, and Jascha Sohl-Dickstein. 2017. Learned optimizers that scale and generalize. In *International Conference on Machine Learning*, pages 3751–3760.

Adina Williams, Nikita Nangia, and Samuel Bowman. 2018. A broad-coverage challenge corpus for sentence understanding through inference. In *Proceedings of the 2018 Conference of the North American Chapter of the Association for Computational Linguistics: Human Language Technologies, Volume 1 (Long Papers)*, pages 1112–1122, New Orleans, Louisiana. Association for Computational Linguistics.

Qianhui Wu, Zijia Lin, Guoxin Wang, Hui Chen, Börje F Karlsson, Biqing Huang, and Chin-Yew Lin. 2019. Enhanced meta-learning for cross-lingual named entity recognition with minimal resources. *arXiv preprint arXiv:1911.06161*.

Shijie Wu and Mark Dredze. 2019. Beto, bentz, becas: The surprising cross-lingual effectiveness of BERT. In *Proceedings of the 2019 Conference on Empirical Methods in Natural Language Processing and the 9th International Joint Conference on Natural Language Processing (EMNLP-IJCNLP)*, pages 833–844, Hong Kong, China. Association for Computational Linguistics.

Zhilin Yang, Ruslan Salakhutdinov, and William W. Cohen. 2017. Transfer learning for sequence tagging with hierarchical recurrent networks. In *International Conference on Learning Representations*.

Katherine Yu, Haoran Li, and Barlas Oguz. 2018. Multilingual seq2seq training with similarity loss for cross-lingual document classification. In *Proceedings of The Third Workshop on Representation Learning for NLP*, pages 175–179. Association for Computational Linguistics.

Barret Zoph and Quoc V Le. 2016. Neural architecture search with reinforcement learning. *arXiv preprint arXiv:1611.01578*.

Barret Zoph, Vijay Vasudevan, Jonathon Shlens, and Quoc V Le. 2018. Learning transferable architectures for scalable image recognition. In *Proceedings of the IEEE conference on computer vision and pattern recognition*, pages 8697–8710.

Zero-Shot Compositional Concept Learning

Guangyue Xu
Michigan State University
xuguang3@msu.edu

Parisa Kordjamshidi
Michigan State University
kordjams@msu.edu

Joyce Y. Chai
University of Michigan
chaijy@umich.edu

Abstract

In this paper, we study the problem of recognizing compositional *attribute-object* concepts within the zero-shot learning (ZSL) framework. We propose an episode-based cross-attention (EpiCA) network which combines merits of cross-attention mechanism and episode-based training strategy to recognize novel compositional concepts. Firstly, EpiCA bases on cross-attention to correlate *concept-visual* information and utilizes the gated pooling layer to build contextualized representations for both images and concepts. The updated representations are used for a more in-depth multi-modal relevance calculation for concept recognition. Secondly, a two-phase episode training strategy, especially the transductive phase, is adopted to utilize unlabeled test examples to alleviate the low-resource learning problem. Experiments on two widely-used zero-shot compositional learning (ZSCL) benchmarks have demonstrated the effectiveness of the model compared with recent approaches on both conventional and generalized ZSCL settings.

1 Introduction

Humans can recognize novel concepts through composing previously learnt knowledge - known as compositional generalization ability (Lake et al., 2015; Lake and Baroni, 2018). As a key critical capacity to build modern AI systems, this paper investigates the problem of zero-shot compositional learning (ZSCL) focusing on recognizing novel compositional *attribute-object* pairs appeared in the images. For example in Figure 1, suppose the training set has images with compositional concepts *sliced-tomato, sliced-cake, ripe-apple, peeled-apple*, etc. Given a new image, our goal is to assign a novel compositonal concept *sliced-apple* to the image by composing the element concepts, *sliced* and *apple*, learned from the training data. Although *sliced* and *apple* have appeared

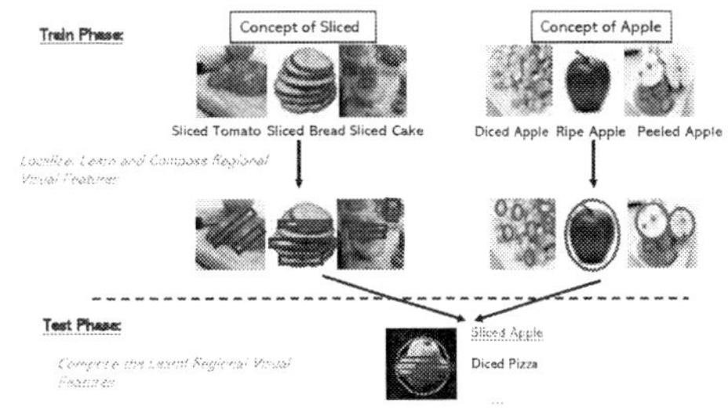

Figure 1: Given the concepts of *sliced* and *apple* in the training phase, our target is to recognize the novel compositional concept *slice apple* which doesn't appear in the training set by decomposing, grounding and composing concept-related visual features.

with other objects or attributes, the combination of this attribute-object pair is not observed in the training set.

This is a challenging problem, because objects with different attributes often have a significant diversity in their visual features. While *red apple* has similar visual features as the *apple* prototype, *sliced apple* presents rather different visual features as shown in Fig 1. Similarly, same attributes can have different visual effects depending on the modified objects. For example, *old* has different visual effect in objects of *old town* compared to objects of *old car*.

Despite recent progress (Misra et al., 2017; Li et al., 2020), previous works still suffer several limitations: (1) Most existing methods adopt metric learning framework by projecting concepts and images into shared latent space, and focus on regularizing the structure of the latent space by adding principled constraints without considering the relationship between concepts and visual features. Our work brings a new perspective, the relevance-based framework inspired by Sung et al., to conduct compositional concept learning. (2)Previous works represent concept and image by the same vector regardless of the context it occurs. However, cross

Proceedings of the 1st Workshop on Meta Learning and Its Applications to Natural Language Processing (MetaNLP 2021), pages 19–27
Bangkok, Thailand (online), August 5, 2021.

concept-visual representation often provides more grounded information to help in recognizing objects and attributes which will consequently help in learning their compositions.

Motivated by the above discussions, we propose an Episode-based Cross Attention (EpiCA) network to capture multi-modal interactions and exploit the visual clues to learn novel compositional concepts. Specifically, within each episode, we first adopt cross-attention encoder to fuse the concept-visual information and discover possible relationships between image regions and element concepts which corresponds to the localizing and learning phase in Fig.1. Second, gated pooling layer is introduced to obtain the global representation by selectively aggregating the salient element features corresponding to Fig. 1's composing phase. Finally, relevance score is calculated based on the updated features to update EpiCA.

The contribution of this work can be summarized as follows: 1) Different from previous work, EpiCA has the ability to learn and ground the attributes and objects in the image by cross-attention mechanism. 2) Episode-based training strategy is introduced to train the model. Moreover, we are among the first works to employ the transductive training to select confident unlabelled examples to gain knowledge about novel compositional concepts. 3) Empirical results show that our framework achieves competitive results on two benchmarks in conventional ZSCL setting. In the more realistic generalized ZSCL setting, our framework significantly outperforms SOTA and achieves over 2× improved performance on several metrics.

2 Related Work

Compositional Concept Learning. As a specific zero-shot learning (ZSL) problem, zero-shot compositional learning (ZSCL) tries to learn complex concepts by composing element concepts. Previous solutions can mainly be categorized as: (1) classifier-based methods train classifiers for element concepts and combine the element classifiers to recognize compositional concepts (Chen and Grauman, 2014; Misra et al., 2017; Li et al., 2019a). (2) metric-based methods learn a shared space by minimizing the distance between the projected visual features and concept features (Nagarajan and Grauman, 2018; Li et al., 2020). (3) GAN-based methods learn to generate samples from the semantic information and transfer ZSCL into a traditional supervised classification problem (Wei et al., 2019).

Attention Mechanism. The attention mechanism selectively use the salient elements of the data to compose the data representation and is adopted in various visiolinguistic tasks. Cross attention is employed to locate important image regions for text-image matching (Lee et al., 2018). Self-attention and cross-attention are combined at different levels to search images with text feedback (Chen et al., 2020b). More recent works refer Transformer (Vaswani et al., 2017) to design various visiolinguistic attention mechanism (Lu et al., 2019).

Episode-based Training. The data sparsity in low-resource learning problems, including few-shot learning and zero-shot learning, makes the typical fine-tuning strategy in deep learning not adaptable, due to not having enough labeled data and the overfitting problem. Most successful approaches in this field rely on an episode-based training scheme: performing model optimization over batches of tasks instead of batches of data. Through training multiple episodes, the model is expected to progressively accumulate knowledge on predicting the mimetic unseen classes within each episode. Representative work includes Matching network (Vinyals et al., 2016), Prototypical network (Snell et al., 2017) and RelNet (Sung et al., 2018).

The related works to EpiCA are RelNet (Sung et al., 2018) and cvcZSL (Li et al., 2019a). Compared with these methods, we have two improvements including an explicit way to construct episodes which is more consistent with the test scenario and a cross-attention module to fuse and ground more detailed information between the concept space and the visual space.

3 Approach

3.1 Task Definition

Different from the traditional supervised setting where training concepts and test concepts are from the same domain, our problem focuses on recognizing novel compositional concepts of attributes and objects which are not seen during the training phase. Although we have seen all the attributes and objects in the training set, their compositions are novel [1].

We model this problem within the ZSL framework where the dataset is divided into the seen

[1] We refer concept as compositional concept, element concept as the attribute and the object in the rest of the paper.

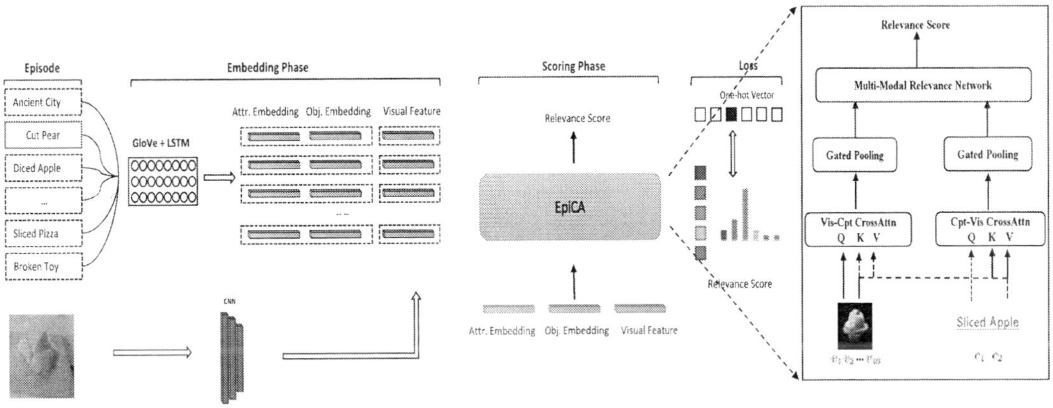

Figure 2: Illustration of the proposed EpiCA framework. It is a two-stage training framwork, including the inductive learning and the transductive learning. Both phases are trained on episodes illustrated in Alg. 1.

domain $\mathcal{S} = \{(v_s, y_s)|v_s \in \mathcal{V}^s, y_s \in \mathcal{Y}^s\}$ for training and the unseen domain $\mathcal{U} = \{(v_u, y_u)|v_u \in \mathcal{V}^u, y_u \in \mathcal{Y}^u\}$ for test, where v is the visual feature of image $\mathcal{I}$ which can be extracted using deep convolution networks and y is the corresponding label which consists of an attribute label a and a object label o as $y = (a, o)$ satisfying $a_u \subseteq a_s$, $o_u \subseteq o_s$ and $\mathcal{Y}_s \cap \mathcal{Y}_u = \phi$. Moreover, we address the problem in both conventional ZSCL setting and generalized ZSCL setting. In conventional ZSCL, we only consider unseen pairs in the test phase and the target is to learn a mapping function $\mathcal{V} \mapsto \mathcal{Y}^u$. In generalized ZSCL, images with both seen and unseen concepts can appear in the test set, and the mapping function changes to $\mathcal{V} \mapsto \mathcal{Y}^s \cup \mathcal{Y}^u$ which is a more general and realistic setting.

3.2 Overall Framework

As summarized in Fig. 2, EpiCA consists of the cross-attention encoder, gated pooling layer and multi-modal relevance network to compute the relevance score between concepts and images. In order to accumulate the knowledge between images and concepts, EpiCA is trained by episodes including the following two phases:

- *Inductive training phase* constructs episodes from the seen concepts and trains EpiCA based on these constructed episodes.
- *Transductive training phase* employs the self-taught methodology to collect confident pseudo-labeled test items to further fine-tune EpiCA.

3.3 Unimodal Representation

Concept Representation. Given a compositonal concept (a, o), we first transform attribute and object using 300-D *GloVe* (Pennington et al., 2014) separately. Then we use one layer BiLSTM (Hochreiter and Schmidhuber, 1997) to obtain contextualized representation for concepts with d_k hidden units. Instead of using the final state, we maintain the output features for both attribute and object and output feature matrix $C \in \mathbb{R}^{2 \times d_k}$ for each compoisitonal concept.

Image Representation. We extract the visual features using pretrained ResNet (He et al., 2016) from a given image. In order to obtain more detailed visual features for concept recognition, we keep the output from the last convolutional layer of ResNet-18 to represent the image and therefore each image is split into $7 \times 7 = 49$ visual blocks with each block as a 512-dim vector denoted as $\mathbf{V} = (\mathbf{v}_1, \mathbf{v}_2, \ldots, \mathbf{v}_{49})$. Each element represents a region in the image. We further convert v_i with a linear transformation $v_i = \mathbf{W}^\top v_i$, where $\mathbf{W} \in \mathbb{R}^{512 \times d_k}$ is the weight matrix to transfer the image into the joint concept-image space.

3.4 Cross Attention Encoder

Motivation. Previous works usually utilize vector representation for both concepts and images and construct a metric space by pushing aligned images and concepts closer to each other. The potential limitation of such frameworks is that the same vector representations without context information will miss sufficient detailed information needed for grounding and recognizing objects and attributes appeared in the images. We observe that certain visual blocks in the image can be more related to certain element concept and certain element concept may highlight different visual blocks. Inspired by this observation, our model addresses the previous limitation by introducing cross-attention encoder and constructs more meaningful cross-modality representation for both images and element concepts for compositional concept recognition.

Cross Attention Layer. To fuse and ground information between visual space and concept space, we first design a correlation layer to calculate the correlation map between the two spaces, which is used to guide the generation of the cross attention map. Given an image and a candidate concept, after extracting unimodal representations, the correlation layer computes the semantic relevance between visual blocks $\{v_i\}_{i=1}^{49}$ and element concepts $\{c_j\}_{j=1}^{2}$ [2] with cosine distance and output the final *image-to-concept* relevance matrix as $R \in \mathbb{R}^{49\times 2}$ with each element r_{ij} calculated using Eq. 1. We can easily have another *concept-to-image* relevance matrix by transposing R.

$$r_{ij} = \left(\frac{v_i}{\|v_i\|_2}\right)^T \left(\frac{c_j}{\|c_j\|_2}\right), i \in [1, 49], j \in [1, 2] \quad (1)$$

In order to obtain attention weights, we need to normalize the relevance score r_{ij} as Eq. 2 as (Chen et al., 2020a).

$$\bar{r}_{ij} = \frac{\text{relu}\,(r_{ij})}{\sqrt{\sum_{j=1}^{n} \text{relu}\,(r_{ij})^2}} \quad (2)$$

After obtaining the normalized attention score, we can calculate the cross-attention representation based on the selected query space Q and the context space V, where $V = K$ in our setting as shown in Fig. 2. Taking *image-to-concept* attention for example, given a visual block feature v_i as query, cross attention encoding is performed over the element concept space C using Eq. 3.

$$\widehat{v}_i = \sum_{j=1}^{n} \alpha_{ij} c_j, \quad \text{s.t.} \quad \alpha_{ij} = \frac{\exp\,(\lambda \bar{r}_{ij})}{\sum_{j=1}^{n} \exp\,(\lambda \bar{r}_{ij})} \quad (3)$$

where λ is the inverse temperature parameter of the softmax function (Chorowski et al., 2015) to control the smoothness of the attention distribution.

Visually-Attended Concept Representation. The goal of this module is to align and represent concepts with related visual blocks and help further determine the alignment between element concepts and image regions. We use concept embedding as query and collect visual clues using Eq. 3 and the final visually-attended features for compositional concept is $\widehat{c} \in R^{2\times d_k}$.

Concept-Attended Visual Representation. An image representation grounded with element concept would be beneficial for compositional concept learning. Following the similar procedure as visually-attended concept representation, we take visual block features as query and concept embedding as context. We can calculate the concept-attended visual representation using Eq. 3. The final result $\widehat{v} \in \mathbb{R}^{49\times d_k}$ represents the concept-attended block visual features with the latent space dimension d_k.

3.5 Gated Pooling Layer

After the cross-attention encoder, the output image features $V = [v_1, \ldots, v_{49}] \in \mathbb{R}^{49\times d_k}$ and concept features $C = [c_1, c_2] \in \mathbb{R}^{2\times d_k}$ are expected to contain rich cross-modal information. Our target of gated pooling layer is to combine elements to form the final representation for concepts and images separately. Pooling techniques can be directly deployed to obtain such representation. However, we argue that elements should have different effect on the final concept recognition. For example, background visual blocks shouldn't be paid much attention during concept recognition. To address the assumption, we propose gated pooling layer to learn the relative importance of each element and dynamically control the contribution of each element in the final representation. Specially, We apply one linear layers with parameter $W \in \mathbb{R}^{d_k\times 1}$ on the element feature x_i and normalize the output to calculate an attention weight α_i that indicates the relative importance of each element using Eq. 4.

$$x = \textstyle\sum_i \alpha_i x_i \quad \text{s.t.} \quad \alpha_i = \frac{\exp((Wx_i))}{\sum_{k=1}^{N} \exp((Wx_k))} \quad (4)$$

3.6 Multi-Modal Relevance Network

After obtaining the updated features for both images $\widehat{v}_i$ and concepts $(\widehat{a}, \widehat{o})_j$, we introduce the multimodal relevance network shared the spirit as (Sung et al., 2018) to calculate the relevance score

[2]Each compositional concept only has two elements, attribute and object.

Algorithm 1: Training EpiCA for ZSCL

Input: $\mathcal{D}_{train} = \{(v_m, (a_m, o_m))\}_{m=1}^{|Tr|}$, $\mathcal{D}_{test} = \{v_n\}_{i=n}^{|Ts|}$, task size S, sample interval t

Output: Multi-Modal Rel. Function f

`// Inductive Learning Phase`

for $epoch \leftarrow 1$ **to** E_{ind_max} **do**

  for *each image and the corresponding pair in the training set* **do**

    Construct an episode $[v_p, (a_p, o_p), (a_{n_1}, o_{n_1}), \cdots, (a_{n_s}, o_{n_s})]$.

    Gated Cross-Attention Encoding using Eq. 1, 2, 3 and 4

    Calculating multi-modal relevance score using Eq 5.

    Updating EpiCA.

`// Transductive Learning Phase`

for $epoch \leftarrow 1$ **to** E_{trans_max} **do**

  if $epoch \ \% \ t == 0$ **then**

    Pick confident samples from unseen set by Eq. 7.

  Updating EpiCA by Eq 9.

as shown in Eq. 5

$$s_{i,j} = g_\phi(\text{concat}[(\widehat{v}_i), (\widehat{a}, \widehat{o})_j]) \tag{5}$$

where g is the relevance function implemented by two layer feed-forward network with trainable parameters ϕ.

In order to train EpiCA, we add Softmax activation on the relevance score to measure the probability of image i belonging to concept j within the current episode as Eq. 5 and update EpiCA using cross-entropy loss.

$$p_j(\widehat{v}_i) = \frac{\exp(s_{i,j})}{\sum_{k=1}^{C} \exp(s_{i,k})} \tag{6}$$

3.7 Training and Prediction

Inductive Training. For each image and the corresponding pair label, we randomly sample negative pairs to form an episode which consists of an image v_p, a positive pair (a_p, o_p) and a predefined number n_t of negative pairs in the form of $[v_p, (a_p, o_p), (a_{n_1}, o_{n_1}), \cdots, (a_{n_t}, o_{n_t})]$. Then within each episode, we calculate the relevance score between image and all candidate pairs using Eq. 5. Finally, we calculate the cross entropy loss using Eq. 6 and update EpiCA as shown in Alg. 1.

Transductive Training. The disjointness of the seen/unseen concept space will result in domain shift problems and cause the predictions biasing towards seen concepts as pointed by (Pan and Yang, 2009). Transductive training utilizes the unlabeled test set to alleviate the problem (Dhillon et al., 2019). Specifically, transductive training has a sampling phase to select confident test samples and utilize the generalized cross entropy loss as Eq. 8 to update EpiCA.

Following previous work (Li et al., 2019b), we use threshold-based method as Eq. 7 to pick up confident examples.

$$\frac{p_1(\widehat{v}_i)}{p_2(\widehat{v}_i)} > \gamma \tag{7}$$

where p is calculated by Eq. 6 and the threshold is the fraction of the highest label probability $p_1(\widehat{v}_i)$ and the second highest label probability $p_2(\widehat{v}_i)$ which measures the prediction peakiness in current episode. Only confident instances are employed to update EpiCA which is controlled by γ.

Moreover, the recently proposed generalized cross-entropy loss (Zhang and Sabuncu, 2018) is used to calculate the loss for pseudo-labeled test examples as Eq. 8.

$$\mathcal{L}_u = \sum_{(v_i,(a,o)_j)\in\mathcal{U}} \frac{1 - (p_j(\widehat{v}_i))^q}{q} \tag{8}$$

where $p_j(\widehat{v}_i)$ is the probability of $\widehat{v}_i$ belonging to pair $(\widehat{a}, \widehat{o})_j$ calculated using Eq. 6. $q \in (0, 1]$ is the hyper-parameter related to the noise level of the pseudo labels, with higher noisy pseudo labels requiring larger q.

Finally, the transductive loss is calculated as Eq. 9, where $\mathcal{L}_u$ corresponds to the generalized cross entropy loss from pseudo-labeled test examples and $\mathcal{L}_s$ is the cross entropy loss for the training examples

$$\mathcal{L} = \mathcal{L}_u + \mathcal{L}_s. \tag{9}$$

Prediction. Given a new image with extracted feature v_i, we iterate over all the candidate pairs and select the pair with the highest relevance score as $(\hat{a}, \hat{o}) = \text{argmax}_{\hat{a},\hat{o}}\, s_{i,j}(v_i, (\hat{a}, \hat{o})_j)$ as Eq. 5 using EpiCA.

4 Experiments

Dataset. We use similar dataset as in (Nagarajan and Grauman, 2018; Purushwalkam et al., 2019) for both conventional and generalized ZSCL settings with the split shown in Tab. 1. Notably, generalized ZSCL setting has additional validation set for both benchmarks which allows cross-validation to set the hyperparameters. The generalized ZSCL evaluates the models on both seen/unseen sets.

- MIT-States (Isola et al., 2015) has 245 objects and 115 attributes. In conventional ZSCL, the pairs are split into two disjoint sets with 1200 seen pairs and 700 unseen pairs. In generalized ZSCL, the validation set has 600 pairs with 300 pairs seen in the training set and 300 pairs unseen during training and the test set has 800 pairs with 400 pairs seen and remaining 400 pairs unseen in the training set.
- UT-Zappos (Yu and Grauman, 2017) contains images of 12 shoe types as object labels and 16 material types as attribute labels. In conventional ZSCL, the dataset is split into disjoint seen set with 83 pairs and unseen set with 33 pairs. In generalized ZSCL, the 36 pairs in the test set consists 18 seen and 18 unseen pairs. 15 seen pairs and 15 unseen pairs composes the validation set.

Implementation Details. We develop our model based on *PyTorch*. For all experiments, we adopt ResNet-18 pre-trained on ImageNet as the backbone to extract visual features. For *attr-obj* pairs, we encode attributes and objects with 300-dim *GloVe* and fix it during the training process. We randomly sample 50 negative pairs to construct episodes. We use Adam with 10^{-3} as the initial learning rate and multiply the learning rate by 0.5 every 5 epoch and train the network for total 25 epochs. We report the accuracy at the last epoch for conventional ZSCL. For generalized ZSCL, the accuracy is reported based on the validation set. Moreover, the batch size is set to 64, λ in Eq. 3 is set to 9, q in Eq. 8 is set to 0.5 and the threshold in Eq. 7 is set to 10.

Baselines. We compare EpiCA with the following SOTA methods: 1) Analog (Chen and Grauman, 2014) trains a linear SVM classifier for the seen pairs and utilizes Bayesian Probabilistic Tensor Factorization to infer the unseen classifier weights. 2) Redwine (Misra et al., 2017) leverages the compatibility between visual features v and concepts semantic representation to do the recognition. 3) AttOperator (Nagarajan and Grauman, 2018) models composition by treating attributes as matrix operators to modify object state to score the compatibility. 4) GenModel (Nan et al., 2019) adds reconstruction loss to boost the metric-learning performance. 5) TAFE-Net (Wang et al., 2019) extracts visual features based on the pair semantic representation and utilizes a shared classifier to recognize novel concepts. 6) SymNet (Li et al., 2020) builds a transformation framework and adds group theory constraints to its latent space to recognize novel concepts. We report the results according to the papers and the released official code [3] [4] of the aforementioned baselines.

	Conventional ZSCL		Generalized ZSCL	
	MIT-States	Zappos	MIT-States	Zappos
# Attr.	115	16	115	16
# Obj.	245	12	245	12
# Train Pair	1262	83	1262	83
# Train Img.	34562	24898	30338	22998
# Test Pair	700	33	800	36
# Test Img.	19191	4228	12995	2914
# Val. Pair			600	30
# Val. Img.			10420	3214

Table 1: Conventional and Generalized Data Split for MIT-States and Zappos Datasets.

Methods	MIT-States(%)	UT-Zappos(%)
Random	0.14	3.0
ANALOG	1.4	18.3
REDWINE	12.5	40.3
ATTOPERATOR	14.2	46.2
GenModel	17.8	48.3
TAFE-Net	16.4	33.2
SymNet	**19.9**	52.1
EpiCA(Inductive)	15.68	**52.56**
EpiCA(Transductive)	18.13	**55.48**

Table 2: Results of Conventional ZSCL setting

4.1 Conventional ZSCL Setting

Quantitive Results. Top-1 accuracy metric is reported in this setting to compare different methods. The top-1 accuracy of the unseen *attr-obj* pairs for conventional ZSCL is presented in Tab. 2. EpiCA outperforms all baselines on Zappos benchmark and exceeds the state-of-the-art by 3.3%. It achieves comparable performance on MITStates benchmark. We will empirically analyze the model's behavior in later sections.

4.2 Generalized ZSCL Setting

In this setting, following the related work (Purushwalkam et al., 2019), we measure the performance

[3]https://github.com/Tushar-N/attributes-as-operators

[4]https://github.com/ucbdrive/tafe-net.git

Model Top k →	Mit-States Val AUC 1	2	3	Mit-States Test AUC 1	2	3	UT-Zappos Val AUC 1	2	3	UT-Zappos Test AUC 1	2	3
AttOperator	2.5	6.2	10.1	1.6	4.7	7.6	21.5	44.2	61.6	25.9	51.3	67.6
RedWine	2.9	7.3	11.8	2.4	5.7	9.3	30.4	52.2	63.5	27.1	54.6	68.8
LabelEmbed+	3.0	7.6	12.2	2.0	5.6	9.4	26.4	49.0	66.1	25.7	52.1	67.8
TMN	3.5	8.1	12.4	2.9	7.1	11.5	36.8	57.1	69.2	29.3	**55.3**	69.8
SymNet	4.3	9.8	14.8	3.0	7.6	12.3	\	\	\	\	\	\
Inductive EpiCA	7.73	12.19	22.93	6.55	13.07	20.01	25.13	50.19	61.97	25.59	50.06	63.08
Transductive EpiCA	**9.01**	**17.63**	**24.01**	**7.18**	**14.02**	**21.31**	**53.18**	**68.71**	**77.89**	**35.04**	54.83	**70.02**

Table 3: AUC in percentage (multiplied by 100) on MIT-States and UT-Zappos. Our *EpiCA* model outperforms the previous methods by a large margin on MIT-States based on most of the metrics on UT-Zappos.

with AUC metric. AUC introduces the concept of calibration bias which is a scalar value added to the predicting scores of unseen pairs. By changing the values of the calibration bias, we can draw an accuracy curve for seen/unseen sets. The area below the curve is the AUC metric as a measurement for the generalized ZSCL system.

Quantitative results. Tab. 3 provides comparisons between our EpiCA model and the previous methods on both the validation and testing sets. As Tab. 3 shows, the EpiCA model outperforms the previous methods by a large margin. On the challenging MIT-States dataset which has about 2000 attribute-object pairs, all the baseline methods have a relatively low AUC score while our model is able to double the performance of the previous methods, indicating its effectiveness.

4.3 Ablation Study

We conduct ablation study on EpiCA and compare its performance in different settings.

Importance of Transductive Learning. The experimental results in Tab. 2 and Tab. 3 show the importance of transductive learning. There are about 2% and 3% performance gains for MIT-States and UT-Zappos in conventional ZSCL. A significant improvement is observed for both datasets in generalized ZSCL. This is within our expectation because 1) our inductive model has accumulated knowledge about the elements of the concept and has the ability to pick confident test examples. 2) after training the model with the confident pseudo-labeled test data, it acquires the knowledge about unseen concepts.

Importance of Cross-Attention (CA) Encoder. To analyze the effect of CA encoder, we remove CA (w/o CA) and use unimodal representations for both concepts and images. From Tab. 4, it can be seen that EpiCA does depend on multi-modal information to do concept recognition and the results also verifies the rationale to fuse multi-modal information by cross-attention mechanism.

Importance of Gated Pooling (GP) Layer. We replace GP layer by average pooling (w/o GP). Tab. 4 shows the effectiveness of GP in filtering out noisy information. Instead of treating each element equally, GP help selectively suppress and highlight salient elements within each modality.

Importance of Episode Training. We also conduct experiments by removing both CA and GP (w/o GP and CA). In this setting, we concatenate unimodal representation of images and concepts and use 2-layer MLP to calculate the relevance score. Although simple, it still achieves satisfactory results, showing episode training is vital for our EpiCA model.

EpiCA variants	MIT-States(%)	UT-Zappos(%)
Full EpiCA	15.79	52.56
- w/o cross attention (CA)	12.05	42.77
- w/o gated pooling (GP)	13.46	50.47
- w/o GP and CA	14.13	48.76

Table 4: Ablation study of EpiCA components. The episode training and cross-attention encoder are import to our model. Adding gated pooling layer further boosts the accuracy.

4.4 Qualitative Analysis.

Fig. 3 shows some examples and their predicted labels by EpiCA. Although it gives the correct predictions for the two examples in the first row, EpiCA still struggles in distinguishing the similar, even opposite attributes, like *New* and *Old*. For example, the second highest prediction for the image with true label *new truck* is *old car*. The predicted object is reasonable, but the predicted attribute is opposite. Meanwhile, for the incorrect predictions, the predicted labels are meaningful and remain relevant

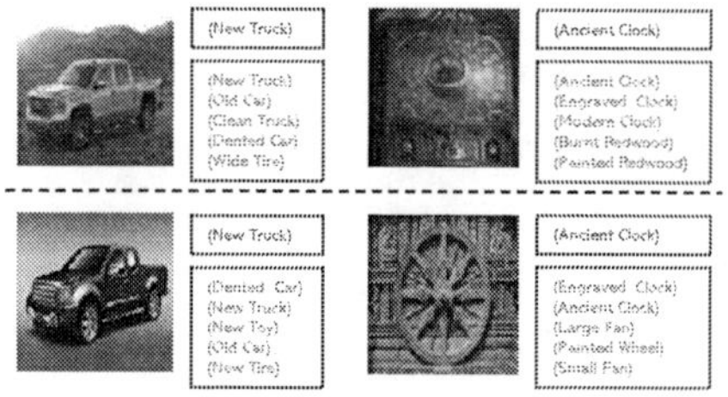

Figure 3: Predicting examples of EpiCA from MIT-States dataset. True label and predicted labels are in red and blue text respectively.

to the image. For example, *Engraved Clock* may be a better label than *Ancient Clock* for the bottom image. These examples show that EpiCA learns the relevance between images and concepts. But the evaluation of the models is hard and in some cases additional information and bias is needed to predict the exact labels occurring in the dataset.

5 Conclusion

In this paper, we propose EpiCA which combines episode-based training and cross-attention mechanism to exploit the alignment between concepts and images to address ZSCL problems. It has led to competitive performance on two benchmark datasets. In generalized ZSCL setting, EpiCA achieves over 2× performance gain compared to the SOTA on several evaluation metrics. However, ZSCL remains a challenging problem. Future work that explores cognitively motivated learning models and incorporates information about relations between objects as well as attributes will be interesting directions to pursue.

References

Chao-Yeh Chen and Kristen Grauman. 2014. Inferring analogous attributes. *Proceedings of the IEEE Conference on Computer Vision and Pattern Recognition*, pages 200–207.

Hui Chen, Guiguang Ding, Xudong Liu, Zijia Lin, Ji Liu, and Jungong Han. 2020a. Imram: Iterative matching with recurrent attention memory for cross-modal image-text retrieval. In *Proceedings of the IEEE/CVF Conference on Computer Vision and Pattern Recognition*, pages 12655–12663.

Yanbei Chen, Shaogang Gong, and Loris Bazzani. 2020b. Image search with text feedback by visiolinguistic attention learning. pages 3001–3011.

Jan K Chorowski, Dzmitry Bahdanau, Dmitriy Serdyuk, Kyunghyun Cho, and Yoshua Bengio. 2015. Attention-based models for speech recognition. *Advances in neural information processing systems*, 28:577–585.

Guneet S Dhillon, Pratik Chaudhari, Avinash Ravichandran, and Stefano Soatto. 2019. A baseline for few-shot image classification. *arXiv preprint arXiv:1909.02729*.

Kaiming He, Xiangyu Zhang, Shaoqing Ren, and Jian Sun. 2016. Deep residual learning for image recognition. *Proceedings of the IEEE conference on computer vision and pattern recognition*, pages 770–778.

Sepp Hochreiter and Jürgen Schmidhuber. 1997. Long short-term memory. *Neural computation*, 9(8):1735–1780.

Phillip Isola, Joseph J Lim, and Edward H Adelson. 2015. Discovering states and transformations in image collections.

Brenden Lake and Marco Baroni. 2018. Generalization without systematicity: On the compositional skills of sequence-to-sequence recurrent networks. *International Conference on Machine Learning*, pages 2873–2882.

Brenden M Lake, Ruslan Salakhutdinov, and Joshua B Tenenbaum. 2015. Human-level concept learning through probabilistic program induction. *Science*, 350(6266):1332–1338.

Kuang-Huei Lee, Xi Chen, Gang Hua, Houdong Hu, and Xiaodong He. 2018. Stacked cross attention for image-text matching. pages 201–216.

Kai Li, Martin Renqiang Min, and Yun Fu. 2019a. Rethinking zero-shot learning: A conditional visual classification perspective. *The IEEE International Conference on Computer Vision (ICCV)*.

Xinzhe Li, Qianru Sun, Yaoyao Liu, Qin Zhou, Shibao Zheng, Tat-Seng Chua, and Bernt Schiele. 2019b. Learning to self-train for semi-supervised few-shot classification. *Advances in Neural Information Processing Systems*, pages 10276–10286.

Yong-Lu Li, Yue Xu, Xiaohan Mao, and Cewu Lu. 2020. Symmetry and group in attribute-object compositions. *Proceedings of the IEEE/CVF Conference on Computer Vision and Pattern Recognition*, pages 11316–11325.

Jiasen Lu, Dhruv Batra, Devi Parikh, and Stefan Lee. 2019. Vilbert: Pretraining task-agnostic visiolinguistic representations for vision-and-language tasks. pages 13–23.

Ishan Misra, Abhinav Gupta, and Martial Hebert. 2017. From red wine to red tomato: Composition with context. *Proceedings of the IEEE Conference on Computer Vision and Pattern Recognition*, pages 1792–1801.

Tushar Nagarajan and Kristen Grauman. 2018. Attributes as operators. *ECCV.*

Zhixiong Nan, Yang Liu, Nanning Zheng, and Song-Chun Zhu. 2019. Recognizing unseen attribute-object pair with generative model. *Proceedings of the AAAI Conference on Artificial Intelligence*, 33:8811–8818.

Sinno Jialin Pan and Qiang Yang. 2009. A survey on transfer learning. *IEEE Transactions on knowledge and data engineering*, 22(10):1345–1359.

Jeffrey Pennington, Richard Socher, and Christopher Manning. 2014. Glove: Global vectors for word representation. *Proceedings of the 2014 conference on empirical methods in natural language processing (EMNLP)*, pages 1532–1543.

Senthil Purushwalkam, Maximilian Nickel, Abhinav Gupta, and Marc'Aurelio Ranzato. 2019. Task-driven modular networks for zero-shot compositional learning. *arXiv preprint arXiv:1905.05908.*

Jake Snell, Kevin Swersky, and Richard Zemel. 2017. Prototypical networks for few-shot learning. *Advances in neural information processing systems*, pages 4077–4087.

Flood Sung, Yongxin Yang, Li Zhang, Tao Xiang, Philip HS Torr, and Timothy M Hospedales. 2018. Learning to compare: Relation network for few-shot learning. *Proceedings of the IEEE Conference on Computer Vision and Pattern Recognition*, pages 1199–1208.

Ashish Vaswani, Noam Shazeer, Niki Parmar, Jakob Uszkoreit, Llion Jones, Aidan N Gomez, Łukasz Kaiser, and Illia Polosukhin. 2017. Attention is all you need. *Advances in neural information processing systems*, pages 5998–6008.

Oriol Vinyals, Charles Blundell, Timothy Lillicrap, Daan Wierstra, et al. 2016. Matching networks for one shot learning. *Advances in neural information processing systems*, pages 3630–3638.

Xin Wang, Fisher Yu, Ruth Wang, Trevor Darrell, and Joseph E Gonzalez. 2019. Tafe-net: Task-aware feature embeddings for low shot learning. *Proceedings of the IEEE Conference on Computer Vision and Pattern Recognition*, pages 1831–1840.

Kun Wei, Muli Yang, Hao Wang, Cheng Deng, and Xianglong Liu. 2019. Adversarial fine-grained composition learning for unseen attribute-object recognition. pages 3741–3749.

Aron Yu and Kristen Grauman. 2017. Semantic jitter: Dense supervision for visual comparisons via synthetic images. *Proceedings of the IEEE International Conference on Computer Vision*, pages 5570–5579.

Zhilu Zhang and Mert Sabuncu. 2018. Generalized cross entropy loss for training deep neural networks with noisy labels. *Advances in neural information processing systems*, pages 8778–8788.

Multi-Pair Text Style Transfer for Unbalanced Data via Task-Adaptive Meta-Learning

Xing Han
University of Texas at Austin
Austin, TX, 78712
aaronhan223@utexas.edu

Jessica Lundin
Salesforce
San Francisco, CA, 94105
jlundin@salesforce.com

Abstract

Text-style transfer aims to convert text given in one domain into another by paraphrasing the sentence or substituting the keywords without altering the content. By necessity, state-of-the-art methods have evolved to accommodate nonparallel training data, as it is frequently the case there are multiple data sources of unequal size, with a mixture of labeled and unlabeled sentences. Moreover, the inherent style defined within each source might be distinct. A generic bidirectional (e.g., formal ⇔ informal) style transfer regardless of different groups may not generalize well to different applications. In this work, we developed a task adaptive meta-learning framework that can simultaneously perform a multi-pair text-style transfer using a single model. The proposed method can adaptively balance the difference of meta-knowledge across multiple tasks. Results show that our method leads to better quantitative performance as well as coherent style variations. Common challenges of unbalanced data and mismatched domains are handled well by this method.

1 Introduction

Text-style transfer is a fundamental challenge in natural language processing. Applications include non-native speaker assistants, child education, personalization and generative design (Fu et al., 2017; Zhou et al., 2017; Yang et al., 2018a; Gatys et al., 2016b,a; Zhu et al., 2017; Li et al., 2017). Figure 1 shows a prominent example on applying style transfer into a hypothetical online shopping platform, where the generated style variations can be used for personalized recommendations. However, compared with other domains, the lack of parallel corpus and quality training data is currently an obstacle for text-style transfer research. For example, assume one supports a multi-tenant service platform including tenant-specific text data, but there is no guarantee that each tenant will provide sufficient amount of data for model training. To build a multi-task language model that matches the text-style of each tenant is more practical and efficient than training individual models. This single-model approach might also have relatively favorable empirical performance.

Existing works on text style transfer have addressed different applications such as sentiment transfer (Shen et al., 2017), word decipherment (Knight et al., 2006), and author imitation (Xu et al., 2012). If parallel training data is available, a wide range of supervised techniques in machine translation (e.g., Seq2Seq models (Bahdanau et al., 2014) and Transformers (Vaswani et al., 2017)) can also be applied to style transfer problems. For non-parallel data, He et al. (2020) proposed a probabilistic formulation that models non-parallel data from two domains as a partially observed parallel corpus, and learn the style transfer model in a completely unsupervised fashion. Unsupervised machine translation method has also been adapted to this setting (Zhang et al., 2018). In recent research focused on learning disentangled content and style representations using adversarial training (John et al., 2018; Yang et al., 2018b; Shen et al., 2017), models are designed for non-parallel data while preserving content. Lample et al. (2018) argued that the adversarial models are not really doing disentanglement, and proposed a denoising auto-encoding approach instead. Another way to approach this problem is through identifying and substituting style-related sub-sentences (Li et al., 2018; Sudhakar et al., 2019), where the unchanged part guarantees consistency over content. Additionally, state-of-the-art language models (BERT (Devlin et al., 2018), GPT-2 (Radford et al., 2019), CTRL (Keskar et al., 2019), etc.) and text-to-text models (Raffel et al., 2019) achieve good performance generating text

Proceedings of the 1st Workshop on Meta Learning and Its Applications to Natural Language Processing (MetaNLP 2021), pages 28–35
Bangkok, Thailand (online), August 5, 2021.

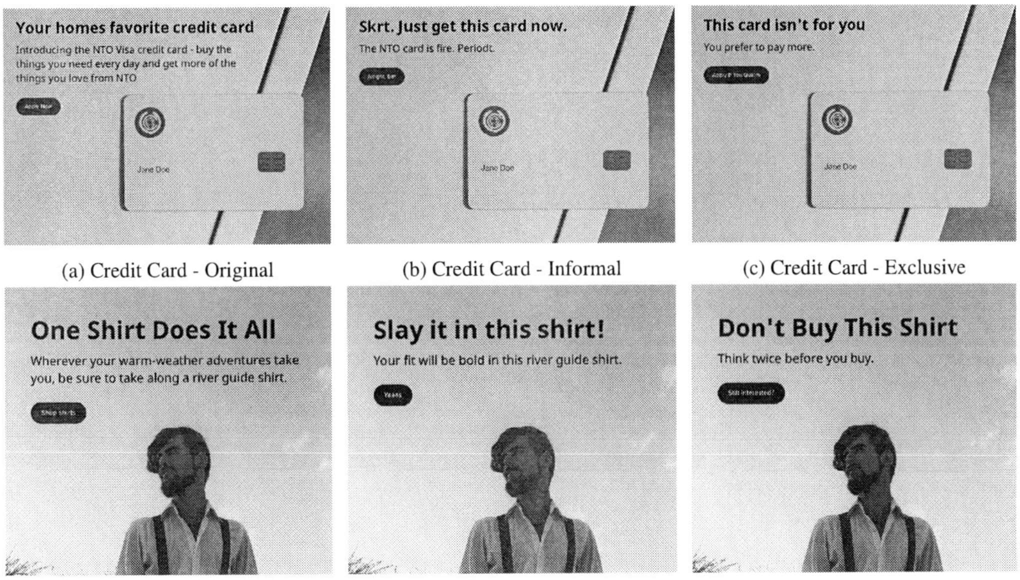

(a) Credit Card - Original (b) Credit Card - Informal (c) Credit Card - Exclusive

(d) Shirt - Original (e) Shirt - Informal (f) Shirt - Exclusive

Figure 1: Text style transfer examples in generative design: the original text is meta-data from e-commerce websites. Two target style variations are predefined for certain groups of customers.

in different styles on multiple tasks (Dathathri et al., 2019; Wolf et al., 2019).

Building upon previous work, we aim to bridge real applications while accounting for the aforementioned data problems. Specifically, we wish to design an efficient training method for a style transfer model that 1. quickly learns and adapts to different style domains with limited data; 2. handling class-imbalance and out-of-distribution tasks. To achieve this, we introduce meta-learning into the style-transfer problem.

Meta-learning (Schmidhuber, 1987) is a method to enable generalization ability to a model over a distribution of tasks. We focus on optimization-based meta-learning for our applications. MAML (Finn et al., 2017) learns a common initialization parameter for each task using a few gradient steps. This standard MAML approach has been applied to text style transfer problems with low resources (Chen and Zhu, 2020) and achieved better performance in this situation. However, this method did not take into account the internal variations between tasks. A similar algorithm called Reptile (Nichol et al., 2018) achieves better performance by maximizing the inner product between gradient of different mini-batches from the same task in its update. Recent works (Qiao et al., 2018; Lee and Choi, 2018) improved a single meta-learner to task-adaptive meta-learning models, which includes task-specific parameters to help generalize better between tasks. Bayesian meta-learning is another active area of research: Finn et al. (2018) proposed a probabilistic version of MAML, where the variational inference framework utilizes a task-specific gradient update. More recently, Lee et al. (2019) incorporated a Bayesian framework into task-adaptive meta-learning. Specifically, they introduce balancing variables for task and class-specific learning and leverage the uncertainties of these parameters derived from training data statistics. In this paper, we will adapt the Bayesian task adaptive meta-learning (TAML) for our application shown in Figure 2 overview.

2 Balancing Variations between Tasks

A common challenge in aforementioned real application is that data from multiple sources may suffer from different problems, such as insufficient training samples, unbalanced class labels, or domain mismatch. However, simply ignore these differences and concatenate all tenants' data for model training will not lead to ideal results.

Meta-learning is one of the most relevant approaches for generalized learning from few samples of different tasks. Assume a task distribution $p(\tau)$ that randomly generates task τ consisting of training set $\mathcal{D}^\tau = \{X^\tau, \overline{X}^\tau\}$ and a test set

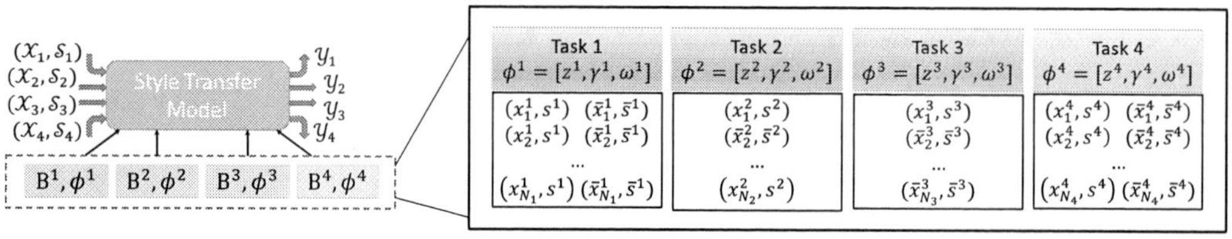

Figure 2: An overview of our multi-pair style transfer method: assume learning from each tenant's data is a task, and the training data available for each task varies. The style transfer model can adaptively learn tasks using our method and the resulting model performs style transfer across multiple domains.

$\mathcal{D}^{\mathcal{T}}_{\text{test}} = \{X^{\mathcal{T}}_{\text{test}}, \overline{X}^{\mathcal{T}}_{\text{test}}\}$. If parallel training data is not available, then we only have $\mathcal{D}^{\mathcal{T}} = X^{\mathcal{T}}$ and $\mathcal{D}^{\mathcal{T}}_{\text{test}} = X^{\mathcal{T}}_{\text{test}}$. The MAML algorithm initialize task-specific parameter $\theta^{\mathcal{T}}$ using a few gradient steps on a small amount of data. In this case, the optimized parameters can generalize to new tasks. Specifically, we have the loss minimization

$$\min_{\theta} \sum_{\mathcal{T}\sim p(\mathcal{T})} \mathcal{L}(\theta - \alpha \nabla_{\theta} \mathcal{L}(\theta; \mathcal{D}^{\mathcal{T}}); \mathcal{D}^{\mathcal{T}}_{\text{test}}), \quad (1)$$

where α is the step size when learning each task. The initial parameter of each task then becomes $\theta^{\mathcal{T}} = \theta - \alpha \nabla_{\theta} \mathcal{L}(\theta; \mathcal{D}^{\mathcal{T}})$, which has been proved to minimize the test loss $\mathcal{L}(\theta^{\mathcal{T}}; \mathcal{D}^{\mathcal{T}}_{\text{test}})$. The training set $\mathcal{D}^{\mathcal{T}}$ may consist of only a few samples.

Eq (1) is effective in numerous applications, yet insufficient in addressing our data problems, as it treats the initialization and learning parameters with equal importance for each task. Inspired by Lee et al. (2019), we now introduce three balancing variables: $z^{\mathcal{T}}, \gamma^{\mathcal{T}}, \omega^{\mathcal{T}}$ for every task $\mathcal{T}$.

Let $\omega^{\mathcal{T}} = (\omega^{\mathcal{T}}_1, ..., \omega^{\mathcal{T}}_C) \in [0, 1]^C$ be the multiplier of each of the class specific gradients to vary the learning rate for each class. In real applications, we often have a style transfer problem with unbalanced training data. For instance, when training formality style transfer models, the number of formal/positive sentences is normally much larger than the number of informal/exclusive sentences. Also, denote $\gamma^{\mathcal{T}} = (\gamma^{\mathcal{T}}_1, ..., \gamma^{\mathcal{T}}_L) \in [0, \infty)^L$ to be the multipliers of the original learning-rate α, where the new learning rate becomes $\gamma^{\mathcal{T}}_1\alpha, \gamma^{\mathcal{T}}_2\alpha, ..., \gamma^{\mathcal{T}}_L\alpha$. Note that the value of γ is task-dependent (e.g., sample size of the training data from each task), and is meant to deal with the small data problem in multi-pair text style transfer. Moreover, since the text data collected from every source or tenant is very hard to be aligned, it is common to have training data with significantly different context. We can treat this as an out of distribution problem and this can be reflected on the value of initial parameters. We use $z^{\mathcal{T}}$ to modulate the initial parameter θ for each task. Specifically, $z^{\mathcal{T}}$ relocates the initial θ to a task-dependent starting point prior to the learning process. We unify these properties as the learning framework below:

$$\theta_0 = \theta * z^{\mathcal{T}}, \quad \text{and for } k = 1, ..., \mathsf{K}:$$

$$\theta_k = \theta_{k-1} - \gamma^{\mathcal{T}} \circ \alpha \circ \sum_{c=1}^{C} \omega^{\mathcal{T}}_c \nabla_{\theta_{k-1}} \mathcal{L}(\theta_{k-1}; \mathcal{D}^{\mathcal{T}}_c), \quad (2)$$

where ω_c and $\mathcal{D}_c$ are class-specific parameters and data; K is the total number of iterations for updating parameters. We currently assume $C = 2$ in the following discussions of this paper, since pair-wise style transfer is the primary problem of interest so far.

3 Learning the Balancing Variables through Variational Inference

We now discuss how to find the most suitable value of each balancing variable. We employ the variational inference framework from probabilistic MAML (He et al., 2020) and TAML (Lee et al., 2019) to extract the task-specific information. The variational inference framework is used to compute posterior distributions for the balancing variables $z^{\mathcal{T}}, \gamma^{\mathcal{T}}, \omega^{\mathcal{T}}$. Assume the training data $X^{\mathcal{T}} = \{x^{\mathcal{T}}_n\}^{N_{\mathcal{T}}}_{n=1}$, $\overline{X}^{\mathcal{T}} = \{\overline{x}^{\mathcal{T}}_n\}^{N_{\mathcal{T}}}_{n=1}$; test data $X^{\mathcal{T}}_{\text{test}} = \{x^{\mathcal{T}}_m\}^{M_{\mathcal{T}}}_{m=1}$, $\overline{X}^{\mathcal{T}}_{\text{test}} = \{\overline{x}^{\mathcal{T}}_m\}^{M_{\mathcal{T}}}_{m=1}$, and $\phi^{\mathcal{T}} = \{\tilde{\omega}^{\mathcal{T}}, \tilde{\gamma}^{\mathcal{T}}, \tilde{z}^{\mathcal{T}}\}$ to be a collection of three balancing variables. The goal of learning for each task $\mathcal{T}$ is to maximize the conditional log-likelihood of the joint dataset $\mathcal{D}^{\mathcal{T}}_{\text{test}}$ and $\mathcal{D}^{\mathcal{T}}$: $\log p(\overline{X}^{\mathcal{T}}_{\text{test}}, \overline{X}^{\mathcal{T}} | X^{\mathcal{T}}_{\text{test}}, X^{\mathcal{T}}; \theta)$. To solve the optimization problem requires determining the true posterior $p(\phi^{\mathcal{T}} | \mathcal{D}^{\mathcal{T}}, \mathcal{D}^{\mathcal{T}}_{\text{test}})$, which is intractable. We resort to variational inference with a tractable

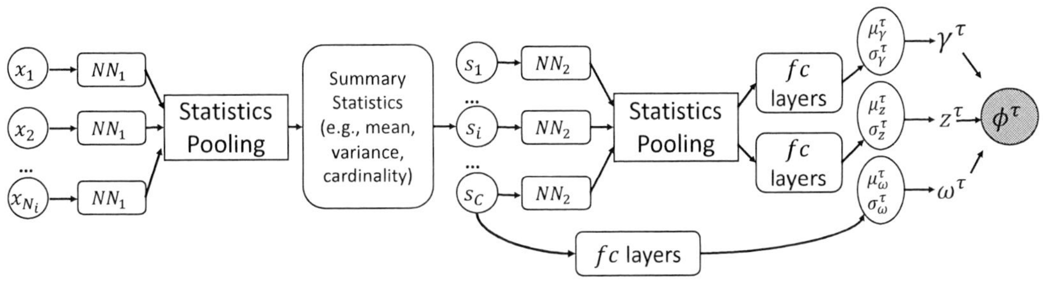

Figure 3: The inference network for generating posterior distribution of balancing variables γ, z, and ω for task i.

form of approximate posterior $q(\phi^\tau|\mathcal{D}^\tau, \mathcal{D}^\tau_{\text{test}}; \psi)$ parameterized by ψ. In order to make the inference network of meta training and meta testing consistent, we drop the dependency of $\mathcal{D}^\tau_{\text{test}}$ since the test labels are unknown in meta-testing. Hence the approximate posterior becomes $q(\phi^\tau|\mathcal{D}^\tau; \psi)$. We now have the approximated lower bound for task adaptive meta learning:

$$\mathcal{L}^\tau_{\theta,\psi} = \frac{N_\tau + M_\tau}{M_\tau} \sum_{m=1}^{M_\tau} E_{q(\phi^\tau|\mathcal{D}^\tau;\psi)} \\ [\log p(\tilde{y}^\tau_m|\tilde{x}^\tau_m, \phi^\tau; \theta)] - \mathsf{KL}[q(\phi^\tau|\mathcal{D}^\tau; \psi)\|p(\phi^\tau)]. \tag{3}$$

Given that each balancing variable is independent, $q(\phi^\tau|\mathcal{D}^\tau; \psi)$ can therefore be fully factorized

$$q(\phi^\tau|\mathcal{D}^\tau; \psi) = \\ \prod_c q(\omega^\tau_c|\mathcal{D}^\tau; \psi) \prod_l q(\gamma^\tau_l|\mathcal{D}^\tau; \psi) \prod_i q(z^\tau_i|\mathcal{D}^\tau; \psi).$$

We assume each single dimension of $q(\phi^\tau|\mathcal{D}^\tau; \psi)$ follows a uni-variate Gaussian distribution with trainable mean and variance. Given $\phi^\tau_s \sim q(\phi^\tau|\mathcal{D}^\tau; \psi)$, we then use the Monte-Carlo approximation on Eq (3) as a new objective:

$$\min_{\theta,\psi} \frac{1}{M_\tau} \sum_{m=1}^{M_\tau} \frac{1}{S} \sum_{s=1}^{S} -\log p(\tilde{y}^\tau_m|\tilde{x}^\tau_m, \phi^\tau_s; \theta) \\ + \frac{1}{N_\tau + M_\tau} \mathsf{KL}[q(\phi^\tau|\mathcal{D}^\tau; \psi)\|p(\phi^\tau)]. \tag{4}$$

To better model the variational distribution $q(\phi^\tau|\mathcal{D}^\tau; \psi)$, an informative representation encoded from the training dataset $\mathcal{D}^\tau$ is necessary. In this case, the inference network can capture all useful statistical information in $\mathcal{D}^\tau$ to recognize its imbalances. We use a two-stage hierarchical set encoder, for a given text style transfer task, we first encodes each class, and then encodes the whole set of classes. Define the encoder $\mathsf{StatisticsPooling}(\cdot)$ that generates concatenation of the class statistics such as mean, variance and cardinality. The two-stage encoder first encodes all text sentences of each class into s_c, followed by encoding representations of the whole set of classes:

$$v^\tau = \mathsf{StatisticsPooling}\left(\{\mathsf{NN_2(s_c)}\}_{\mathsf{c=1}}^{\mathsf{C}}\right), \\ s_c = \mathsf{StatisticsPooling}\left(\{\mathsf{NN_1(x)}\}_{\mathsf{x \in X^\tau_c}}\right),$$

where $c = 1, ..., C$ represents classes; X^τ_c is the collection of class c examples in task τ; $\mathsf{NN_1}$ and $\mathsf{NN_2}$ are some neural networks parameterized by ψ. Therefore, the summarized feature vectors of $\mathcal{D}^\tau$ can be used to infer the Gaussian distribution parameters of balancing variables ω^τ, z^τ and γ^τ to be further applied in the update of meta-learning. Note that since the balancing variable ω is class-specific, inference its distributional parameters does not need to go through the second stage of encoding. The overall structure of the inference network is shown in Figure 3.

4 Task-Adaptive Style Transfer

We discuss formulation of multi-pair text-style transfer problem using the TAML framework. An overview of our method is shown in Figure 2. We assume training data in each task could either be parallel (task 1 and 4) or non-parallel (task 2 and 3). The number of training samples in task i is represented by N_i, which is not necessarily equal for each task. In addition, the class distribution in non-parallel training data is heavily skewed.

We now formulate our problem as follows. Given a distribution of similar tasks $p(\tau)$, each task represents performing text style transfer on a certain dataset $\mathcal{D}^\tau$. Define a generic loss function $\mathcal{L}$ and shared parameters θ within tasks, the

Algorithm 1 Multi-Pair Text Style Transfer via TAML

Input: style pair for each task τ, $\{(s^\tau, \overline{s}^\tau)\}_{\tau=1}^{\mathcal{T}}$, parameters α, β,
Meta-training procedure:
while not done **do**
  for each style pair $(s^\tau, \overline{s}^\tau)$ **do**
    Train inference network $q(\phi^\tau|\mathcal{D}^\tau;\psi)$ by minimizing objective (4)
    Obtain balancing variables $\{z^\tau, \gamma^\tau, \omega^\tau\} \sim q(\phi^\tau|\mathcal{D}^\tau;\psi)$
    Initialize sub-learner with $\theta_0^\tau = \theta * z^\tau$
    for step in 1, ..., K **do**
      Sample batch data from $\mathcal{D}_s^\tau$
      Update parameters for task τ using $\theta_k^\tau = \theta_{k-1}^\tau - \gamma^\tau \circ \alpha \circ \sum_{c=1}^{2} \omega_c^\tau \nabla_{\theta_{k-1}^\tau} \mathcal{L}(\theta_{k-1}^\tau, \mathcal{D}_s^\tau)$
    end for
    Sample batch data from $\mathcal{D}_t^\tau$
    Evaluate $\mathcal{L}(\theta_{\mathsf{K}}^\tau, \mathcal{D}_t^\tau)$
  end for
  Update meta-learner f_θ with $\theta = \theta - \beta\nabla_\theta \sum_{\tau=1}^{\mathcal{T}} \mathcal{L}(\theta^\tau, \mathcal{D}_t^\tau)$
end while
Meta testing: $Y^\tau \leftarrow f_\theta(X_{\text{test}}^\tau, \mathcal{S}_{\text{test}}^\tau)$

goal is to jointly learn a task-agnostic model $f_\theta : (X^\tau, \mathcal{S}^\tau) \mapsto Y^\tau$, where for each τ, $\mathcal{S}^\tau$ is the corresponding set of style labels of original text X^τ, and Y^τ is the resulting style transformed text. Ideally, Y^τ should be consistent with $\overline{X}^\tau$, the corresponding input text sentence in another style domain which may or may not be available in model training. In fine-tuning with a new task, the parameters are initialized accounting for the imperfect nature of the given dataset. Similar to the standard meta-learning approach, the training data of task τ is divided into a support set $\mathcal{D}_s^\tau$ and a query set $\mathcal{D}_t^\tau$, where $\mathcal{D}_s^\tau$ is used to update each sub-task and $\mathcal{D}_t^\tau$ is used to evaluate the loss, and later used for meta-learner updates. A detailed description can be found in Algorithm 1.

5 Experiments

We conduct experiments on multiple style-transfer datasets: Shakespeare (Xu et al., 2012), Yelp reviews (Shen et al., 2017) and an internal dataset from a company that contains formal/informal text sentences. Performing style transfer on each of the above dataset defines a unique task. The Shakespeare dataset contains 21k parallel sentences, which includes original text style and Shakespeare's style. The maximum length of the sentences is 20. The Yelp dataset contains around 252k sentences of positive and negative restaurant reviews, where we use a maximum length of 15 to conduct the experiment. We evaluate our method using state-of-the-art transformers including BERT, GPT-2, T5, and VAE (John et al., 2018) designed for style transfer by learning disentangled representations. Our baseline method includes regular model training without distinguishing the difference between tasks, and the MAML method in Eq (1) to fine-tune the style transfer models on multiple distinct tasks, which has also been proposed by Chen and Zhu (2020). We then employ Algorithm 1 to adaptively fine-tune the style transfer models for each task.

The unbalanced training data is created by sampling from each class at different rate (75% positive class, 25% negative class). We use the pretrained transformers in Huggingface library (Wolf et al., 2020) as our initial style transfer models. Specifically, we build a two-head model (Figure 4) on top of the decoders where each head is composed of multiple dense layers. We do not perform end-to-end training for the entire transformer but only train the two-head model. The model input is the sentence and style pairs $(X^\tau, \mathcal{S}^\tau)$ while the forward propagation of transformer's output to each model head is dependent on the style labels. The resulting output sentences are style dependent, and one can perform text-style transfer by flipping the style labels during the inference phase. Similarly, we use both baseline and TAML to train VAE and obtain disentangled style and content representations, and replace the style embedding during the inference stage to get style transferred sentences. Note that we focus on improving the fine-tuning part of text style transfer models, while we do not modify the model structure themselves. In terms of content preservation, the objective function of the VAE model proposed by (John et al., 2018) contains a content-oriented loss, while for other transformer-based models, we designed the loss $\mathcal{L}$ to be the cross entropy loss

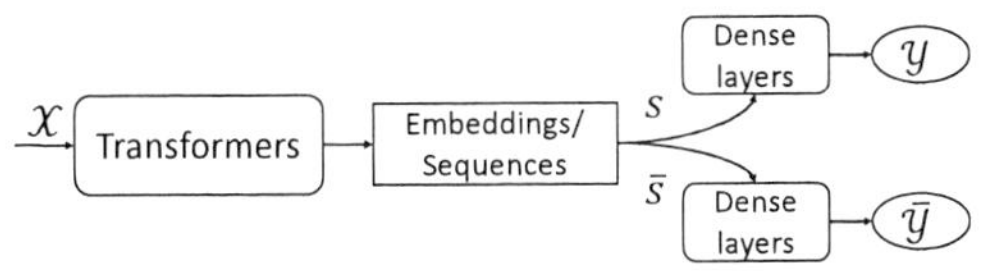

Figure 4: Two-head architecture

Model	Shakespeare			Yelp		
	BLEU↑	PPL↓	ACC↑	BLEU↑	PPL↓	ACC↑
BERT	12.04	26.43	78.77	9.56	15.31	74.68
GPT-2	2.83	38.47	74.45	4.81	45.49	76.67
T5	3.65	59.39	82.58	5.22	39.41	75.14
VAE	14.36	22.29	81.92	10.81	10.65	77.27
MAML-BERT	16.31	21.09	79.34	10.87	15.02	74.98
MAML-GPT-2	7.01	36.94	75.25	5.04	41.76	77.06
MAML-T5	4.77	50.44	83.02	6.46	33.72	75.86
MAML-VAE	15.52	21.45	81.96	11.74	11.04	77.24
TAML-BERT	17.56	**19.36**	79.34	11.02	16.82	75.22
TAML-GPT-2	7.42	36.67	76.02	5.63	37.66	77.18
TAML-T5	4.81	47.23	**83.45**	6.92	32.30	75.64
TAML-VAE	**17.98**	20.14	82.61	**12.31**	**10.59**	**77.33**

Table 1: Evaluations of multiple text style transfer models on testing set of the listed data. TAML-based model training methods achieve better performance on multi-task text style transfer.

between Y^τ and $\overline{X}^\tau$, or between Y^τ and X^τ in non-parallel situations.

For BERT, GPT-2, and T5, we use the built-in vocabulary within the transformers library. Adam optimizer is used with learning of 5×10^{-4} to train the model. The batch size is set to 16 and the model is trained for 100 epochs. We build the two-head model by using 6 fully connected layers with hidden size of 256 and ReLU activation function. The parameters are chosen empirically with the best performance. For VAE approach, we use the same parameter settings as reported in (John et al., 2018). As for NN_1 in inference network, we used two consecutive blocks of 3×3 convolution layer followed by 2×2 max pooling layer, the output is then fed into one fully connected layer for statistics pooling. We then use two fully connected layers for NN_2. All the activation functions are ReLU.

We evaluate competing methods on quality and accuracy of style transfer. The adopted metrics are common choices among recent works.

`BLEU`: We use BLEU (Papineni et al., 2002) score to evaluate the content preservation, the scores are calculated using ScareBLEU (Post, 2018). When parallel sentences are available, we compute the BLEU score between the style transferred sentences Y^τ and the ground truth sentences $\overline{X}^\tau$. Otherwise, we use the original sentences X^τ instead.

`PPL`: We implemented a bigram language model (Kneser and Ney, 1995) to quantitatively evaluate the fluency of a sentence. The language model is trained on the target-style domain, and we report the PPL of the generated sentences.

`Accuracy`: We also trained a TextCNN classifier (Rakhlin, 2016) simultaneously while training style transfer models. The trained classifier is then used to evaluate the classification accuracy on the generated sentences.

Table 1 shows our results for each method. By applying task-adaptive meta learning on each style-transfer model, the performance with respect to every metric is generally improved on the datasets we evaluated. We observe that the VAE method performs better in style transfer, as other models are not explicitly designed for this goal.

6 Conclusion

In this paper, we investigated meta-learning approaches applied to text-style transfer, for situations with multiple data sources. Given the distinct context and total amount of data, we propose a task-adaptive meta-learning approach to fine-tune style-transfer models. The proposed method introduces three balancing variables with probabilistic distributions, which can be encoded from training data. These balancing variables are then used to solve class and task imbalance problems. Empirically, we found that TAML improves the style-transfer performance on multiple models. In the future, we wish to explore generating style variations in more fine-grained levels (for $C > 2$) with the help of meta-learning.

References

Dzmitry Bahdanau, Kyunghyun Cho, and Yoshua Bengio. 2014. Neural machine translation by jointly learning to align and translate. *arXiv preprint arXiv:1409.0473*.

Xiwen Chen and Kenny Q Zhu. 2020. St^2: Small-data text style transfer via multi-task meta-learning. *arXiv preprint arXiv:2004.11742*.

Sumanth Dathathri, Andrea Madotto, Janice Lan, Jane Hung, Eric Frank, Piero Molino, Jason Yosinski, and Rosanne Liu. 2019. Plug and play language models: a simple approach to controlled text generation. *arXiv preprint arXiv:1912.02164*.

Jacob Devlin, Ming-Wei Chang, Kenton Lee, and Kristina Toutanova. 2018. Bert: Pre-training of deep bidirectional transformers for language understanding. *arXiv preprint arXiv:1810.04805*.

Chelsea Finn, Pieter Abbeel, and Sergey Levine. 2017. Model-agnostic meta-learning for fast adaptation of deep networks. *arXiv preprint arXiv:1703.03400*.

Chelsea Finn, Kelvin Xu, and Sergey Levine. 2018. Probabilistic model-agnostic meta-learning. In *Advances in Neural Information Processing Systems*, pages 9516–9527.

Zhenxin Fu, Xiaoye Tan, Nanyun Peng, Dongyan Zhao, and Rui Yan. 2017. Style transfer in text: Exploration and evaluation. *arXiv preprint arXiv:1711.06861*.

Leon A Gatys, Matthias Bethge, Aaron Hertzmann, and Eli Shechtman. 2016a. Preserving color in neural artistic style transfer. *arXiv preprint arXiv:1606.05897*.

Leon A Gatys, Alexander S Ecker, and Matthias Bethge. 2016b. Image style transfer using convolutional neural networks. In *Proceedings of the IEEE conference on computer vision and pattern recognition*, pages 2414–2423.

Junxian He, Xinyi Wang, Graham Neubig, and Taylor Berg-Kirkpatrick. 2020. A probabilistic formulation of unsupervised text style transfer. *arXiv preprint arXiv:2002.03912*.

Vineet John, Lili Mou, Hareesh Bahuleyan, and Olga Vechtomova. 2018. Disentangled representation learning for non-parallel text style transfer. *arXiv preprint arXiv:1808.04339*.

Nitish Shirish Keskar, Bryan McCann, Lav R Varshney, Caiming Xiong, and Richard Socher. 2019. Ctrl: A conditional transformer language model for controllable generation. *arXiv preprint arXiv:1909.05858*.

Reinhard Kneser and Hermann Ney. 1995. Improved backing-off for m-gram language modeling. In *1995 international conference on acoustics, speech, and signal processing*, volume 1, pages 181–184. IEEE.

Kevin Knight, Anish Nair, Nishit Rathod, and Kenji Yamada. 2006. Unsupervised analysis for decipherment problems. In *Proceedings of the COLING/ACL 2006 Main Conference Poster Sessions*, pages 499–506.

Guillaume Lample, Sandeep Subramanian, Eric Smith, Ludovic Denoyer, Marc'Aurelio Ranzato, and Y-Lan Boureau. 2018. Multiple-attribute text rewriting. In *International Conference on Learning Representations*.

Hae Beom Lee, Hayeon Lee, Donghyun Na, Saehoon Kim, Minseop Park, Eunho Yang, and Sung Ju Hwang. 2019. Learning to balance: Bayesian meta-learning for imbalanced and out-of-distribution tasks. *arXiv preprint arXiv:1905.12917*.

Yoonho Lee and Seungjin Choi. 2018. Gradient-based meta-learning with learned layerwise metric and subspace. *arXiv preprint arXiv:1801.05558*.

Juncen Li, Robin Jia, He He, and Percy Liang. 2018. Delete, retrieve, generate: A simple approach to sentiment and style transfer. *arXiv preprint arXiv:1804.06437*.

Yanghao Li, Naiyan Wang, Jiaying Liu, and Xiaodi Hou. 2017. Demystifying neural style transfer. *arXiv preprint arXiv:1701.01036*.

Alex Nichol, Joshua Achiam, and John Schulman. 2018. On first-order meta-learning algorithms. *arXiv preprint arXiv:1803.02999*.

Kishore Papineni, Salim Roukos, Todd Ward, and Wei-Jing Zhu. 2002. Bleu: a method for automatic evaluation of machine translation. In *Proceedings of the 40th annual meeting of the Association for Computational Linguistics*, pages 311–318.

Matt Post. 2018. A call for clarity in reporting BLEU scores. In *Proceedings of the Third Conference on Machine Translation: Research Papers*, pages 186–191, Belgium, Brussels. Association for Computational Linguistics.

Siyuan Qiao, Chenxi Liu, Wei Shen, and Alan L Yuille. 2018. Few-shot image recognition by predicting parameters from activations. In *Proceedings of the IEEE Conference on Computer Vision and Pattern Recognition*, pages 7229–7238.

Alec Radford, Jeffrey Wu, Rewon Child, David Luan, Dario Amodei, and Ilya Sutskever. 2019. Language models are unsupervised multitask learners. *OpenAI blog*, 1(8):9.

Colin Raffel, Noam Shazeer, Adam Roberts, Katherine Lee, Sharan Narang, Michael Matena, Yanqi Zhou, Wei Li, and Peter J Liu. 2019. Exploring the limits of transfer learning with a unified text-to-text transformer. *arXiv preprint arXiv:1910.10683*.

A Rakhlin. 2016. Convolutional neural networks for sentence classification. *GitHub*.

Jürgen Schmidhuber. 1987. *Evolutionary principles in self-referential learning, or on learning how to learn: the meta-meta-... hook*. Ph.D. thesis, Technische Universität München.

Tianxiao Shen, Tao Lei, Regina Barzilay, and Tommi Jaakkola. 2017. Style transfer from non-parallel text by cross-alignment. In *Advances in neural information processing systems*, pages 6830–6841.

Akhilesh Sudhakar, Bhargav Upadhyay, and Arjun Maheswaran. 2019. Transforming delete, retrieve, generate approach for controlled text style transfer. *arXiv preprint arXiv:1908.09368*.

Ashish Vaswani, Noam Shazeer, Niki Parmar, Jakob Uszkoreit, Llion Jones, Aidan N Gomez, Lukasz Kaiser, and Illia Polosukhin. 2017. Attention is all you need. In *Advances in neural information processing systems*, pages 5998–6008.

Thomas Wolf, Lysandre Debut, Victor Sanh, Julien Chaumond, Clement Delangue, Anthony Moi, Pierric Cistac, Tim Rault, Rémi Louf, Morgan Funtowicz, Joe Davison, Sam Shleifer, Patrick von Platen, Clara Ma, Yacine Jernite, Julien Plu, Canwen Xu, Teven Le Scao, Sylvain Gugger, Mariama Drame, Quentin Lhoest, and Alexander M. Rush. 2019. Huggingface's transformers: State-of-the-art natural language processing. *ArXiv*, abs/1910.03771.

Thomas Wolf, Lysandre Debut, Victor Sanh, Julien Chaumond, Clement Delangue, Anthony Moi, Pierric Cistac, Tim Rault, Rémi Louf, Morgan Funtowicz, Joe Davison, Sam Shleifer, Patrick von Platen, Clara Ma, Yacine Jernite, Julien Plu, Canwen Xu, Teven Le Scao, Sylvain Gugger, Mariama Drame, Quentin Lhoest, and Alexander M. Rush. 2020. Transformers: State-of-the-art natural language processing. In *Proceedings of the 2020 Conference on Empirical Methods in Natural Language Processing: System Demonstrations*, pages 38–45, Online. Association for Computational Linguistics.

Wei Xu, Alan Ritter, Bill Dolan, Ralph Grishman, and Colin Cherry. 2012. Paraphrasing for style. In *Proceedings of COLING 2012*, pages 2899–2914.

Cheng Yang, Maosong Sun, Xiaoyuan Yi, and Wenhao Li. 2018a. Stylistic chinese poetry generation via unsupervised style disentanglement. In *Proceedings of the 2018 Conference on Empirical Methods in Natural Language Processing*, pages 3960–3969.

Zichao Yang, Zhiting Hu, Chris Dyer, Eric P Xing, and Taylor Berg-Kirkpatrick. 2018b. Unsupervised text style transfer using language models as discriminators. In *Advances in Neural Information Processing Systems*, pages 7287–7298.

Zhirui Zhang, Shuo Ren, Shujie Liu, Jianyong Wang, Peng Chen, Mu Li, Ming Zhou, and Enhong Chen. 2018. Style transfer as unsupervised machine translation. *arXiv preprint arXiv:1808.07894*.

Ganbin Zhou, Ping Luo, Rongyu Cao, Fen Lin, Bo Chen, and Qing He. 2017. Mechanism-aware neural machine for dialogue response generation. In *Thirty-First AAAI Conference on Artificial Intelligence*.

Jun-Yan Zhu, Taesung Park, Phillip Isola, and Alexei A Efros. 2017. Unpaired image-to-image translation using cycle-consistent adversarial networks. In *Proceedings of the IEEE international conference on computer vision*, pages 2223–2232.

On the cross-lingual transferability of multilingual prototypical models across NLU tasks

Oralie Cattan[1,2] **Christophe Servan**[1] **Sophie Rosset**[2]

[1]QWANT
61 rue de Villier,
92200 Neuilly-sur-Seine, France
inital.lastname@qwant.com

[2]Université Paris-Saclay,
CNRS, LISN,
91405, Orsay, France
lastname@lisn.fr

Abstract

Supervised deep learning-based approaches have been applied to task-oriented dialog and have proven to be effective for limited domain and language applications when a sufficient number of training examples are available. In practice, these approaches suffer from the drawbacks of domain-driven design and under-resourced languages. Domain and language models are supposed to grow and change as the problem space evolves. On one hand, research on transfer learning has demonstrated the cross-lingual ability of multilingual Transformers-based models to learn semantically rich representations. On the other, in addition to the above approaches, meta-learning have enabled the development of task and language learning algorithms capable of far generalization. Through this context, this article proposes to investigate the cross-lingual transferability of using synergistically few-shot learning with prototypical neural networks and multilingual Transformers-based models. Experiments in natural language understanding tasks on MultiATIS++ corpus shows that our approach substantially improves the observed transfer learning performances between the low and the high resource languages. More generally our approach confirms that the meaningful latent space learned in a given language can be can be generalized to unseen and under-resourced ones using meta-learning.

1 Introduction

Traditionally, Natural Language Understanding (NLU) is an intermediate module between the user interface and the dialogue management module in a dialogue system. It aims to extract semantic information from a user's query or utterance to fill slots in a domain specific semantic frame. Domain classification, intent detection and slot filling are three core components belonging to the NLU. They are in charge of determining the domain or service of a users query, its underlying goal or intent and associating utterance segments with conceptual labels, called slots, similar to named entity recognition.

NLU is usually defined as a supervised learning problem, involving conventional machine learning models on massive amount of annotated training data, which are language dependent. This prerequisite has prevented its widespread adoption for poorly endowed languages and for small technology companies that do not benefit from millions of users to gather data. Besides the requirement of a large amount of annotated data being available, domains, intents and slots are language dependent. Consequently, in practice, the resulting systems are hardly adaptable to expand to new languages.

As a solution to this problem, cross-lingual transfer approaches were developed to leverage the knowledge from well-resourced languages, with task specific data available to under-resourced languages with little or no data. Recent efforts focused on training Transformer models multilingually such as the multilingual version of BERT (Devlin et al., 2019). While earlier work demonstrated the effectiveness of multilingual models to learn representations which are transferable across languages, they show limitations when applied to low-resource languages (Pires et al., 2019; Conneau et al., 2020). From another perspective low-shot learning such as few-shot and zero-shot, aims to transfer knowledge learned from one language to another when the training data is limited or is missing some task labels.

As a core contribution, we explore the potential for cross-lingual transferability of multilingual Transformer-based model (Vaswani et al., 2017) (mBERT) combined with a few-shot learning algorithm based on prototypical representations. We also introduce a zero-shot scenario, where models are trained on multiple languages and evaluated on another. Our proposed approach relies on appending a mBERT encoder module to the prototypical neural network, which is a proven few-shot model,

Proceedings of the 1st Workshop on Meta Learning and Its Applications to Natural Language Processing (MetaNLP 2021), pages 36–43
Bangkok, Thailand (online), August 5, 2021. ©2021 Association for Computational Linguistics

originally designed for image classification. Our experimental results show that the generated model trained with a limited number of annotated training examples outperforms the transfer learning based approach on MultiATIS++ dataset (Xu et al., 2020; Upadhyay et al., 2018) and can be applied to unseen languages directly with decent performance.

2 Related work

The availability of large datasets has enabled deep learning methods to achieve great success in a variety of fields. However, most of these successes are based on supervised learning approaches, which require lots of labeled data to train. Most datasets are only available in English. Only a few other languages are supported, and most of them are considered as under-resourced languages.

Recently, meta-learning approaches have enabled the development of task-agnostic learning algorithms capable of far generalizations (cross-domain or cross-lingual) in the context of having a low-data regime. Because literature on low-shot learning is vast and diverse, only the most relevant approaches to this work are presented and we refer the reader to Vanschoren (2019) and Wang et al. (2019) for a surveys of earlier work.

2.1 Low-shot learning

Humans manifest a capacity of learning new concepts from few stimuli quickly and efficiently by utilizing prior knowledge and experience. Inspired by this ability, there has been a resurgence of interest in designing specialized models to perform low-shot learning. An example of this form of learning is metric-based approaches founded on the simple idea of learning a discriminative metric space in which similar samples are mapped close to each other and dissimilar ones distant. Siamese (Koch, 2015), Matching (Vinyals et al., 2016) or Prototypical (Snell et al., 2017) networks belong to this category.

2.1.1 Supervised generalization

In recent years, several approaches have been introduced and refined to overcome the issue of data-limited regime. As an example, the Prototypical Neural Networks (PNNs), developed by Snell et al. (2017) originally for image classification, were used to extract representative characteristics of the data by mapping data points into an embedding space where each sample will cluster around their respective prototype representation. Fort (2017) proposed to extend their work by adding a confidence region around prototypes with the help of Gaussian covariance models.With the aim of improving the generalization capacity of metric-based methods, Wang et al. (2018) proposed to enforce a large margin between the class prototypes by modifying the standard softmax loss function.

2.1.2 Semi-supervised generalization

Other approaches, closely related to the aforementioned ones, proposed to take advantage of labeled and unlabeled data. Among them, Boney and Ilin (2017) extended PNNs to address semi-supervised image classification problems. They applied a hard clustering to assign the class for the unlabeled examples within the latent space learned by the PNNs. A close method was developed by Ren et al. (2018) to refine the prototype generation process with clustering. The authors introduced distractor classes with the aim of handling unlabeled samples not belonging to any of the known classes.

Most of these approaches have mainly been explored in the field of computer vision, and a few of them were applied to NLP fields, such like Natural Language Understanding (NLU).

2.2 NLU using low-shot learning

A number of different deep learning approaches have been applied to the problem of language understanding in recent years. For a thorough overview of deep learning methods in conversational language understanding, we refer the readers to Gao et al. (2018). In the context of relying on limited training resources, few-shot learning has been used for NLU tasks. Yazdani and Henderson (2015) proposes a method to leverage unlabeled data in order to find the separating hyperplanes that divide the utterances with the same label from those with different labels. Sun et al. (2019) extended PNNs for intent classification using hierarchical attention mechanisms when generating the prototype representations.

Slot filling using few-shot models has also been explored. Ferreira et al. (2015) presented a zero-shot approach based on a knowledge base and on word representations learned from unlabeled data. Fritzler et al. (2019) applied PNNs to few-shot named entity recognition by training a separate model for each entity type and Hou et al. (2019) proposed a conditional random forest-based approach enhanced with transfer mechanisms that implicitly incorporate label dependencies and similarities. More recently, Dou et al. (2019), Bansal et al. (2020a) and Bansal et al. (2020b) applied various meta-learned models to few-shot NLU across domains and tasks.

Finally, besides the approaches of Gu et al. (2018) and Zhang et al. (2020) that focus on handling new and low-resource languages for machine translation, to the best of our knowledge, there are no approaches that combine cross-lingual transfer and meta-learning methods for NLU tasks.

3 Approach

In this section, we present the design of a Prototypical Neural Network and its episodic training procedure before introducing our approach.

3.1 Prototypical Neural Networks

Prototypical Neural Networks (Snell et al., 2017) or PNNs are based on the computation of distance measures between seen-class prototypes to unseen ones. More specifically, a D-dimensional embedding is generated for each example $x \in \mathbb{R}^D$ using a neural network based function $f(\cdot)$ parameterized by Θ. This function enhances the encoding process with better separability properties through a non-linear mapping $f_\Theta : \mathbb{R}^D \rightarrow \mathbb{R}^M$. The M-dimensional prototype of each class is formed as the centroid c_i of their embedded support points as seen in Equation (1):

$$c_i = \frac{1}{|S_i|} \sum_{(x_j, y_j) \in S_i} f_\Theta(x_j), \qquad (1)$$

where S_i represents the set of examples labeled with class i and y_j the corresponding label of x_j. Equation (2) shows how, given a query (that is, a new and an unlabeled sample) q_i, the probability distribution over the prototypes is computed from $d(\cdot, \cdot)$, an arbitrary similarity measures function such as the squared euclidean distance or cosine similarity.

$$p_\Theta(y_i|q_i) = \frac{exp(-d(f_\Theta(q_i), c_i))}{\sum_{i'} exp(-d(f_\Theta(q_i), c_{i'}))} \qquad (2)$$

Finally, the class with the highest probability is chosen by a softmax over the distances and at optimization time, the negative log-probability $J(\Theta) = -\log p_\Theta(y_i|q_i)$ of the true class of each query point is minimized by stochastic gradient descent during an episodic learning process described in the next subsection.

3.2 Episodic learning

With the aim of generalizing unseen classes from zero to few training examples per class, PNNs is trained from a collection of N-way, k-shot classification tasks through an episodic training procedure (Vinyals et al., 2016). Specifically, each episode is one mini-batch consisting of k examples from each of the N classes (both randomly sampled), used to form a labeled (support S) and an unlabeled set of examples (query Q). The parameter k often takes a very small value, meaning we have zero-to-k labeled samples. During training, the model is fed with S to construct the class prototypes using Equation (1). Its parameters are learned in order to minimize the prototypical loss of its predictions for the examples in the given Q according to Equation (3) of Section 3.1. The evaluation is done by averaging the classification performances on query sets of many testing episodes.

3.3 Transformer-based PNNs

Studies have demonstrated that contextualized representations produced by language models such as ELMo (Peters et al., 2018) or BERT (Devlin et al., 2019) gave neural networks a better training initializations. Rather than training the initialized encoder of PNNs with feature extractors such as convolution or recurrent networks we propose to induce robustness of the pre-trained multilingual BERT (mBERT) to test the distinctiveness of the representation of each class accross languages. The embedding layer is initialized with the pre-trained mBERT embeddings and fine-tuned together with a dense linear layer that defines the embedding space where the prototype-based classifier operates. This latent space is used to learn prototypes of each class by estimating their mean and the chosen class is derived from the output layer of the network based on a softmax over distance to the class prototypes. The motivation behind fine-tuning the encoder with prototypical loss is to induce better generalization properties at test-time to new class labels not seen during training given only a few examples.

3.4 The cross-lingual way

As introduced earlier, even though recent works demonstrate strong cross-lingual transfer capability of multilingual pretrained BERT, they exhibit limitations when applied to low-resource languages (Pires et al., 2019; Conneau et al., 2020). To enable cross-lingual transfer according to our few-shot

Language	# utterances			# tokens			# intents	# slot types
	train	dev	test	train	dev	test		
English				50755	5445	9164		
Spanish				55197	5927	10338		
Portuguese				55052	5909	10228		
German	4488	490	893	51111	5517	9383	18	84
French				55909	5769	10511		
Chinese				88194	9652	16710		
Japanese				133890	14416	25939		
Hindi	1440	160	893	16422	1753	9755	17	75
Turkish	578	60	715	6132	686	7683	17	71

Table 1: Details of the MultiATIS++ corpus.

scenario, we construct mutiple episodic batches E. From the available data, we draw the task sets by sampling a subset of labels to form a support set from data in the high-resources languages and a query set from data in the low-resource languages to be evaluated. NLU data consists of utterances composed of sentence-level intent labels and sequences of slot labels annotated in BIO format (Ramshaw and Marcus, 1995) to define the boundary of slots. The N-way k-shot NLU task is then defined as follows: given an input query utterance in a new language q_i and a k-shot support set S as references, find the most appropriate intent label or slot label sequence y:

$$\underset{\theta}{argmax_E} \sum_{(q_i,y_i)\in Q} \log p_\theta(y_i|q_i,S). \tag{3}$$

4 Experiments

Our NLU experiments in cross-lingual and few-shot learning for under-resources languages are conducted on MultiATIS++ (Xu et al., 2020; Upadhyay et al., 2018) corpus, whose description follows.

4.1 The MultiATIS++ corpus

MultiATIS++ (Upadhyay et al., 2018; Xu et al., 2020) is the multilingual extension of the ATIS corpus (Hemphill et al., 1990), which belongs to the air travel planning domain. Originally in English (en), it has been human translated to 8 different other (distant and close) languages i.e., Spanish (es), German (de), French (fr), Portuguese (pt), Hindi (hi), Chinese (zh), Japanese (ja), and Turkish (tr). It contains 37,084 training examples and 7,859 test examples. Details of subsets statistics in terms of the number of utterances, intents and slots are shown in Table 1. Our main concerns about this corpus are the Hindi and Turkish portions of the data, which are smaller than the other languages, covering only a subset of intents and slots and containing extremely few labeled examples.

4.2 Models

We use the fine-tuning procedure (Devlin et al., 2019) of the original mBERT model as our baseline. In sequence-level and token-level classification tasks, it takes the final hidden states (the last layer output of the multi-head Transformer) of the first [CLS] sequence token or each individual token representation as input of the prediction layer to compute classification scores. Since we plan to use transfer learning in the context of PNNs, we fine-tune the pre-trained mBERT model together with a dense linear layer that defines the embedding space (Section 3.3).

4.3 Training configurations

We perform three sets of experiments: *target only*, *multilingual* and *multilingual zero-shot*.

- **target only**: this configuration consists of using only the target language data.

We also considered two cross-lingual classification tasks with a varying quantity of data between source and target languages to investigate the behaviour of different types of knowledge transfer.

- **multilingual**: where the training strategy aims to train a network on the concatenation of all of the nine languages and testing the model for each target language.

- **multilingual zero-shot**: where the training relies on the concatenation of all training

config.	encoder	en	es	de	zh	ja	pt	fr	hi	tr
target only	**mBERT**	98.54	**97.31**	98.43	**97.09**	**97.20**	**97.54**	**98.88**	90.93	83.36
	mBERT + PNN (5w1s)	97.46	95.14	97.18	96.35	95.53	96.80	97.11	84.95	85.17
	mBERT + PNN (5w10s)	**98.77**	96.97	**98.54**	97.0	96.64	97.42	97.98	**91.33**	**89.33**
multilingual	**mBERT**	98.42	97.98	98.59	97.65	97.45	**98.3**	98.46	95.33	**93.93**
	mBERT + PNN (5w1s)	95.33	93.71	95.93	95.89	94.42	94.00	94.78	91.4	90.91
	mBERT + PNN (5w10s)	**99.87**	**98.54**	**98.60**	**98.67**	**98.54**	**98.32**	**98.66**	**95.49**	92.61
multilingual (zero shot)	**mBERT**	96.42	**97.98**	**97.54**	96.71	**97.45**	97.42	**97.87**	**94.37**	**91.61**
	mBERT + PNN (5w1s)	93.73	92.02	93.27	95.62	91.73	93.51	93.28	90.51	89.92
	mBERT + PNN (5w10s)	**96.47**	97.87	96.86	**97.65**	96.64	**98.10**	97.45	93.17	90.67

Table 2: Averaged intent accuracies obtained with PNNs on 5-way k-shot classification $k \in [1, 10]$ (best scores are marked in bold) and baseline results.

datasets from all languages except the one we want to test.

This works only for the baseline approach (*mBERT*), but with our PNNs approach (*mBERT+PNN*), we performs few-shot learning. This means we use only a few training data in the considered language (*target only* and *multilingual* configurations).

For instance, when we evaluate our approach in the English task, we consider only a fraction of the English training dataset to train our *mBERT+PNN* model in the *target only*. In the *multilingual* configuration, our few-shot approach (*mBERT+PNN*) is trained using only a fraction of all the examples provided for each language.

4.4 Training details

For all the baseline models built, we use the publicly available mBERT models pre-trained on over a hundred different languages (Devlin et al., 2019). We trained it using 20 epochs like Xu et al. (2020).

PNNs training was done using a number of 1000 episodes using Euclidean distance as suggested by the original authors (Snell et al., 2017). We consider a configuration parameter and tried a 5-way k-shot intent classification with $k \in [1, 10]$ (5w1s and 5w10s) and 5-way 10-shots slot filling.

For all approaches we use AdamW optimizer (Loshchilov and Hutter, 2017) using a learning rate of 5e-5 to apply gradients with respect to the loss and weight decay.

All results are reported using the average performances of over 30 runs for intent classification and over 5 runs for slot filling (fewer amount of runs because of higher training time).

4.5 Results

Our experimental findings are summarized in Tables 2 and 3 for the intent classification and the slot-filling tasks, respectively.

4.5.1 Intent classification results

Using the *target only* configuration, the baseline obtains optimal scores when applied to high resource languages, e.g. *English* (en), *French* (fr) or *German* (de) reaching nearly identical high scores. We obtain the highest baseline scores with an accuracy of 98.8 on the French model, followed by the English model with an accuracy of 98.5. Unlike other mainstream languages, the baseline is less accurate on under-resourced languages, with a loss of 7 to 15 points for intent classification on *Hindi* (hi) and *Turkish* (tr) respectively.

In *multilingual* configuration, baseline models perform reasonably well over all the high-resource languages with a significant performance boost due to the availability of additional data. The *mBERT + PNN (5w10s)* models outperformed the baseline for all languages, except for the Turkish (tr) language.

When transferring from all languages to an unseen one (*multilingual zero-shot* configuration) we observe the best results for the *mBERT* model, except *Portuguese* (pt) and *English* (en) languages, in which the *mBERT + PNN (5w10s)* is 0.5 points better.

Finally, within the framework of the intent classification task, the *mBERT + PNN (5w10s)* model achieves better overall performances in the *multilingual* configuration, especially in the case of under-resourced languages with a gain up to 9 points of accuracy, compared to the *target-only* configuration and an average of one point compared to the best model in the *multilingual zero-shot* configuration.

4.5.2 Slot-filling results

Slot-filling result trends in the *target only* configuration are about one point better of F1 score for the *mBERT + PNN (5w10s)* model compared to the baseline model (*mBERT*). The *mBERT + PNN*

config.	encoder	en	es	de	zh	ja	pt	fr	hi	tr
target only	**mBERT**	95.64	85.52	94.88	92.93	93.13	91.71	92.78	85.12	78.22
	mBERT + PNN (5w10s)	**95.76**	**87.40**	**95.63**	**93.45**	**93.93**	**92.22**	**93.13**	**85.70**	**82.67**
multilingual	**mBERT**	96.02	88.03	95.03	93.63	93.01	92.31	91.18	87.39	86.83
	mBERT + PNN (5w10s)	**98.40**	**92.09**	**97.12**	**95.50**	**97.24**	**95.81**	**96.80**	**89.59**	**88.39**
multilingual (zero shot)	**mBERT**	**94.10**	**87.14**	**94.23**	**92.17**	**92.61**	**91.59**	**90.79**	86.14	85.86
	mBERT + PNN (5w10s)	93.25	86.99	93.57	91.82	92.38	91.19	90.39	**87.49**	**86.83**

Table 3: Averaged slot F1s obtained with PNNs on 5-way 10-shot and baseline results (highest scores are marked in bold).

(5w10s) model even outperformed the baseline by more than 4 points of F1 in the Turkish task (tr).

We can observe the same trend in the *multilingual* configuration: our approach outperformed the baseline in all languages.

On the contrary, the *mBERT + PNN (5w10s)* fails in most of language tasks in the *multilingual zero-shot* configuration, except for the *Hindi* (hi) and the *Turkish* (tr) languages.

Finally, like the intent classification task, the *mBERT + PNN (5w10s)* model achieves better overall performance in the *multilingual* configuration for all languages.

4.6 Result analysis

First, our baseline results are on par with those obtained by Qin et al. (2019) and Xu et al. (2020) when they trained BERT-based models using only English training data (en) with intent accuracy scores of 97.5% and 96.08% while we obtain 98.5%. This is the same in our slot-filling experiment in which they report 94.7 F1 points while we obtain 95.6. This difference comes from our results averaging between 30 and 5 runs for intent classification and slot filling, while previous works only performed 5 runs. We also observe that, just like Xu et al. (2020), slot filling on *Spanish* (es) leads to lower results, similar to those obtained in our few-shot setting.

When transferring from all languages to an unseen one (*multilingual zero-shot configuration* in both tables 2 and 3) we obtained lower scores than the *multilingual* configurations. This means the multilingual representation captured in mBERT is efficient enough when data is available in several languages and none are available in the target considered language. But, in both cases, the combination of mBERT+PNN performs better when fewer data is available using the few-shot approach (the *multilingual* configuration). This means that our approach quickly adapts to the considered target language with only a few examples available and enhances the mBERT multilingual transfer learning capabilities. This is especially true in the case of slot filling with gains in terms of F1-scores ranging from 2 to 5 points.

Finally, using the mBERT baseline model, transfer learning to *French* or *German* has performance scores similar to *English* while using the *Turkish* (tr) or *Hindi* (hi) yielded significant loss. This leads us to the same conclusion as Xu et al. (2020): exploiting language interrelationships learnt with transfer learning improve the model performances. This may come from the fact that French, English and German are similar and share some vocabulary while Turkish or Hindi are dissimilar to European languages (Hock and Joseph, 2019).

A detailed inspection of the PNNs results shows that in the *target only* and in the *multilingual* configurations, there is an overall and important reduction in recall values, which is balanced by an improvement of the precision values. If we analyze deeper the mislabeled examples we can observe that applying PNNs help to prevent overlapping and annotation mismatch cases that occur in the data.

We observed that MultiAtis++ corpus seems to be a highly unbalanced labeled dataset with the number of training examples per class varying from 1 to 3300. This impacts the model performance, and it could explain why we observe a lower recall and an improvement in precision using our approach, since it is based on the reduction of the amount of data.

5 Conclusions

In this paper, we demonstrate the opportunities in leveraging mBERT-based modeling using few-shot learning for both intent classification and slot filling tasks on under-resource languages. We found that our approach model is a highly effective technique for training models for low-resource languages. This illustrates the performance gains that can be achieved by exploiting language interrelationships learnt with transfer learning, a conclusion further emphasised by the fact that multilingual results outperformed other configuration models (target only and specifically multilingual zero-shot) regardless of the approach. Overall, PNNs models outperform mBERT-based transfer learning approach, enabling us to train competitive NLU systems for under-resources languages with only a fraction of training examples.

From this work a new challenge naturally comes up and a possible direction is to adapt a few-shot setting to a joint approach of intent detection and slot filling, like in Zhang and Wang (2016), Liu and Lane (2016) and Zhang et al. (2019), which demonstrates that performing these two tasks jointly improves the performance of both of them.

References

Trapit Bansal, Rishikesh Jha, and Andrew McCallum. 2020a. Learning to few-shot learn across diverse natural language classification tasks. In *Proceedings of the 28th International Conference on Computational Linguistics*, pages 5108–5123, Barcelona, Spain (Online). International Committee on Computational Linguistics.

Trapit Bansal, Rishikesh Jha, Tsendsuren Munkhdalai, and Andrew McCallum. 2020b. Self-supervised meta-learning for few-shot natural language classification tasks. In *Proceedings of the 2020 Conference on Empirical Methods in Natural Language Processing (EMNLP)*, pages 522–534, Online. Association for Computational Linguistics.

Rinu Boney and Alexander Ilin. 2017. Semi-supervised few-shot learning with prototypical networks. In *Workshop on Meta-Learning 2017 (NIPS 2017)*.

Alexis Conneau, Kartikay Khandelwal, Naman Goyal, Vishrav Chaudhary, Guillaume Wenzek, Francisco Guzmán, Edouard Grave, Myle Ott, Luke Zettlemoyer, and Veselin Stoyanov. 2020. Unsupervised cross-lingual representation learning at scale. In *Proceedings of the 58th Annual Meeting of the Association for Computational Linguistics*, pages 8440–8451, Online. Association for Computational Linguistics.

Jacob Devlin, Ming-Wei Chang, Kenton Lee, and Kristina Toutanova. 2019. BERT: Pre-training of deep bidirectional transformers for language understanding. In *Proceedings of the 2019 Conference of the North American Chapter of the Association for Computational Linguistics: Human Language Technologies, Volume 1 (Long and Short Papers)*, pages 4171–4186, Minneapolis, Minnesota. Association for Computational Linguistics.

Zi-Yi Dou, Keyi Yu, and Antonios Anastasopoulos. 2019. Investigating meta-learning algorithms for low-resource natural language understanding tasks. In *Proceedings of the 2019 Conference on Empirical Methods in Natural Language Processing and the 9th International Joint Conference on Natural Language Processing (EMNLP-IJCNLP)*, pages 1192–1197, Hong Kong, China. Association for Computational Linguistics.

Emmanuel Ferreira, Bassam Jabaian, and Fabrice Lefèvre. 2015. Online adaptative zero-shot learning spoken language understanding using word-embedding. *IEEE International Conference on Acoustics, Speech and SP*.

Stanislav Fort. 2017. Gaussian prototypical networks for few-shot learning on omniglot. In *Workshop on Bayesian Deep Learning (NIPS 2017)*.

Alexander Fritzler, Varvara Logacheva, and Maksim Kretov. 2019. Few-shot classification in named entity recognition task. In *Proceedings of the 34th ACM/SIGAPP Symposium on Applied Computing*, SAC '19, page 993–1000, New York, NY, USA. Association for Computing Machinery.

Jianfeng Gao, Michel Galley, and Lihong Li. 2018. Neural approaches to conversational ai. In *The 41st International ACM SIGIR Conference on Research and Development in Information Retrieval*, SIGIR '18, page 1371–1374, New York, NY, USA. Association for Computing Machinery.

Jiatao Gu, Yong Wang, Yun Chen, Victor O. K. Li, and Kyunghyun Cho. 2018. Meta-learning for low-resource neural machine translation. In *Proceedings of the 2018 Conference on Empirical Methods in Natural Language Processing*, pages 3622–3631, Brussels, Belgium. Association for Computational Linguistics.

Charles T Hemphill, John J Godfrey, and George R Doddington. 1990. The atis spoken language systems pilot corpus. In *Speech and Natural Language: Proceedings of a Workshop Held at Hidden Valley, Pennsylvania, June 24-27, 1990*.

Hans Henrich Hock and Brian D Joseph. 2019. *Language history, language change, and language relationship: An introduction to historical and comparative linguistics*. Walter de Gruyter GmbH & Co KG.

Yutai Hou, Zhihan Zhou, Yijia Liu, Ning Wang, Wanxiang Che, Han Liu, and Ting Liu. 2019. Few-shot sequence labeling with label dependency transfer. *CoRR*, abs/1906.08711.

Gregory R. Koch. 2015. Siamese neural networks for one-shot image recognition. In *ICML Deep Learning Workshop*.

Bing Liu and Ian Lane. 2016. Attention-based recurrent neural network models for joint intent detection and slot filling. *INTERSPEECH*, pages 685–689.

Ilya Loshchilov and Frank Hutter. 2017. Fixing weight decay regularization in adam. *CoRR*, abs/1711.05101.

Matthew E. Peters, Mark Neumann, Mohit Iyyer, Matt Gardner, Christopher Clark, Kenton Lee, and Luke Zettlemoyer. 2018. Deep contextualized word representations. In *Proc. of NAACL*.

Telmo Pires, Eva Schlinger, and Dan Garrette. 2019. How multilingual is multilingual BERT? In *Proceedings of the 57th Annual Meeting of the Association for Computational Linguistics*, pages 4996–5001, Florence, Italy. Association for Computational Linguistics.

Libo Qin, Wanxiang Che, Yangming Li, Haoyang Wen, and Ting Liu. 2019. A stack-propagation framework with token-level intent detection for spoken language understanding. In *Proceedings of the 2019 Conference on Empirical Methods in Natural Language Processing and the 9th International Joint Conference on Natural Language Processing (EMNLP-IJCNLP)*, pages 2078–2087, Hong Kong, China. Association for Computational Linguistics.

Lance Ramshaw and Mitch Marcus. 1995. Text chunking using transformation-based learning. In *Third Workshop on Very Large Corpora*.

Mengye Ren, Sachin Ravi, Eleni Triantafillou, Jake Snell, Kevin Swersky, Josh B. Tenenbaum, Hugo Larochelle, and Richard S. Zemel. 2018. Meta-learning for semi-supervised few-shot classification. In *International Conference on Learning Representations*.

Jake Snell, Kevin Swersky, and Richard Zemel. 2017. Prototypical networks for few-shot learning. In I. Guyon, U. V. Luxburg, S. Bengio, H. Wallach, R. Fergus, S. Vishwanathan, and R. Garnett, editors, *Advances in Neural Information Processing Systems 30*, pages 4077–4087. Curran Associates, Inc.

Shengli Sun, Qingfeng Sun, Kevin Zhou, and Tengchao Lv. 2019. Hierarchical attention prototypical networks for few-shot text classification. In *Proceedings of the 2019 Conference on Empirical Methods in Natural Language Processing and the 9th International Joint Conference on Natural Language Processing (EMNLP-IJCNLP)*, pages 476–485, Hong Kong, China. Association for Computational Linguistics.

Shyam Upadhyay, Manaal Faruqui, Gokhan Tür, Hakkani-Tür Dilek, and Larry Heck. 2018. (almost) zero-shot cross-lingual spoken language understanding. In *2018 IEEE International Conference on Acoustics, Speech and Signal Processing (ICASSP)*, pages 6034–6038. IEEE.

Joaquin Vanschoren. 2019. *Meta-Learning*, pages 35–61. Springer International Publishing, Cham.

Ashish Vaswani, Noam Shazeer, Niki Parmar, Jakob Uszkoreit, Llion Jones, Aidan N. Gomez, undefinedukasz Kaiser, and Illia Polosukhin. 2017. Attention is all you need. In *Proceedings of the 31st International Conference on Neural Information Processing Systems*, NIPS'17, page 6000–6010, Red Hook, NY, USA. Curran Associates Inc.

Oriol Vinyals, Charles Blundell, Timothy Lillicrap, Koray Kavukcuoglu, and Daan Wierstra. 2016. Matching networks for one shot learning. In *Proceedings of the 30th International Conference on Neural Information Processing Systems*, NIPS'16, page 3637–3645, Red Hook, NY, USA. Curran Associates Inc.

Wei Wang, Vincent W. Zheng, Han Yu, and Chunyan Miao. 2019. A survey of zero-shot learning: Settings, methods, and applications. *ACM Trans. Intell. Syst. Technol.*, 10(2).

Yong Wang, Xiao-Ming Wu, Qimai Li, Jiatao Gu, Wangmeng Xiang, Lei Zhang, and Victor O. K. Li. 2018. Large margin few-shot learning. *CoRR*, abs/1807.02872.

Weijia Xu, Batool Haider, and Saab Mansour. 2020. End-to-end slot alignment and recognition for cross-lingual NLU. In *Proceedings of the 2020 Conference on Empirical Methods in Natural Language Processing (EMNLP)*, pages 5052–5063, Online. Association for Computational Linguistics.

Majid Yazdani and James Henderson. 2015. A model of zero-shot learning of spoken language understanding. In *Proceedings of the 2015 Conference on Empirical Methods in Natural Language Processing*, pages 244–249, Lisbon, Portugal. Association for Computational Linguistics.

Biao Zhang, Philip Williams, Ivan Titov, and Rico Sennrich. 2020. Improving massively multilingual neural machine translation and zero-shot translation. In *Proceedings of the 58th Annual Meeting of the Association for Computational Linguistics*, pages 1628–1639, Online. Association for Computational Linguistics.

Chenwei Zhang, Yaliang Li, Nan Du, Wei Fan, and Philip Yu. 2019. Joint slot filling and intent detection via capsule neural networks. In *Proceedings of the 57th Annual Meeting of the Association for Computational Linguistics*, pages 5259–5267, Florence, Italy. Association for Computational Linguistics.

Xiaodong Zhang and Houfeng Wang. 2016. A joint model of intent determination and slot filling for spoken language understanding. In *Proceedings of the Twenty-Fifth International Joint Conference on Artificial Intelligence*, IJCAI'16, page 2993–2999. AAAI Press.

Meta-Learning for Few-Shot Named Entity Recognition

Cyprien de Lichy
Amazon, Alexa AI
101 Main St
Cambridge, MA, USA
cllichy@amazon.com

Hadrien Glaude
Amazon, Alexa AI
101 Main St
Cambridge, MA, USA
hglaude@amazon.com

William Campbell
Amazon, Alexa AI
101 Main St
Cambridge, MA, USA
cmpw@amazon.com

Abstract

Meta-learning has recently been proposed to learn models and algorithms that can generalize from a handful of examples. However, applications to structured prediction and textual tasks pose challenges for meta-learning algorithms. In this paper, we apply two meta-learning algorithms, Prototypical Networks and Reptile, to few-shot Named Entity Recognition (NER), including a method for incorporating language model pre-training and Conditional Random Fields (CRF). We propose a task generation scheme for converting classical NER datasets into the few-shot setting, for both training and evaluation. Using three public datasets, we show these meta-learning algorithms outperform a reasonable fine-tuned BERT baseline. In addition, we propose a novel combination of Prototypical Networks and Reptile.

1 Introduction

The usage of Natural Language Understanding (NLU) technologies has spread widely in the last decade thanks to the recent jump in accuracy due to Deep Neural Networks (DNN). In addition, DNN libraries have made easier than ever the productization of NLU technologies. Applications have spread in quality and quantity with the broadened usage of chat bots by customer services, the development of virtual assistants (e.g. Amazon Alexa, Google Home, Apple's Siri or Microsoft Cortana) and the need of document parsing (e.g. medical reports, receipts, tweets, news articles) for data extraction. These applications often rely on NER to locate and classify named entities in text. NER aims at extracting named entities (e.g. "artist", "city" or "restaurant_type") from a sequence of words. This problem is often approached (McCallum and Li, 2003) as a sequence labeling task that assigns to each word one of the different entity types or the "other" label for words that do not belong to any named entity.

The wide variety of applications has made the need for domain specific data the main bottleneck to train or fine-tune statistical models. This data is often acquired by running the application itself and collecting user inputs. Then, the annotation effort can be significantly reduced using active learning (Peshterliev et al., 2019) or semi-supervised learning (Cho et al., 2019b). However, to reach this bootstrapping stage, statistical models have to perform reasonably before being exposed to users. Indeed, low performing models can turn away users or shift the input distribution as users lose engagement with features that do not work.

Transfer learning (Do and Gaspers, 2019) is an efficient way to cope with the data shortage by extracting task-agnostic high-level features. In particular, for NER, fine-tuning language models (Peters et al., 2018; Devlin et al., 2018; Conneau and Lample, 2019) allows achieving state-of-the-art performances (Wang et al., 2018a). However, fine tuning to specific tasks still requires a reasonable amount of data, especially for a task like NER with large structured label spaces. In certain cases, for example to learn personalized models or for products with restricted budgets, only a handful "reference" examples are available. As we will show, in such scenarios where very few training examples are available, transfer learning has its limitations.

Few-Shot Learning (FSL) is a rapidly growing field of research, reviewed in Section 2, that aims at building models that can generalize from very few examples as detailed in (Miller et al., 2000; Koch et al., 2015). This area of research is motivated by the ability of humans and animals to learn object categories from few examples, and at a rapid pace. In particular, inductive bias (Mitchell, 1980) has been identified for a long time as a key component to fast generalization to new inputs. Previous work has suggested that meta-learning (Schmidhuber, 1987) can help quickly acquire knowledge from few examples by learning an inductive bias from

Proceedings of the 1st Workshop on Meta Learning and Its Applications to Natural Language Processing (MetaNLP 2021), pages 44–58
Bangkok, Thailand (online), August 5, 2021.

a distribution of similar tasks but with different categories.

In this paper, we leverage recent progress made in transfer learning and meta-learning to address few-shot NER. First, we provide a novel definition of few-shot NER in Section 3.1 where few-shot NER aims at building models to solve NER tasks given only a handful of labeled utterances per entity type. Then, in Section 3.2, we define a transfer learning baseline consisting in fine-tuning a pre-trained language model (BERT Devlin et al., 2018) using only few examples. In addition, we introduce an extension of Prototypical Networks (Snell et al., 2017), a metric-based model, capable of handling structured prediction. In particular, we detail how it can be combined with Conditional Random Fields (CRF) (Lafferty et al., 2001). In Section 3.3, we explain how such models can be trained using meta-learning. In addition, we introduce the application of an optimization-based algorithm to NER, Reptile (Nichol et al., 2018), capable of meta-learning a better initialization model. We also propose a novel combination of Prototypical Networks and Reptile that brings the best of both worlds, performance and the ability to handle a different number of classes between training and testing. Finally, in Section 3.4, we show how to generate diverse and realistic FSL tasks, corresponding to the bootstrapping phase of NER systems, from classical NER datasets either for meta-training or meta-testing.

In Section 4, we conduct an extensive evaluation on three public datasets: SNIPS (Coucke et al., 2018), Task Oriented Parsing (TOP Gupta et al., 2018) and Google Schema-Guided Dialogue State Tracking (DSTC8 Rastogi et al., 2019) where we compare our three meta-learning approaches to the transfer learning baseline. Source code and datasets will be made available online.

2 Related Work

Few-shot learning has been addressed using metric-learning, data augmentation and meta-learning. Metric-learning relies on learning how to compare pairs (Koch et al., 2015) or triplets (Ye and Guo, 2018) of examples and use that distance function to classify new examples. Data augmentation through deformation has been known to be effective in image recognition tasks. More advanced approaches rely on generative models (Gupta, 2019; Hou et al., 2018; Zhao et al., 2019; Guu et al., 2018; Yoo et al., 2018), paraphrasing (Cho et al., 2019a) or machine translation (Johnson et al., 2019). All the methods above rely somewhat on transfer learning with the hope that representations learned in one domain can be applied to another one.

Meta-learning takes a different approach by trying to learn an inductive bias on a distribution of similar tasks that can be utilized to build models from very few examples. There are four common approaches. Model-based meta-learning relies on a meta-model to update or predict the weights of a task specific model (Munkhdalai and Yu, 2017). Generation-based meta-learning (Zhang et al., 2018; Schwartz et al., 2018) produces generative models able to quickly learn how to generate task specific examples, often in the feature space (Kumar et al., 2019). The other two approaches are explained in detail below.

Metric-based meta-learning is similar to nearest neighbors algorithms. In particular, several metric-based meta-learning methods (Vinyals et al., 2016; Snell et al., 2017; Rippel et al., 2015) have been proposed for few-shot classification where an embedding space or a metric is meta-learned and used at test time to embed the few support examples of new categories and the queries. Prediction is performed by comparing embedded queries and support examples. In many cases, the loss function is based on a distance between the supports and the queries. More advanced losses have been proposed in (Triantafillou et al., 2017; Wang et al., 2018b; Sung et al., 2018) for example based on triplet, ranking and max-margin losses. One of the issues with approaches listed above is that the distance is the same for all categories. Thus, Fort (2017); Hilliard et al. (2018) have explored scaling the distance for new categories.

Optimization-based meta-learning explicitly meta-learns an update rule or weight initialization that enables fast learning during meta-testing. In Ravi and Larochelle (2017), they use an LSTM meta-learner trained to be an optimization algorithm. However, this approach incurs a high complexity. In Finn et al. (2017), the authors explored with success using ordinary gradient descent in the learner and meta-learning the initialization weights. However, this algorithm named MAML, requires to back propagate through gradient updates and so rely on second order derivatives which are expensive to compute. They also proposed an algorithm, FOMAML, relying only on first order derivatives. This idea has been extended by Nichol et al. (2018) to propose an algorithm, Reptile, that does not need a training-test split for each task as explained in Section 3.3. Note that, Triantafillou et al. (2019) gives an overview of many meta-learning algorithms and propose a set of benchmarks to evaluate them. Finally, instead of just learning a model initialization, Li et al. (2017) propose to learn a full-stack Stochastic Gradient Descent (SGD), including update direction, and learning rate.

Few-Shot Learning on textual data has been explored recently, mostly for text classification tasks. Yu et al. (2018) propose to meta-learn a set of distances and learn a task-specific weighted combination of those. Jiang et al. (2018) build on top of MAML and attention mechanisms to propose an algorithm for text classification. Geng et al. (2019) focuses on sentiment and intent classification. Cheng et al. (2019) propose to use metric-based meta-learning to learn task-specific metrics that can handle imbalanced datasets. Recently, Bansal et al. (2019) proposed a new optimization-based meta-learning algorithm, LEOPARD, that outperforms strong baselines on several text classification problems (entity typing, natural language inference, sentiment analysis). Few-shot relation classification has also attracted some attention in the past two years, thanks to Han et al. (2018) who proposed a new dataset and using Prototypical Networks. Several works built on top of this to combine Prototypical Networks with attention models (Sun et al., 2019; Ye and Ling, 2019).

NER has been addressed in several works. In (Fritzler et al., 2019; Yang and Katiyar, 2020) the task of interest consists of recognizing one class of named entities, for tag set extension or domain transfer. In our work, we extend the N-way K-shot setting to structured prediction. (Hou et al., 2020) propose a CRF with coarse-grained transitions between abstract classes. In (Krone et al., 2020) the authors propose a task sampling algorithm based on intents which can result in leakage between meta-training and meta-testing sets. In (Hofer et al., 2018) the authors don't use pre-trained language models. As we will show subsequently our work differs significantly from those. First, our task sampling method, that can generate a very large amount of tasks, is key to learn efficiently an inductive bias. Second, we utilize pre-trained language models. Third, using a fine-grained CRF, amenable to meta-learning, our model can learn sequential dependencies between labels. Fourth, we fine-tune our meta-learned Prototypical Network per task and even utilize optimization-based meta-learning to improve the fine-tuning. Those contributions are central in achieving the best performance on few-shot NER as shown in Section 4.

3 Few-Shot Named Entity Recognition

3.1 Task Definition

We define the few-shot NER problem by describing what is a task. A task is defined by a set of N target entity types (examples of entity types could be "song", "city" or "date"), a small training set of $N \times K$ utterances (with their labels) called support set and another disjoint set of labeled utterances called query set. Similarly to Triantafillou et al. (2019), we refer to this setting as N-way-K-shot with the difference that we have a total of $N \times K$ support utterances rather than K examples for each of the N entity types, which is not feasible as one utterance might contain several entities. Thus, the number of mentions per entity type can be imbalanced. In addition, the support set follows the same distribution as the query set. Evaluation is performed by sampling a set of tasks from the meta-testing set. For each task, an NER model is learned from the support set. This model is evaluated on the query set. The performance is finally averaged across tasks. During meta-training, an additional set of meta-training tasks is available with disjoint entity types from the meta-testing set. Queries are used to train the meta-model. At meta-testing, this meta-model is tailored to the task using the support examples as mentioned above.

3.2 Prototypical Networks for NER

This paper builds on top of Prototypical Networks, introduced by Snell et al. (2017). Their model embeds support and query examples into a vector space. Then, one prototype per category is computed by taking the mean of its supports. Finally, queries are compared to prototypes using the euclidean distance. The distances are converted to probabilities using a Gibbs distribution. The model is meta-trained to predict the query labels using only few examples. This Section details the architecture of Prototypical Networks for sequence labeling. The next Section explains how the embedding function is meta-learned. Without meta-learning the architecture of Prototypical Networks does not bring any advantage over classical ones.

For a sequence labeling task, like NER, the difference is that to each word is assigned one label. Let $S = \{(\mathbf{x}^1, \mathbf{y}^1), \ldots, (\mathbf{x}^n, \mathbf{y}^n)\}$ be a small support set of n labeled sequences where $\mathbf{x}^i = (x_1^i, \ldots, x_L^i)$ is an utterance of length L and $\mathbf{y}^i = (y_1^i, \ldots, y_L^i)$ a sequence of entity labels. For each entity type k, we compute a prototype c_k by embedding all words tagged as k using an embedding function f_θ where θ represents the meta-learned parameters. The fundamental difference with the common implementation of Prototypical Networks is that the embedding function f_θ utilizes the context of the current word to compute its representation in a vector space. Although, we should formally note $f_\theta(x_j^i; \mathbf{x}^i)$ the representation of x_j^i in the embedding space, we will just write $f_\theta(x_j^i)$ in the sequel to not overload equations. Thus, prototypes are defined by

$$c_k = \frac{1}{|S_k|} \sum_{x \in S_k} f_\theta(x), \tag{1}$$

where $S_k = \{x_j^i \mid y_j^i = k, (\mathbf{x}^i, \mathbf{y}^i) \in S\}$, i.e. the set of all tokens with a particular label k. Note that we compute one prototype per entity type and also one for "other". As mentioned in Section 5, we leave better handling of "other" for future work.

In this paper, we use BERT to generate embeddings for each word. More specifically, we used the pre-trained English BERT Base uncased model from (Wolf et al., 2019). This BERT model has 12 layers, 768 hidden states, and 12 heads. Then, we followed recommendation from Souza et al. (2019) to fine-tune BERT. Since BERT uses WordPiece sub-word units and NER labels are aligned to words, we elected to pick the last sub-word representation of a word as the final word representation. Then, we sum the outputs of the last 4 layers to get a word-level representation and then add dropout and a linear layer. [1] For our baseline model, the linear layer output size is the number of entity types plus "other". When using Prototypical Networks, the linear layer output size is 64. Then, distances to prototypes are computed for every word, giving the same output size than for the baseline model.

Finally, in our experiments, we tried two different decoders. For the first one, we simply feed the distances into a SoftMax layer and use the negative log-likelihood (NLL) summed over all positions for the loss function, as follow,

$$p(y_t = k \mid \mathbf{x}) = \frac{e^{-\|f_\theta(x_t) - c_k\|^2}}{\sum_{k'} e^{-\|f_\theta(x_t) - c_{k'}\|^2}}, \tag{2}$$

$$p(\mathbf{y} \mid \mathbf{x}) = \prod_t p(y_t \mid \mathbf{x}, \{c_k\}). \tag{3}$$

For our second decoder, we use a CRF, as Lample et al. (2016) have shown they are effective for NER when combined with neural networks. Using a CRF instead of making independent tagging decisions allows to model the dependencies between labels by considering a transition score between labels in addition to the standard emission scores to obtain a probability distribution,

$$p(\mathbf{y} \mid \mathbf{x}) = \frac{\exp\left(\sum_t \left[U(x_t, y_t) + T(y_t, y_{t+1})\right]\right)}{\mathcal{Z}(\mathbf{x})}, \tag{4}$$

$$Z(x) = \sum_{\mathbf{y}'} \exp\left(\sum_t U(x_t, y_t') + T(y_t', y_{t+1}')\right) \tag{5}$$

where, T is a transition matrix, U the emission network and $\mathcal{Z}$ the partition function - a normalization factor used so that the probabilities sum to 1, equal to the sum of the scores over all label sequences. The loss function is the standard NLL. The emission network is the same as the SoftMax decoder.

For our baseline, the transition matrix is just a parameter of our network. However, estimating transitions between labels in the FSL setting is very prone to over-fitting as many transition pairs are likely to be absent from the limited training data. This intuition will be confirmed empirically in Section 4. Hence, we make use of prototypes and transfer learning to estimate the transition matrix. More specifically,

$$U(x_t, y_t) = -\|f_\theta(x_t) - c_{y_t}\|^2 \text{ and} \tag{6}$$

$$T(y_t, y_{t+1}) = g_\psi(c_{y_t}, c_{y_{t+1}}), \tag{7}$$

where the weights ψ of our neural network g are learned across tasks during meta-training and eventually fine-tuned during meta-testing. In our experiments, g is implemented as a feed-forward neural

[1] In our experiments, we also tried an alternative architecture consisting of a frozen BERT model topped with three ELU-activation linear layers with dropout (Clevert et al., 2016), motivated by the fact that fine-tuning a large capacity model with very few examples might degrade the performances. As the first architecture worked better by a significant margin for the baseline, we did not pursue further this alternative.

network on stacked prototype representation with one hidden layer of size 64 and ELU activation function. Looking only at the learning of the transition matrix during meta-training, this setting is equivalent to a standard training procedure that uses classes, represented by prototypes, as training examples and tries to predict transitions between them. Hence, we rely on the generalization capability of our transition DNN during meta-testing to handle new classes. We will see in Section 4, that using our Prototypical CRF decoder is very beneficial compared to a standard CRF.

3.3 Meta-Learning

In this Section, we introduce meta-learning and how it can be used to meta-learn initialization weights for the baseline architecture using Reptile, the embedding function in Prototypical Networks or both. In most cases, meta-learning algorithms, i.e. algorithms that learn how to learn, are typically comprised of two processes. The inner process is a traditional learning process capable of learning quickly using only a small number of task-specific examples. The outer loop, or meta-learning loop, slowly learns the inductive bias across a set of tasks. Thus, the objective of the outer loop is to improve generalization during the inner learning process. This is often achieved thanks to a meta-model. For Prototypical Networks the meta-model is the embedding function that defines the prototypes and the distance. For Reptile, the meta-model are the initialization weights that will be fine-tuned during meta-testing. During meta-testing, task specific models are derived from the meta-model and the support examples, for example by building prototypes or by gradient descent. Then, all queries are used to evaluate the task-specific model.

Meta-training runs in episodes. For each episode, a task or a batch of tasks is sampled. In our setting, we are only considering one task at a time. Then, from the current meta-model, a task specific model is built using the inner process and the support examples. The loss is computed using the queries and back-propagated through the inner process to update the meta-model. Good performance is often achieved when the inner process at meta-training and meta-testing are alike.

In the case of Prototypical Networks for sequence labeling, the meta-learner learns a representation amenable to generalization where queries can be compared to prototypes built from few support examples. Hence, the inner process just builds one prototype per entity type $k \in \mathcal{E}$, where $\mathcal{E}$ is the set of entity types for this task (including "other") as described in Algorithm 1.

Algorithm 1 ProtoNet

```
INITIALIZE θ
while has not converged do
    E, S, Q ← SAMPLETASK(T, K, N)
    for all entity type k in E do
        c_k ← 1/|S_k| Σ_{x∈S_k} f_θ(x) as in eq. (1)
    end for
    L ← NLL(p, BATCH(Q)) where p is defined
    in eq. (3) or eq. (4)
    θ ← UPDATE(θ, ∂L/∂θ)
end while
```

During meta-testing, we can simply compute the prototypes from the support examples as in eq. (1), in that case training is done without any backpropagation. However, in our experiments, see Section 4, we found that fine-tuning the meta-model using the task-specific supports was improving the performance. To fine-tune the model we further split the supports into two subsets using 80% to build the prototypes and the remaining to compute the loss and backpropagating it to update the model. By introducing this additional fine-tuning step at test time, the inner process now differs between meta-training and meta-testing. Similarly, for our baseline, we fine-tune our BERT-based model using the support utterances at meta-test time. In both cases, to better align meta-training and meta-testing, we turned to optimization-based meta-learning. Optimization-based meta-learning encompasses methods where the inner process consists in fine-tuning the meta-model. Back-propagating through the inner optimization loop allows computing a meta-gradient to update the meta-model as done in MAML. However doing so requires to compute second order derivatives. Instead, Reptile builds a first order approximation as shown in Algorithm 2, where T is the number of steps used to compute the first order approximation.

In addition, for MAML, the inner-loop optimization uses support examples, whereas the loss is computed using the queries. This way MAML optimizes for generalization. However, Reptile does not require a query-support split to compute the meta-gradient, which makes it a better candidate to be combined with Prototypical Networks.

Algorithm 2 Reptile

```
INITIALIZE θ_0
while has not converged do
    E, S, Q ← SAMPLETASK(T, K, N)
    for t ∈ 1..T do
        L ← NLL(p, BATCH(S ∪ Q))
        θ_t ← UPDATE(θ_{t-1}, ∂L/∂θ_{t-1})
    end for
    θ_0 ← UPDATE(θ_0, θ_T − θ_0)
end while
```

To combine MAML and Prototypical Networks, Triantafillou et al. (2019) use the same support examples to compute prototypes and to compute the loss for backpropagation in the MAML inner loop. However, having two disjoints support sets is preferable so as not to compare examples to prototypes computed from the same examples. With Reptile, this issue is alleviated altogether as shown in Algorithm 3.

Algorithm 3 Proto-Reptile

```
INITIALIZE θ_0
while has not converged do
    E, S, Q ← SAMPLETASK(T, K, N)
    for all entity type k in E do
        c_k ← 1/|S_k| Σ_{x∈S_k} f_θ(x) as in eq. (1)
    end for
    for t ∈ 1..T do
        L ← NLL(p, BATCH(Q))
        θ_t ← UPDATE(θ_{t-1}, ∂L/∂θ_{t-1})
    end for
    θ_0 ← UPDATE(θ_0, θ_T − θ_0)
end while
```

In Algorithms 1 to 3, NLL stands for the negative log-likelihood function, BATCH for a function that samples a batch. $\mathcal{T}$ is the training set, K the number of shots, N the number of ways, S the support set and Q the query set, T is the number of steps in Reptile. In addition, UPDATE can be any optimizer, such that SGD or Adam (Kingma and Ba, 2015). In our experiments, we use Adam in Algorithm 1, and in the inner loop of Algorithm 3. For the outer loop of Algorithm 3, we use the classical SGD update rule without any momentum. Note that, each loop has its own learning rate. In addition, we used different learning rates for the BERT encoder and the rest of the network.

3.4 Generating Tasks for Training or Testing

To generate training and testing data from classical NER datasets, we first randomly partition entity types and utterances to either the train, the validation or the test split. Utterances are assigned based on the majority split of its entity types, counted per word. In other words, for a given utterance we count the number of words for entity types that are in each split and utterances are assigned to the partition that was the most represented in that utterance. In case of tie, priority is given to the test split, then the valid split and finally to the train split. Any entity contained in an utterance that is not in the corresponding partition is replaced with "other" to ensure, e.g., no test entities are seen during training. Finally, utterances with no entities are dropped. This task sampling procedure can both simulate a realistic few-shot NER testing setting and generate a large number of training tasks. During meta-training, having a diverse enough distribution of training tasks is crucial to learn an inductive bias effectively, similarly to having many examples helps generalization.

4 Experiments

4.1 Datasets and Pre-Processing

Experiments were conducted on the SNIPS (Coucke et al., 2018), Task Oriented Parsing (TOP Gupta et al., 2018) and Google Schema-Guided Dialogue State Tracking (DSTC8 Rastogi et al., 2019) datasets. For evaluation, we sampled 50 tasks from the meta-test set to average the Micro F1 across tasks. We use the Micro F1 metric introduced in (Tjong Kim Sang, 2002) that does not give any credit to partial matches. For SNIPS, we combine B and I labels from the BIO (Ramshaw and Marcus, 1995) encoding into a single label. For DSTC8, we used utterances from both the system and user, we discarded utterances containing more than 1 frame. For the TOP dataset, which contains hierarchical labels for slot labels and intents, we used the finest-grained entity types (the leaf nodes) as labels and discarded intents. We did not adhere to any pre-defined train, valid and test partitions, but followed our own task-based procedure defined in Section 3.4. Additional details about data preparation and datasets statistics are given in the appendix.

4.2 Hyper-Parameter Tuning

During meta-testing, only a few support examples are available to fine-tune the task specific model derived from the meta-model. As such, it is impractical to set aside some as a validation set for early stopping. However, early stopping is really important in the few-shot setting as the model can easily overfit. Hence, we find the best number of fine-tuning epochs on the validation split and then use it during meta-testing. For the baseline, this is the only purpose of meta-training.

For each algorithm (Baseline, ProtoNet, Reptile, Proto-Reptile) and decoder (SoftMax or CRF), we conducted an extensive hyper-parameter optimization (HPO) procedure using the built-in Bayesian optimization of AWS SageMaker (Amazon Web Services, 2017) on the SNIPS meta-validation dataset. The search space, the best hyper-parameters, the best performance and the training times are given in the appendix. We used the same hyper-parameters in all our experiments. However, after HPO, we retrained all our models with a number of meta updates and updates manually tuned per algorithm on each meta-validation dataset to avoid (meta-)stopping too early. All results on the meta-validation set and training times can be found in the appendix.

4.3 Results

We conducted four types of experiments. First, we compared all approaches on the three datasets using $N = 4$ and $K = 10$ in Table 1. Fine-tuning produces the largest gains, especially on SNIPS and TOP (less on DSTC8). Indeed, starting with the baseline, fine-tuning a pre-trained BERT model with aggressive dropout (0.9) is quite effective. Chen et al. (2019); Tian et al. (2020) also observed that transfer learning baselines are often competitive and neglected in FSL works. We also evaluated Prototypical Networks without fine-tuning at meta-test time using the supports. We refer to those algorithms by ProtoNet* and Proto-Reptile*. Compared to previous work on image recognition (Chen et al., 2019), fine-tuning the Prototypical Network seems to be extremely beneficial for textual application that builds on top of pre-trained language models instead of solely building the prototypes. Hence, combining optimization-based and metric-based meta-learning sounds a natural idea.

Comparing ProtoNet and Reptile, we can see that the Prototypical Network architecture helps generalization in the low data regime thanks to being instance-based. In addition, gains are even larger when combined with a CRF, with or without fine-tuning, in particular on DSTC8. Indeed, the CRF can only be slightly beneficial compared to using a simple SoftMax decoder for the Baseline and for Reptile. On the other hand, using our Prototypical CRF achieves a significant jump in Micro F1, especially on DSTC8, demonstrating that the transition network can generalize to new classes unseen at meta-training. We believe that, Reptile's meta-learning approach is inefficient because the initialization weights of the transition matrix do not have enough capacity to encode an inductive bias. Maybe other optimization-based meta-learning methods relying on external neural networks with larger capacity, e.g. a network that predicts the update direction as proposed by Li et al. (2017), could be more efficient than relying solely on the initialization weights to learn the inductive bias.

Comparing Reptile to Baseline and Proto-Reptile to ProtoNet, we see that optimization-based meta-learning can help significantly with fine-tuning. Although the gap is less impressive between Proto-Reptile to ProtoNet, Proto-Reptile obtains the best result in most cases. Comparing results between datasets, DSTC8 high diversity seems to be a real game changer for meta-learning. Indeed, all meta-learning approaches achieve twice or more the Baseline Micro F1. We argue that, the richer the task distribution, the better the learned inductive bias.

In our second experiment, we evaluated cross-domain transfer learning of the inductive bias by meta-training on TOP or DTSC8 and meta-testing on SNIPS. Note that early stopping was calibrated on the source meta-validation set, which gives an unfair advantage to the baseline to avoid overfitting. On inductive bias transfer, Proto and Proto-Reptile outperform the baseline by a small but statistically significant margin. As already observed, DTCS8 diversity is better to learn an inductive bias that can transfer across domain. Showing that task diversity is key to meta-learning.

In the third experiment, we varied N and K on the DSTC8 dataset to observe the performance gap between Proto-Reptile and the baseline. Results are plotted in the first row of Figure 1. As expected, Micro F1 increases when there are fewer entity types to discriminate (smaller N) or more examples

Meta-train dataset		SNIPS	TOP	DSTC8	TOP	DSTC8
Meta-test dataset		SNIPS	SNIPS	SNIPS	TOP	DSTC8
Baseline	CRF	76.84 ± 3.75	N/A	N/A	51.09 ± 5.06	34.57 ± 4.70
	SoftMax	73.68 ± 3.41	N/A	N/A	48.18 ± 4.78	35.18 ± 3.27
ProtoNet	CRF	**89.67 ± 0.63**	78.78 ± 1.14	82.88 ± 0.99	64.99 ± 3.51	75.69 ± 2.53
	SoftMax	87.11 ± 1.26	78.49 ± 1.37	80.37 ± 1.51	62.08 ± 3.58	66.39 ± 2.73
ProtoNet*	CRF	58.56 ± 1.78	44.75 ± 1.92	52.97 ± 2.04	29.53 ± 4.40	71.49 ± 3.81
	SoftMax	54.52 ± 1.82	43.23 ± 2.08	45.77 ± 1.26	28.34 ± 3.74	60.07 ± 2.62
Reptile	CRF	80.08 ± 3.58	74.85 ± 3.47	75.06 ± 3.32	57.18 ± 6.02	70.50 ± 2.60
	SoftMax	80.00 ± 3.51	75.82 ± 3.48	75.14 ± 3.45	57.64 ± 5.96	71.06 ± 2.77
Proto-Reptile	CRF	89.20 ± 0.89	**80.50 ± 1.24**	**82.96 ± 1.19**	**67.34 ± 3.87**	**78.96 ± 1.60**
	SoftMax	88.09 ± 0.90	77.53 ± 1.30	79.83 ± 1.74	64.06 ± 3.75	62.56 ± 2.14
Proto-Reptile*	CRF	49.98 ± 2.02	48.09 ± 1.85	51.63 ± 1.37	33.78 ± 3.41	75.22 ± 2.44
	SoftMax	58.41 ± 1.63	44.14 ± 1.88	37.93 ± 1.23	24.63 ± 3.68	58.09 ± 2.55

Table 1: Micro F1 averaged over 50 tasks. Results are reported with a Gaussian 95% confidence interval. Asterisks indicate that prototypes were not finetuned. The best result per column is in bold.

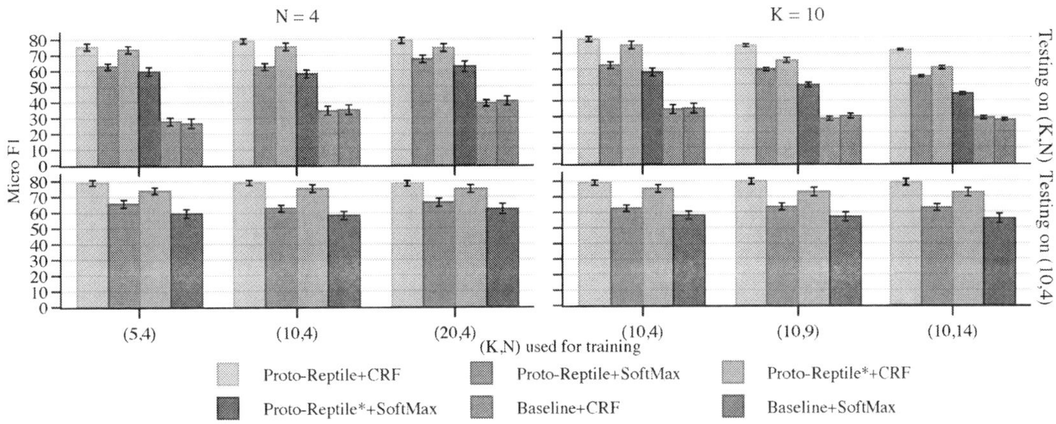

Figure 1: Micro F1 averaged over 50 tasks on N-way-K-shot DTSC8 for different value of (K, N). Error bars represent Gaussian 95% confidence intervals. In the first row of plots, (K, N) match between training and testing. In the second row, models trained on different N-way-K-shot settings are tested on 4-way-10-shot.

for each entity type (larger K). Indeed, either the problem becomes easier — fewer entity types to discriminate — or we get more data per entity type. Nevertheless, the Micro F1 increases faster with K for the baseline. We expect that, in the high data regime (very large K), the baseline would catch up to our approach. However, comparing those approaches in the high data regime would not be very relevant and the meta-learning would not scale.

Finally, we looked at meta-training on N-way-K-shot datasets but meta-testing on the 4-way-10-shot dataset in the second row of Figure 1. Training with more shots or more ways does not seem to improve or decrease performances significantly for Proto-Reptile. This demonstrate our approach is robust to variations in the meta-testing scheme, compared to what is usually observed in the few-shot literature. This is probably because we sample imbalanced support sets. All results in Figure 1 are reported numerically in the appendix.

5 Conclusions

In this paper, we have proposed a new definition of few-shot learning for NER, not relying a coarse-grain approach, like in (Fritzler et al., 2019), based on the intent to generate tasks. We have shown that, combining fine-tuning language models, CRF, diverse task generation, optimization-based and metric-based meta-learning, can significantly and consistently outperform transfer learning on three datasets. Also, our combination of Prototypical Network and Reptile is quite robust to mismatches in the number of shots or ways between meta-training and meta-testing. Thus, our approaches are effective to bootstrap NLU systems.

For future works, one specificity of few-shot NER has not been properly addressed yet. Although different in every tasks, the definition of the background class ("other") is partially shared between tasks. This assumption could be better leveraged in our approaches to transfer some of that knowledge across tasks instead of treating the background class as a different entity type in every tasks. Another interesting direction to explore is few-shot integration, when we have to build a model that performs well on tasks made of entity types seen and unseen during meta-training.

References

Amazon Web Services. 2017. AWS SageMaker. https://aws.amazon.com/sagemaker/.

Trapit Bansal, Rishikesh Jha, and Andrew McCallum. 2019. Learning to few-shot learn across diverse natural language classification tasks. *arXiv preprint arXiv:1911.03863*.

Wei-Yu Chen, Yen-Cheng Liu, Zsolt Kira, Yu-Chiang Frank Wang, and Jia-Bin Huang. 2019. A closer look at few-shot classification. In *7th International Conference on Learning Representations, ICLR 2019, New Orleans, LA, USA, May 6-9, 2019*. OpenReview.net.

Yu Cheng, Mo Yu, Xiaoxiao Guo, and Bowen Zhou. 2019. Few-shot learning with meta metric learners. In *Proceedings of the 3rd Workshop on Meta-Learning (MetaLearn 2019)*.

Eunah Cho, He Xie, and William M Campbell. 2019a. Paraphrase generation for semi-supervised learning in nlu. In *Proceedings of the Workshop on Methods for Optimizing and Evaluating Neural Language Generation*.

Eunah Cho, He Xie, John P Lalor, Varun Kumar, and William M Campbell. 2019b. Efficient semi-supervised learning for natural language understanding by optimizing diversity. In *Proceedings of the 2019 IEEE Automatic Speech Recognition and Understanding Workshop, ASRU 2019, Singapore, December 14-18, 2019*. IEEE.

Djork-Arné Clevert, Thomas Unterthiner, and Sepp Hochreiter. 2016. Fast and accurate deep network learning by exponential linear units (elus). In *4th International Conference on Learning Representations, ICLR 2016, San Juan, Puerto Rico, May 2-4, 2016, Conference Track Proceedings*.

Alexis Conneau and Guillaume Lample. 2019. Cross-lingual language model pretraining. In H. Wallach, H. Larochelle, A. Beygelzimer, F. dÁlché Buc, E. Fox, and R. Garnett, editors, *Advances in Neural Information Processing Systems 32*, pages 7059–7069. Curran Associates, Inc.

Alice Coucke, Alaa Saade, Adrien Ball, Théodore Bluche, Alexandre Caulier, David Leroy, Clément Doumouro, Thibault Gisselbrecht, Francesco Caltagirone, Thibaut Lavril, et al. 2018. Snips voice platform: an embedded spoken language understanding system for private-by-design voice interfaces. *arXiv preprint arXiv:1805.10190*.

Jacob Devlin, Ming-Wei Chang, Kenton Lee, and Kristina Toutanova. 2018. Bert: Pre-training of deep bidirectional transformers for language understanding. *arXiv preprint arXiv:1810.04805*.

Quynh Do and Judith Gaspers. 2019. Cross-lingual transfer learning with data selection for large-scale spoken language understanding. In *Proceedings of the 2019 Conference on Empirical Methods in Natural Language Processing and the 9th International Joint Conference on Natural Language Processing (EMNLP-IJCNLP)*, pages 1455–1460.

Jesse Dodge, Suchin Gururangan, Dallas Card, Roy Schwartz, and Noah A. Smith. 2019. Show your work: Improved reporting of experimental results. In *Proceedings of the 2019 Conference on Empirical Methods in Natural Language Processing and the 9th International Joint Conference on Natural Language Processing (EMNLP-IJCNLP)*, pages 2185–2194, Hong Kong, China. Association for Computational Linguistics.

Chelsea Finn, Pieter Abbeel, and Sergey Levine. 2017. Model-agnostic meta-learning for fast adaptation of deep networks. In *Proceedings of the 34th International Conference on Machine Learning*. JMLR.org.

Stanislav Fort. 2017. Gaussian prototypical networks for few-shot learning on omniglot. *arXiv preprint arXiv:1708.02735*.

Alexander Fritzler, Varvara Logacheva, and Maksim Kretov. 2019. Few-shot classification in named entity recognition task. In *Proceedings of the 34th ACM/SIGAPP Symposium on Applied Computing*, pages 993–1000.

Ruiying Geng, Binhua Li, Yongbin Li, Xiaodan Zhu, Ping Jian, and Jian Sun. 2019. Induction networks for few-shot text classification. In *Proceedings of the 2019 Conference on Empirical Methods in Natural Language Processing and the 9th International Joint Conference on Natural Language Processing (EMNLP-IJCNLP)*, pages 3895–3904.

Rahul Gupta. 2019. Data augmentation for low resource sentiment analysis using generative adversarial networks. In *IEEE International Conference on Acoustics, Speech and Signal Processing*.

Sonal Gupta, Rushin Shah, Mrinal Mohit, Anuj Kumar, and Mike Lewis. 2018. Semantic parsing for task oriented dialog using hierarchical representations. *arXiv preprint arXiv:1810.07942*.

Kelvin Guu, Tatsunori B Hashimoto, Yonatan Oren, and Percy Liang. 2018. Generating sentences by editing prototypes. *Transactions of the Association of Computational Linguistics*.

Xu Han, Hao Zhu, Pengfei Yu, Ziyun Wang, Yuan Yao, Zhiyuan Liu, and Maosong Sun. 2018. FewRel: A large-scale supervised few-shot relation classification dataset with state-of-the-art evaluation. In *Proceedings of the 2018 Conference on Empirical Methods in Natural Language Processing*, pages 4803–4809, Brussels, Belgium. Association for Computational Linguistics.

Nathan Hilliard, Lawrence Phillips, Scott Howland, Artëm Yankov, Courtney D Corley, and Nathan O Hodas. 2018. Few-shot learning with metric-agnostic conditional embeddings. *arXiv preprint arXiv:1802.04376*.

Maximilian Hofer, A. Kormilitzin, Paul Goldberg, and A. Nevado-Holgado. 2018. Few-shot learning for named entity recognition in medical text. *ArXiv*, abs/1811.05468.

Yutai Hou, Wanxiang Che, Yongkui Lai, Zhihan Zhou, Yijia Liu, Han Liu, and Ting Liu. 2020. Few-shot slot tagging with collapsed dependency transfer and label-enhanced task-adaptive projection network. In *Proceedings of the 58th Annual Meeting of the Association for Computational Linguistics*.

Yutai Hou, Yijia Liu, Wanxiang Che, and Ting Liu. 2018. Sequence-to-sequence data augmentation for dialogue language understanding. *arXiv preprint arXiv:1807.01554*.

Xiang Jiang, Mohammad Havaei, Gabriel Chartrand, Hassan Chouaib, Thomas Vincent, Andrew Jesson, Nicolas Chapados, and Stan Matwin. 2018. Attentive task-agnostic meta-learning for few-shot text classification. In *Proceedings of the 2nd Workshop on Meta-Learning (MetaLearn 2018)*.

Andrew Johnson, Penny Karanasou, Judith Gaspers, and Dietrich Klakow. 2019. Cross-lingual transfer learning for japanese named entity recognition. In *Proceedings of the 2019 Conference of the North American Chapter of the Association for Computational Linguistics: Human Language Technologies, Volume 2 (Industry Papers)*, pages 182–189.

Diederik P. Kingma and Jimmy Ba. 2015. Adam: A method for stochastic optimization. In *3rd International Conference on Learning Representations, ICLR 2015, San Diego, CA, USA, May 7-9, 2015, Conference Track Proceedings*.

Gregory Koch, Richard Zemel, and Ruslan Salakhutdinov. 2015. Siamese neural networks for one-shot image recognition. In *ICML Deep Learning Workshop*.

Jason Krone, Yi Zhang, and Mona Diab. 2020. Learning to classify intents and slot labels given a handful of examples. In *Proceedings of the 2nd Workshop on Natural Language Processing for Conversational AI*.

Varun Kumar, Hadrien Glaude, Cyprien de Lichy, and Wlliam Campbell. 2019. A closer look at feature space data augmentation for few-shot intent classification. In *Proceedings of the 2nd Workshop on Deep Learning Approaches for Low-Resource NLP (DeepLo 2019)*, pages 1–10, Hong Kong, China. Association for Computational Linguistics.

John D. Lafferty, Andrew McCallum, and Fernando C. N. Pereira. 2001. Conditional random fields: Probabilistic models for segmenting and labeling sequence data. In *Proceedings of the Eighteenth International Conference on Machine Learning (ICML 2001), Williams College, Williamstown, MA, USA, June 28 - July 1, 2001*, pages 282–289. Morgan Kaufmann.

Guillaume Lample, Miguel Ballesteros, Sandeep Subramanian, Kazuya Kawakami, and Chris Dyer. 2016. Neural architectures for named entity recognition. In *Proceedings of the 2016 Conference of the North American Chapter of the Association for Computational Linguistics: Human Language Technologies*.

Zhenguo Li, Fengwei Zhou, Fei Chen, and Hang Li. 2017. Meta-sgd: Learning to learn quickly for few-shot learning. *arXiv preprint arXiv:1707.09835*.

Andrew McCallum and Wei Li. 2003. Early results for named entity recognition with conditional random fields, feature induction and web-enhanced lexicons. In *Proceedings of the Seventh Conference on Natural Language Learning, CoNLL 2003, Held in cooperation with HLT-NAACL 2003, Edmonton, Canada, May 31 - June 1, 2003*, pages 188–191. ACL.

Erik G Miller, Nicholas E Matsakis, and Paul A Viola. 2000. Learning from one example through shared densities on transforms. In *Proceedings IEEE Conference on Computer Vision and Pattern Recognition. CVPR 2000 (Cat. No. PR00662)*, volume 1, pages 464–471. IEEE.

Tom M. Mitchell. 1980. The need for biases in learning generalizations. Technical report, Rutgers University, New Brunswick, NJ.

Tsendsuren Munkhdalai and Hong Yu. 2017. Meta networks. In *Proceedings of the 34th International Conference on Machine Learning*.

Alex Nichol, Joshua Achiam, and John Schulman. 2018. On first-order meta-learning algorithms.

Stanislav Peshterliev, John Kearney, Abhyuday Jagannatha, Imre Kiss, and Spyros Matsoukas. 2019. Active learning for new domains in natural language understanding. In *Proceedings of the 2019 Conference of the North American Chapter of the Association for Computational Linguistics: Human Language*

Technologies, Volume 2 (Industry Papers), pages 90–96, Minneapolis, Minnesota. Association for Computational Linguistics.

Matthew E Peters, Mark Neumann, Mohit Iyyer, Matt Gardner, Christopher Clark, Kenton Lee, and Luke Zettlemoyer. 2018. Deep contextualized word representations. In *Proceedings of NAACL-HLT*, pages 2227–2237.

Lance Ramshaw and Mitch Marcus. 1995. Text chunking using transformation-based learning. In *Third Workshop on Very Large Corpora*.

Abhinav Rastogi, Xiaoxue Zang, Srinivas Sunkara, Raghav Gupta, and Pranav Khaitan. 2019. Towards scalable multi-domain conversational agents: The schema-guided dialogue dataset. *arXiv preprint arXiv:1909.05855*.

Sachin Ravi and Hugo Larochelle. 2017. Optimization as a model for few-shot learning. In *In International Conference on Learning Representations*.

Oren Rippel, Manohar Paluri, Piotr Dollar, and Lubomir Bourdev. 2015. Metric learning with adaptive density discrimination. *arXiv preprint arXiv:1511.05939*.

Jurgen Schmidhuber. 1987. Evolutionary principles in self-referential learning. on learning now to learn: The meta-meta-meta...-hook. Diploma thesis, Technische Universitat Munchen, Germany, 14 May.

Eli Schwartz, Leonid Karlinsky, Joseph Shtok, Sivan Harary, Mattias Marder, Abhishek Kumar, Rogerio Feris, Raja Giryes, and Alex Bronstein. 2018. Delta-encoder: an effective sample synthesis method for few-shot object recognition. In *Advances in Neural Information Processing Systems*.

Jake Snell, Kevin Swersky, and Richard Zemel. 2017. Prototypical networks for few-shot learning. In I. Guyon, U. V. Luxburg, S. Bengio, H. Wallach, R. Fergus, S. Vishwanathan, and R. Garnett, editors, *Advances in Neural Information Processing Systems 30*, pages 4077–4087. Curran Associates, Inc.

Fábio Souza, Rodrigo Nogueira, and Roberto Lotufo. 2019. Portuguese Named Entity Recognition using BERT-CRF. *arXiv e-prints*.

Shengli Sun, Qingfeng Sun, Kevin Zhou, and Tengchao Lv. 2019. Hierarchical attention prototypical networks for few-shot text classification. In *Proceedings of the 2019 Conference on Empirical Methods in Natural Language Processing and the 9th International Joint Conference on Natural Language Processing (EMNLP-IJCNLP)*, pages 476–485, Hong Kong, China. Association for Computational Linguistics.

Flood Sung, Yongxin Yang, Li Zhang, Tao Xiang, Philip HS Torr, and Timothy M Hospedales. 2018. Learning to compare: Relation network for few-shot learning. In *Proceedings of the IEEE Conference on Computer Vision and Pattern Recognition*, pages 1199–1208.

Yonglong Tian, Yue Wang, Dilip Krishnan, Joshua B. Tenenbaum, and Phillip Isola. 2020. Rethinking few-shot image classification: a good embedding is all you need? *CoRR*, abs/2003.11539.

Erik F. Tjong Kim Sang. 2002. Introduction to the CoNLL-2002 shared task: Language-independent named entity recognition. In *COLING-02: The 6th Conference on Natural Language Learning 2002 (CoNLL-2002)*.

Eleni Triantafillou, Richard Zemel, and Raquel Urtasun. 2017. Few-shot learning through an information retrieval lens. In *Advances in Neural Information Processing Systems*.

Eleni Triantafillou, Tyler Zhu, Vincent Dumoulin, Pascal Lamblin, Utku Evci, Kelvin Xu, Ross Goroshin, Carles Gelada, Kevin Swersky, Pierre-Antoine Manzagol, et al. 2019. Meta-dataset: A dataset of datasets for learning to learn from few examples. *arXiv preprint arXiv:1903.03096*.

Oriol Vinyals, Charles Blundell, Timothy Lillicrap, koray kavukcuoglu, and Daan Wierstra. 2016. Matching networks for one shot learning. In D. D. Lee, M. Sugiyama, U. V. Luxburg, I. Guyon, and R. Garnett, editors, *Advances in Neural Information Processing Systems 29*, pages 3630–3638. Curran Associates, Inc.

Alex Wang, Amanpreet Singh, Julian Michael, Felix Hill, Omer Levy, and Samuel Bowman. 2018a. Glue: A multi-task benchmark and analysis platform for natural language understanding. In *Proceedings of the 2018 EMNLP Workshop BlackboxNLP: Analyzing and Interpreting Neural Networks for NLP*, pages 353–355.

Yong Wang, Xiao-Ming Wu, Qimai Li, Jiatao Gu, Wangmeng Xiang, Lei Zhang, and Victor O. K. Li. 2018b. Large margin few-shot learning.

Thomas Wolf, Lysandre Debut, Victor Sanh, Julien Chaumond, Clement Delangue, Anthony Moi, Pierric Cistac, Tim Rault, R'emi Louf, Morgan Funtowicz, and Jamie Brew. 2019. Huggingface's transformers: State-of-the-art natural language processing. *ArXiv*, abs/1910.03771.

Yi Yang and Arzoo Katiyar. 2020. Simple and effective few-shot named entity recognition with structured nearest neighbor learning. In *Proceedings of the 2020 Conference on Empirical Methods in Natural Language Processing (EMNLP)*.

Meng Ye and Yuhong Guo. 2018. Deep triplet ranking networks for one-shot recognition. *arXiv preprint arXiv:1804.07275*.

Zhi-Xiu Ye and Zhen-Hua Ling. 2019. Multi-level matching and aggregation network for few-shot relation classification. In *Proceedings of the 57th Annual Meeting of the Association for Computational*

Linguistics, pages 2872–2881, Florence, Italy. Association for Computational Linguistics.

Kang Min Yoo, Youhyun Shin, and Sang goo Lee. 2018. Data augmentation for spoken language understanding via joint variational generation.

Mo Yu, Xiaoxiao Guo, Jinfeng Yi, Shiyu Chang, Saloni Potdar, Yu Cheng, Gerald Tesauro, Haoyu Wang, and Bowen Zhou. 2018. Diverse few-shot text classification with multiple metrics. In *Proceedings of the North American Chapter of the Association for Computational Linguistics*.

Ruixiang Zhang, Tong Che, Zoubin Ghahramani, Yoshua Bengio, and Yangqiu Song. 2018. Metagan: An adversarial approach to few-shot learning. In *Advances in Neural Information Processing Systems*.

Zijian Zhao, Su Zhu, and Kai Yu. 2019. Data augmentation with atomic templates for spoken language understanding. *arXiv preprint arXiv:1908.10770*.

6 Appendix

6.1 Dataset preparation and statistics

This Section details how data was prepared. First, utterances without any named entities and the ones that are longer than 40 sub-word units (given by the BERT tokenizer) were removed. For each dataset, less than 1% of utterances were longer than 40 subwords. Removing long utterances allowed us to increase the computation efficiency significantly without impacting the results too much. datasets statistics are given in Table 2. For SNIPS, we used the data preprocessed in `https://github.com/MiuLab/SlotGated-SLU/`.

6.2 Hyper-parameters Tuning

This section describes the search space for hyper-parameters of each algorithm. The dropout parameter is the dropout of the additional layers on trop of BERT. In all settings, we used 0.1 for the BERT dropout and 64 for the batch size. During validation, we fine-tuned the current meta-model for 10 epochs, each epoch consisting of 64 batches, for each tasks. Validation Micro F1 was averaged over 5 sampled tasks with 128 queries each, using the same tasks in-between epochs to reduce the randomness. In the outer loop, we used early stopping with a patience of 4 and a maximum of 12 meta-epochs. At every meta-epoch, we reported the best epoch during the validation fine-tuning, to be used for meta-testing. The number of task per meta-epoch varies per algorithm and so is given in Tables 3 to 6 along with all the other parameters optimized. Bayesian optimization ran with 4 workers in parallel and a total of 30 training jobs, optimizing for the validation Micro F1. For Reptile-based algorithm, the number of steps stands for the number of steps used to compute the first order approximation (T in algorithms 2 and 3 of the main paper). Note that, Reptile was quite sensitive to hyper-parameter tuning and less stable than other approaches.

Training times are reported in Table 8. We used p2.xlarge AWS instances to train our models. Most of the training time actually is spent in validation that requires fine-tuning the meta-model.

In Figure 2, we reported how the performance of the best model increased overtime during hyper-parameters tuning. Because, we used Bayesian optimization instead of random search, it would have been very computationally intensive to compute the expected validation performance as suggested by (Dodge et al., 2019). Indeed, because random search produces i.i.d. trials, they can build an estimator of the validation performance and its variance at no cost. In our case, trials are dependant from the previous ones. We believe, Figure 2 provides a decent estimation of the budget needed for hyper-parameters tuning and how it affects the performance.

The best hyper-parameters per algorithm and per decoder is reported in Table 7 and the best validation Micro F1 is reported in Table 8.

6.3 Number of parameters

All our models used almost the same number of parameters. The differences introduced by the CRFs are negligible compared to BERT (110 millions parameters). Putting aside BERT, without Prototypical Networks, the linear layer on top of BERT adds $768 \times 4 \times N$ parameters and the CRF transition matrix adds $N \times N$ parameters. With Prototypical Networks, the linear layer on top of BERT adds $768 \times 4 \times 64$ parameters and the CRF transition network adds 64×64 parameters.

6.4 Results on the meta-validation set

Table 9 list the validation Micro F1, the training time, the best number of meta-epochs and the best number of epochs that is reused to stop the training during meta-testing. Note that most of the training time of meta-training is spend during validation.

	SNIPS			TOP			DSTC8		
	Train	Valid	Test	Train	Valid	Test	Train	Valid	Test
Utterances	9166	3832	1486	12868	13316	11547	107763	26562	26851
Entity types	27	5	7	20	6	8	84	18	20

Table 2: Datasets statistics.

Hyper-parameter	Range/Values	Scaling
Learning rate	$[5 \times 10^{-5}, 0.001]$	Logarithmic
BERT learning rate	$[1 \times 10^{-5}, 2 \times 10^{-4}]$	Logarithmic
Dropout	$[0.1, 0.9]$	Linear

Table 3: Hyper-parameter search space for the baseline.

Hyper-parameter	Range/Values	Scaling
# tasks	2048	Static
Learning rate	$[5 \times 10^{-5}, 0.001]$	Logarithmic
BERT learning rate	$[1 \times 10^{-5}, 2 \times 10^{-4}]$	Logarithmic
Meta learning rate	$[5 \times 10^{-5}, 0.001]$	Logarithmic
Meta BERT learning rate	$[1 \times 10^{-5}, 2 \times 10^{-4}]$	Logarithmic
Dropout	$[0.1, 0.9]$	Linear

Table 4: Hyper-parameter search space for ProtoNet.

Hyper-parameter	Range/Values	Scaling
# task	1024	Static
Learning rate	$[5 \times 10^{-5}, 0.001]$	Logarithmic
BERT learning rate	$[1 \times 10^{-5}, 2 \times 10^{-4}]$	Logarithmic
Meta learning rate	$[0.1, 1]$	Linear
Meta BERT learning rate	$[0.1, 1]$	Linear
Dropout	$[0.1, 0.9]$	Linear
# steps	[1..10]	Discrete

Table 5: Hyper-parameter search space for the Reptile.

Hyper-parameter	Range/Values	Scaling
# task	512	Static
Learning rate	$[5 \times 10^{-5}, 0.001]$	Logarithmic
BERT learning rate	$[1 \times 10^{-5}, 2 \times 10^{-4}]$	Logarithmic
Meta learning rate	$[0.1, 1]$	Linear
Meta BERT learning rate	$[0.1, 1]$	Linear
Dropout	$[0.1, 0.9]$	Linear
# steps	[1..10]	Discrete

Table 6: Hyper-parameter search space for Proto-Reptile.

Algorithm	Decoder	# steps	Meta LR	Meta BERT LR	LR	BERT LR	Dropout
Baseline	SoftMax	N/A	N/A	N/A	4.35×10^{-4}	8.94×10^{-5}	0.9
	CRF	N/A	N/A	N/A	1×10^{-3}	3.94×10^{-5}	0.897
ProtoNet	SoftMax	N/A	8.2×10^{-4}	6.88×10^{-5}	9.53×10^{-4}	1.99×10^{-5}	0.393
	CRF	N/A	9.73×10^{-4}	6.21×10^{-5}	3.54×10^{-4}	2.24×10^{-5}	0.558
Reptile	SoftMax	10	0.909	0.126	3.32×10^{-4}	7.91×10^{-5}	0.104
	CRF	10	0.107	0.188	7.97×10^{-4}	4.45×10^{-5}	0.71
Proto-Reptile	SoftMax	2	0.641	0.580	4×10^{-4}	1.05×10^{-5}	0.496
	CRF	10	0.847	0.329	6.92×10^{-4}	1.15×10^{-5}	0.446

Table 7: Best hyper-parameters found using Bayesian optimization.

Algorithm	Decoder	Micro F1	Best # meta-epochs	Best # epochs	Training time
Baseline	SoftMax	61.04 ± 5.23	N/A	10	01:33:44
	CRF	59.49 ± 3.12	N/A	9	01:43:42
ProtoNet	SoftMax	70.48 ± 3.83	5	10	11:19:57
	CRF	73.65 ± 2.92	8	5	14:53:58
Reptile	SoftMax	71.88 ± 2.19	8	3	13:57:09
	CRF	70.64 ± 2.30	4	2	16:56:16
Proto-Reptile	SoftMax	70.89 ± 2.98	10	5	10:57:57
	CRF	76.18 ± 4.22	6	8	24:18:03

Table 8: Best validation run found using Bayesian optimization. Micro F1 is averaged over 5 tasks. Results are reported with Gaussian 95% confidence interval. However, note that the same 5 validations tasks are used for every algorithms and models, which introduces a beneficial dependency.

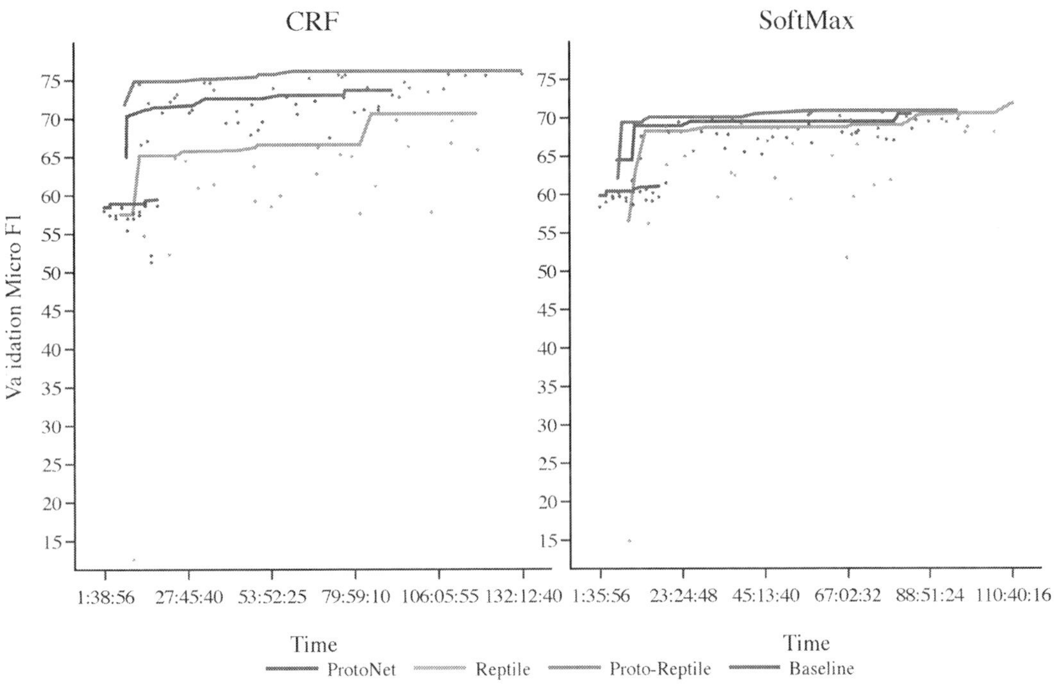

Figure 2: Averaged Micro F1 over the same 5 tasks randomly drawn from the SNIPS validation split during Bayesian optimization of the hyper-parameters. Each dot represents one meta-training. The lines indicate the best model performance overtime.

Dataset	Algorithm	Decoder	Micro F1	# Tasks	# Meta Epochs	# Epochs	Time
SNIPS	ProtoNet	CRF	63.60 ± 5.43	5	9	2	50:31:06
		SoftMax	60.61 ± 5.04	5	11	3	54:30:54
	Reptile	CRF	60.02 ± 5.30	5	20	12	11:55:21
		SoftMax	58.18 ± 4.54	5	20	13	11:14:58
	Proto-Reptile	CRF	67.13 ± 4.01	5	4	13	55:05:08
		SoftMax	62.05 ± 3.38	5	7	13	33:50:06
	Baseline	CRF	48.82 ± 4.37	8	N/A	14	5:16:26
		SoftMax	45.01 ± 4.75	8	N/A	11	4:47:26
TOP	ProtoNet	CRF	71.16 ± 5.77	5	8	1	72:04:31
		SoftMax	67.68 ± 5.05	5	4	4	65:59:54
	Reptile	CRF	59.16 ± 6.38	5	10	10	8:51:06
		SoftMax	60.87 ± 5.55	5	5	4	5:44:05
	Proto-Reptile	CRF	72.29 ± 4.37	5	2	14	72:06:05
		SoftMax	69.90 ± 4.55	5	12	12	72:06:16
	Baseline	CRF	59.16 ± 4.26	8	N/A	14	10:38:27
		SoftMax	55.85 ± 4.61	8	N/A	5	9:31:50
DSTC8	ProtoNet	CRF	82.29 ± 4.13	5	17	15	72:08:26
		SoftMax	73.56 ± 6.46	5	5	8	35:56:08
	Reptile	CRF	75.03 ± 5.62	5	18	2	16:36:53
		SoftMax	75.01 ± 3.35	5	22	5	17:30:08
	Proto-Reptile	CRF	83.83 ± 4.13	5	6	10	72:07:55
		SoftMax	75.87 ± 4.80	5	12	10	33:42:35
	Baseline	CRF	47.08 ± 7.02	8	N/A	14	10:42:08
		SoftMax	42.17 ± 8.23	8	N/A	1	10:00:21

Table 9: Validation Micro F1 with Gaussian 95% confidence interval and training times.

Multi-accent Speech Separation with One Shot Learning

Kuan Po Huang[1⋆], **Yuan-Kuei Wu**[2⋆], **Hung-yi Lee**[3]
[123]National Taiwan University
[1]Graduate Institute of Computer Science and Information Engineering
[23]Graduate Institute of Communication Engineering
{r09922005, f07942100, hungyilee}@ntu.edu.tw*

Abstract

Speech separation is a problem in the field of speech processing that has been studied in full swing recently. However, there has not been much work studying a multi-accent speech separation scenario. Unseen speakers with new accents and noise aroused the domain mismatch problem which cannot be easily solved by conventional joint training methods. Thus, we applied MAML and FOMAML to tackle this problem and obtained higher average Si-SNRi values than joint training on almost all the unseen accents. This proved that these two methods do have the ability to generate well-trained parameters for adapting to speech mixtures of new speakers and accents. Furthermore, we found out that FOMAML obtains similar performance compared to MAML while saving a lot of time.

1 Introduction

Speech separation has been a well-known task to solve in the speech processing field. Many model architectures mentioned in Section 2 have been proposed and achieved high performance. This suggests that deep learning based methods are suitable for the speech separation task.

Despite having promising results, the generalizability of these models is still questionable. The performance of switching to different datasets or environments is not guaranteed. A straightforward solution is to exhaustively collect data under all kinds of environment settings and train a model with these data jointly. Although this may sound reasonable, it is difficult to always consider every situation during training. To make sure that models can be quickly adapted to mixtures spoken by new speakers with not many samples, meta-learning comes to the rescue. Meta-learning has been widely applied on different speech tasks, especially on speech recognition mentioned in Section 2. Nonetheless, there is not much work that applied meta-learning on the speech separation task. In our previous work, (Wu et al., 2020), we first proposed to solve the speech separation problem with meta-learning. Their setting is viewing utterance mixtures of two different speakers as a meta task. These speakers have the same accents. However, we hope that a speech separation model can have the ability to adapt to mixtures with accents never seen before. Thus, besides the setting of two different speakers forming a meta task, we also added a setting that meta tasks with speakers of same accents form an accent task set. Section 4 and 5.1 describe more about the dataset and task construction procedure.

Our contributions are listed below:

- To our best knowledge, we are the first to conduct speech separation experiments on a multi-accent dataset.
- We applied meta-learning to help improve the multi-accent speech recognition task.

The remaining sections of this paper are organized as follows. In Section 2, we give a brief overview of existing works related to speech separation and meta-learning. In Section 3, we elaborate the problem formulation of speech separation in detail. In Section 4, we list out the two phases of MAML, including the meta training phase and meta testing phase. Additionally, we show how FOMAML is modified from MAML. The experimental setup, dataset, and model we used are presented in Section 5. Finally, results and conclusions are given in Section 6 and 7.

*The two first authors made equal contributions.

Proceedings of the 1st Workshop on Meta Learning and Its Applications to Natural Language Processing (MetaNLP 2021), pages 59–66
Bangkok, Thailand (online), August 5, 2021.

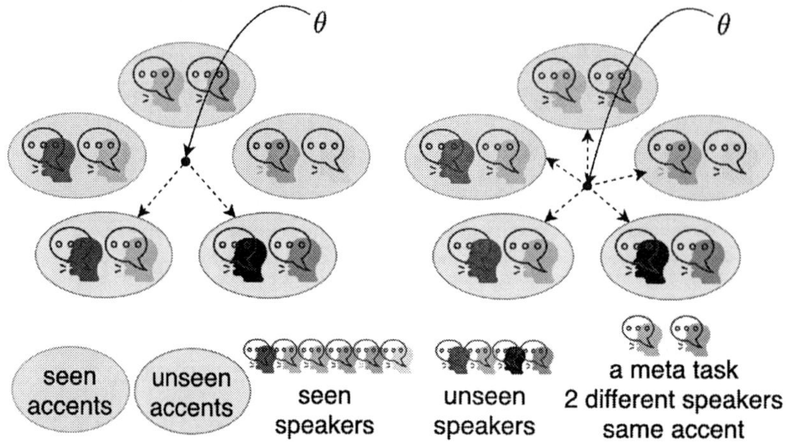

Figure 1: Illustration of joint training and meta-learning for multi-accent speech separation. The oval area is the accent task sets. Each accent task set contains multiple meta tasks. The solid lines are the pretraining process, joint training on the left, and meta-learning on the right. The dashed lines represent the adaptation paths from parameters θ to the unseen accents of unseen speakers. This figure is modified from Gu et al. (2018) and our previous work Wu et al. (2020).

2 Related Work

Speech Separation End-to-end separation models have shown great success in separating speech mixtures of the WSJ0-2mix dataset designed by (Hershey et al., 2016) which is generated from the WSJ0 corpus(Paul and Baker, 1992). (Luo and Mesgarani, 2018) came up with a time-domain audio separation network (TasNet) that takes waveforms as input to alleviate the separation model from dealing with time-frequency representations. They further proposed convolutional TasNet (Luo and Mesgarani, 2019) which substitutes the LSTM layers in TasNet with convolutional layers. This overcame the problem of long temporal dependencies of LSTM and reduced the model size. Before long, they came up will the Dual-path RNN model, which used intra- and inter-blocks to capture local and global information dependencies within the speech mixtures. (Nachmani et al., 2020) utilized the idea of Dual-path RNN and added a speaker identity loss to improve performance on separating mixtures with an unknown number of speakers. (Tzinis et al., 2020) proposed to use a separator constructed with U-ConvBlocks which can not only reduce the number of layers while still having high performance but also require less computational resources and time. This helped the model to more likely be used in real-time speech separation. (Zeghidour and Grangier, 2020) integrated speaker identity information into the separating process, and obtained state-of-the-art performance.

Meta-learning Meta-learning has recently become a trend when it comes to solving multi-task problems. This training method has been widely applied in the computer vision field, for instance, (Vinyals et al., 2016; Rusu et al., 2018; Sun et al., 2019). Meta-learning is also used in the natural language processing field. (Gu et al., 2018) used MAML (Finn et al., 2017) for low-resource neural machine translation (NMT). Moreover, in the speech processing domain, some speech-related problems are solved with meta-learning, too. (Winata et al., 2020) applied meta-transfer learning on code-switched speech recognition. (Xiao et al., 2020; Hsu et al., 2020) applied meta-learning to solve the multilingual low-resource speech recognition problem. (Winata et al., 2019) also used MAML to adapt models to unseen accents on speech recognition. (Indurthi et al., 2019) adopted meta-learning algorithms to perform speech translation on speech-transcript paired low-resource data. (Chen et al., 2021) came up with some improvements of meta-learning to help the speaker verification task.

3 Speech Separation

In this work, we perform single channel speech separation. Given a mixture

$$\mathbf{x} = \sum_{c=1}^{C} \mathbf{s}_c \tag{1}$$

where C is the number of speakers in mixture $\mathbf{x} \in \mathbf{R}^T$ and $\mathbf{s}_c \in \mathbf{R}^T$ are the ground truth sources. For speech separation, the goal is to estimate C sources $\{\hat{\mathbf{s}}_1, \cdots, \hat{\mathbf{s}}_C\} \in \mathbf{R}^T$ such that the estimates sources are as similar as the ground truth sources. The model we used in this work is Conv-TasNet (Luo and Mesgarani, 2019). In their work, the similarity of the estimated sources and ground truth sources are measured by scale-invariant signal-to-noise ratio (Si-SNR) shown in Eq.(4):

$$\mathbf{s}_{\text{proj}} = \frac{\mathbf{s} \cdot \hat{\mathbf{s}}}{||\mathbf{s}||^2}\mathbf{s} \tag{2}$$

$$\text{error} = \hat{\mathbf{s}} - \mathbf{s}_{\text{proj}} \tag{3}$$

$$\text{Si-SNR} = 10 \log_{10} \frac{||\mathbf{s}_{\text{proj}}||^2}{||\text{error}||^2} \tag{4}$$

The Conv-TasNet model is a mask-based model which consists of an encoder, separator, and decoder. The encoder encodes the mixture $\mathbf{x}$ to a latent space as shown in Eq.(5).

$$\mathbf{x}_{\text{enc}} = \text{enc}(\mathbf{x}) \tag{5}$$

$\mathbf{x}_{\text{enc}} \in \mathbf{R}^{H \times T'}$ is the encoder output, where H is the dimension of the latent space and T' is the length of $\mathbf{x}_{\text{enc}}$. The separator then calculates C masks $\mathbf{m}_i \in \mathbf{R}^{H \times T'}$, $i \in \{1, \cdots, C\}$ based on $\mathbf{x}_{\text{enc}}$ shown in Eq.(6).

$$\mathbf{m}_i = \text{sep}(\mathbf{x}_{\text{enc}}) \tag{6}$$

The masks are then multiplied with the encoder output, forming separated features $\mathbf{d}_i$ shown in Eq.(7),

$$\mathbf{d}_i = \mathbf{x}_{\text{enc}} \odot \mathbf{m}_i \tag{7}$$

where $\odot$ is the element-wise multiplication. The separated features $\mathbf{d}_i$ can be viewed as source representations, and are further input to a decoder to estimate separated sources shown in Eq.(8).

$$\hat{\mathbf{s}}_i = \text{dec}(\mathbf{d}_i) \tag{8}$$

At this point, before measuring the estimated sources with Si-SNR, there is a label permutation problem. An align between $\{\hat{\mathbf{s}}_1, \cdots, \hat{\mathbf{s}}_C\}$ and $\{\mathbf{s}_1, \cdots, \mathbf{s}_C\}$ needs to be decided. We used the utterance-level permutation invariant training(uPIT) method described in (Kolbæk et al., 2017) to solve this problem.

4 MAML

The procedure of MAML (Finn et al., 2017) is stated as follows. Given a set of multi-accent tasks $\mathcal{T} = \{\{\mathcal{T}_1^i\}_{i=1}^{tq_1}, \cdots, \{\mathcal{T}_K^i\}_{i=1}^{tq_K}\}$, where K is the number of accents. $\mathcal{T}_k = \{\mathcal{T}_k^i\}_{i=1}^{tq_k}$ is the accent task set containing tasks only with the kth accent and tq_k denotes the task quantity of the kth accent task set. The set of tasks $\mathcal{T}$ is split into the source task set $\mathcal{T}_{source}$ and the target task set $\mathcal{T}_{target}$. The model denoted as f, will be trained on the source task set $\mathcal{T}_{source}$ in the hope of having the ability to quickly adapt to the target task set $\mathcal{T}_{target}$.

4.1 Meta Training Phase

During the meta training phase, the MAML algorithm aims to find initialized parameters θ that can further be quickly adapted to new tasks. Moreover, these initialized parameters should be sensitive to the difference between two different tasks, such that adaptation of the initialized parameters can significantly improve the performance on new tasks sampled from the source task set $\mathcal{T}_{source}$. This is achieved by the inner loop and outer loop optimization. A batch of tasks $\tau_{source} = \{\tau_1, \cdots, \tau_b\}$ is sampled from $\mathcal{T}$ proportional to the task quantity of every accent task set, e.g., for an accent task set $\mathcal{T}_k$, the larger tq_k is, the more likely a task is to be sampled from it. Each task in τ_{source} is further split into a support set τ^{sup} and a query set τ^{qry}. The support set is used to adapt the model parameters by performing a one-step gradient decent, which is known as the inner loop shown in Eq.(9).

$$\theta_j' \leftarrow \theta - \alpha \nabla_\theta \mathcal{L}_{\tau_j^{sup}}(f_\theta) \tag{9}$$

where α is the learning rate. The goal of the inner loop is to minimize the loss of τ_j^{sup} with respect to f_θ. More concisely,

$$\theta_j' = \arg\min_\theta \mathcal{L}_{\tau_j^{sup}}(f_\theta) \tag{10}$$

At this point, the sum of the query loss of each query set in τ_{source} is calculated by

$$\mathcal{L}_{qry} = \sum_{j=1}^{b} \mathcal{L}_{\tau_j^{qry}}(f_{\theta_j'}) \tag{11}$$

The goal of the meta training phase is to minimize the total loss of the query sets. This is also performed by a one-step gradient decent, known as the outer loop shown in Eq.(12).

$$\theta \leftarrow \theta - \beta \nabla_\theta \mathcal{L}_{qry} \tag{12}$$

4.2 Meta Testing Phase

During the meta testing phase, we perform a procedure (see Eq.(13)) similar to the inner loop in the meta training phase. This procedure adapts the parameters θ obtained in the meta training phase to the target tasks $\tau_{target} = \{\tau'_1, \cdots, \tau'_b\}$.

$$\theta_j \leftarrow \theta - \beta \nabla_\theta \mathcal{L}_{\tau'^{sup}_j}(f_\theta) \quad (13)$$

4.3 First-order MAML (FOMAML)

Eq.(14) is the calculation of the gradient in the outer loop, where $\mathcal{L}_{\tau^{qry}_j}$ is denoted as $\mathcal{L}^j$ for simplicity.

$$\nabla_\theta \mathcal{L}_{qry} = \nabla_\theta \sum_{j=1}^{b} \mathcal{L}^j(f_{\theta'_j}) = \sum_{j=1}^{b} \nabla_\theta \mathcal{L}^j(f_{\theta'_j}) \quad (14)$$

When performing the outer loop during the meta training phase, high computational cost is needed to calculate the second-order derivatives with backpropagation. Eq.(15) is the first-order approximation of the second-order derivative,

$$\frac{\partial \mathcal{L}^j(f_{\theta'_j})}{\partial \theta^d} = \sum_{i=1}^{D} \frac{\partial \mathcal{L}^j(f_{\theta'_j})}{\partial \theta'^i_j} \frac{\partial \theta'^i_j}{\partial \theta^d} \approx \frac{\partial \mathcal{L}^j(f_{\theta'_j})}{\partial \theta'^d_j} \quad (15)$$

where θ is a D dimensional parameter, θ^d is the d-th dimension of θ and θ'^i_j is the i-th dimension of θ'_j. The difference between FOMAML and MAML is that this approximation is used instead of the second-order derivatives. Thus, compared to MAML, FOMAML can save a lot of computational time, resulting in a faster gradient calculation.

5 Experiments

5.1 Dataset

The multi-accent speech utterances are collected from the speech accent archive (Weinberger, 2014). This archive currently has more than 200 kinds of accents and 2939 samples. Each native or non-native speaker speaks the same English paragraph. We selected 123 accents that contain more than one speaker since we need utterances of two different speakers to generate mixtures. We split these accents into three sets, 85 accents for generating the training tasks and 19 accents each for generating the developing and testing tasks. The utterance of each speaker is split into segments with a duration of 4 seconds. For each accent, we construct meta tasks by following the task construction method described in (Wu et al., 2020). We select at most 12 speakers for each accent and generate speech mixtures for each pair of speakers with the same accents. Thus, there will be at most $\binom{12}{2} = 66$ meta tasks and at least $\binom{2}{2} = 1$ meta task for each accent. In each meta task, 3 utterance segments are selected from each speaker and mixed with an SNR level randomly selected between 0 to 5 dB and resampled at an 8kHz sample rate. This results in $3 \times 3 = 9$ speech mixtures in one meta task. Fig.(2) is an illustration describing the support set and query set of a meta task. Finally, for the training, developing, and testing set, 22.4, 3.8, and 3.9 hours of speech mixtures are generated.

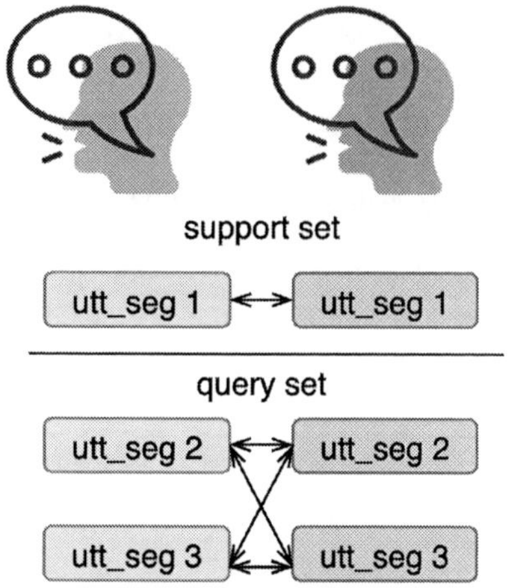

Figure 2: Illustration of a meta task. For two different speakers with the same accent, we sample 3 utterance segments to form a meta task. Thus, there will be 9 mixtures. However, during training, we only sample one mixture to form the support set since our setting is one shot learning. The other 4 mixtures that do not contain the utterance segments in the support set are selected to form the query set.

5.2 Model

The model we used is Conv-TasNet (Luo and Mesgarani, 2019). It consists of an encoder, separator, and a decoder. The encoder is a 1-dim convolution, which transforms the input mixture into a representation. The separator then calculates two masks based on the encoder output. More specifically, it consists of R stacks of temporal convolutional networks (TCN). Each TCN layer consists of M 1-dim exponentially increasing dilated convolutional blocks. These M blocks each have a residual connection and a skip connection. The residual connection is the input of the next block and the skip connection of all blocks are summed together, passing a parametric relu, linear projection, and a sigmoid function to produce two masks. The two masks are multiplied with the representation output from the encoder respectively and further input into the decoder to generate two separate waveforms of the two speakers. The decoder is also a 1-dim convolution. The configuration that we used is the one that obtained the best performance reported in (Luo and Mesgarani, 2019).

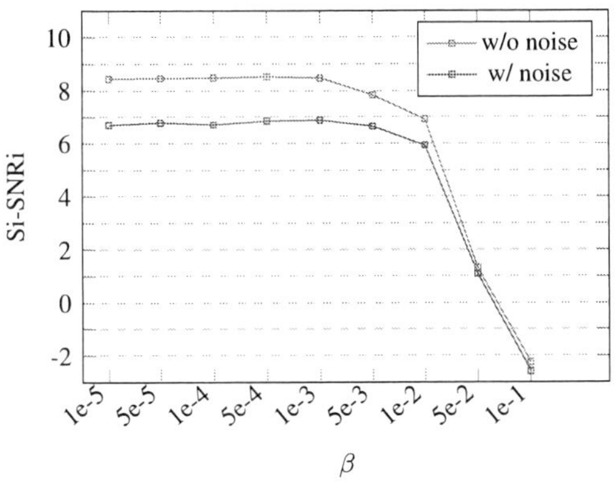

Figure 3: For fine-tuning after joint training, we evaluated the performance by adjusting the learning rate β in the range of 10^{-5} to 10^{-1}.

5.3 Joint Training and Transfer Learning

There are many other works such as (Chen et al., 2020; Tong et al., 2017), that try to solve the domain mismatch problem, where the source domain and target domain datasets do not have a similar distribution. Joint training refers to pretraining a model with different source domain data together. Transfer learning refers to adapting the pretrained model to some partial target domain data and testing the fine-tuned model on the target domain data. The most common adaptation method is fine-tuning. Moreover, the domain mismatch scenario has a low-resource problem if the target domain has only fewer data compared to the scale of the source domain data. There are also several works that tried to solve this problem, such as (Chen and Mak, 2015; Zoph et al., 2016; Hsu et al., 2020). Our jointly trained model is also based on this low-resource scenario.

5.4 MAML and FOMAML

To deal with the domain mismatch and low-resource problem, we applied MAML as our training method in the hope of performing better than joint training. We set the number of the support set in each task as 1, meaning that the model needs to have the ability to adapt to a new task by only seeing one speech mixture of two new different speakers with a new accent never seen before. We also trained our model with FOMAML in order to know whether calculating gradients with first-order approximation still obtains relatively good performance compared to training with MAML.

5.5 Experiment Settings

For both the joint training and MAML methods, we trained the model from randomly initialized parameters for 100 epochs with the Adam optimizer of 0.001 learning rate and 0.00001 weight decay. For the MAML methods, during the meta training phase, we set $\alpha = 0.01$. For joint training, we also fine-tuned the model parameters with the method in Eq.(13). We tested the fine-tuning learning rate β on the testing set, reported it in section 6, and used the learning rates that obtained the best performance for joint training as our baseline. However, for the models trained with MAML methods, the fine-tuning learning rate β is fixed at 0.01 since other values lead to significant performance degradation.

6 Results

6.1 Joint Training

For joint training, we tested the fine-tuning learning rate β on the testing set as shown in Fig.(3), and found out that $\beta = 5e{-4}$ obtained the best performance on the clean testing set, while $\beta = 1e{-3}$ obtained the best performance on the testing set with noise. We use these two experiment settings as our baseline.

6.2 MAML and FOMAML

Comparing models (d), (f) with model (b), we can see that MAML and FOMAML perform better than the joint training baseline. This suggests that the initial model parameters obtained by MAML and FOMAML have the better potential to be adapted to new unseen tasks. Besides, the standard deviation of the testing accent task sets of models (d) and (f) are both less than model (b). This implies that the performance of the models trained with MAML and FOMAML have small dispersion with respect to the mean Si-SNRi value of all the accents compared to the model jointly trained. From Fig.(4), we can see that model (b) performs better

	method	fine-tune	test w/o noise	test w/ noise
(a)	Joint Training	before	8.40 ± 2.25	6.67 ± 2.10
(b)		after	8.52 ± 2.20	6.89 ± 1.84
(c)	FOMAML	before	8.45 ± 3.19	6.66 ± 2.59
(d)		after	**10.13** ± 2.12	8.19 ± 1.62
(e)	MAML	before	-6.19 ± 1.38	-6.85 ± 1.31
(f)		after	10.11 ± 1.86	**8.26** ± 1.52

Table 1: Evaluation results of joint training and MAML methods on the testing accent task sets with and without noise. The two numbers in a cell denote the average Si-SNRi of all the testing tasks and the standard deviation of all the testing accent task sets.

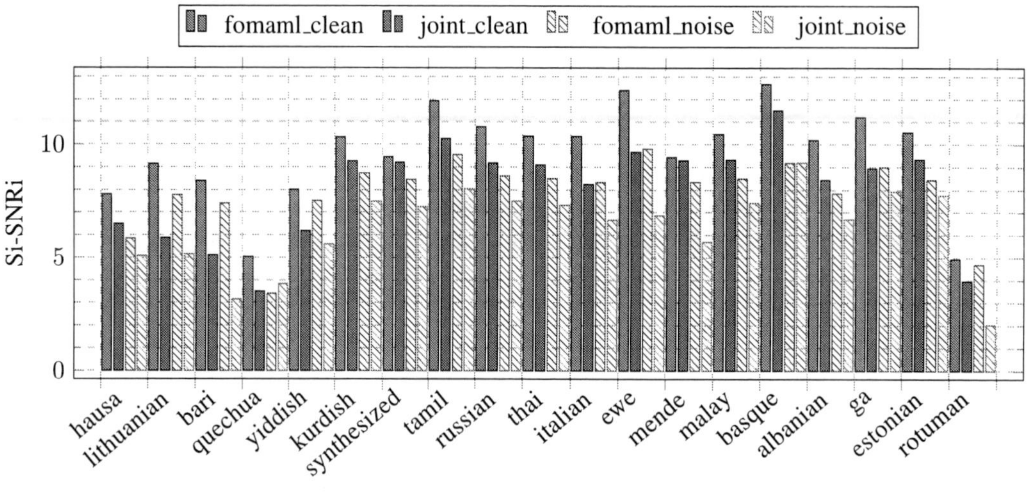

Figure 4: Evaluation results of each testing accent task set for model (b) and (d) in table 1.

on all accents when there is no noise involved and performs better on most of the accents when there is noise in the mixtures.

By comparing models (d) and (f), we found out that these two training methods have similar performance. Model (d) has a slightly higher performance than model (f) under the circumstances that the mixtures are clean in the testing tasks, while model (d) has a slightly lower performance than model (f) under the circumstances that there is noise in the testing tasks. However, MAML requires more than 10 times the training time compared to FOMAML, indicating that the first-order approximation takes advantage over calculating the second-order derivatives by saving a lot of time while still obtaining similar performance. Moreover, FOMAML without fine-tuning (model (c)) has similar performance compared to the baseline model, and yet somehow, initialized parameters obtained by MAML (model (e)) do not have the ability to perform speech separation.

7 Conclusion

Our results show that MAML and FOMAML training methods are effective on multi-accent speech separation. More specifically, it is confirmed that these two methods are better than joint training when adapting to new speakers with new accents and even noisy environments. Besides, FOMAML is shown to be sufficient for dealing with the multi-accent speech separation task and can reduce a large amount of training time. Despite the fact that FOMAML outperforms joint training on the testing set, we can still see that the performance of each accent task set varies a lot from Fig.(4). This is probably due to the task-difficulty imbalance issue described in (Xiao et al., 2020), perhaps some speakers with special accents may be hard to separate. Thus, in the future, we will try to solve this problem with meta sampling methods mentioned in (Xiao et al., 2020).

References

Dongpeng Chen and Brian Kan-Wing Mak. 2015. Multitask learning of deep neural networks for low-resource speech recognition. *IEEE/ACM Transactions on Audio, Speech, and Language Processing*, 23(7):1172–1183.

Yafeng Chen, Wu Guo, and Bin Gu. 2021. Improved meta-learning training for speaker verification. *arXiv preprint arXiv:2103.15421*.

Yi-Chen Chen, Jui-Yang Hsu, Cheng-Kuang Lee, and Hung-yi Lee. 2020. Darts-asr: Differentiable architecture search for multilingual speech recognition and adaptation. *arXiv preprint arXiv:2005.07029*.

Chelsea Finn, Pieter Abbeel, and Sergey Levine. 2017. Model-agnostic meta-learning for fast adaptation of deep networks. In *International Conference on Machine Learning*, pages 1126–1135. PMLR.

Jiatao Gu, Yong Wang, Yun Chen, Kyunghyun Cho, and Victor OK Li. 2018. Meta-learning for low-resource neural machine translation. *arXiv preprint arXiv:1808.08437*.

John R Hershey, Zhuo Chen, Jonathan Le Roux, and Shinji Watanabe. 2016. Deep clustering: Discriminative embeddings for segmentation and separation. In *2016 IEEE International Conference on Acoustics, Speech and Signal Processing (ICASSP)*, pages 31–35. IEEE.

Jui-Yang Hsu, Yuan-Jui Chen, and Hung-yi Lee. 2020. Meta learning for end-to-end low-resource speech recognition. In *ICASSP 2020-2020 IEEE International Conference on Acoustics, Speech and Signal Processing (ICASSP)*, pages 7844–7848. IEEE.

Sathish Indurthi, Houjeung Han, Nikhil Kumar Lakumarapu, Beomseok Lee, Insoo Chung, Sangha Kim, and Chanwoo Kim. 2019. Data efficient direct speech-to-text translation with modality agnostic meta-learning. *arXiv preprint arXiv:1911.04283*.

Morten Kolbæk, Dong Yu, Zheng-Hua Tan, and Jesper Jensen. 2017. Multitalker speech separation with utterance-level permutation invariant training of deep recurrent neural networks. *IEEE/ACM Transactions on Audio, Speech, and Language Processing*, 25(10):1901–1913.

Yi Luo and Nima Mesgarani. 2018. Tasnet: time-domain audio separation network for real-time, single-channel speech separation. In *2018 IEEE International Conference on Acoustics, Speech and Signal Processing (ICASSP)*, pages 696–700. IEEE.

Yi Luo and Nima Mesgarani. 2019. Conv-tasnet: Surpassing ideal time–frequency magnitude masking for speech separation. *IEEE/ACM transactions on audio, speech, and language processing*, 27(8):1256–1266.

Eliya Nachmani, Yossi Adi, and Lior Wolf. 2020. Voice separation with an unknown number of multiple speakers. In *International Conference on Machine Learning*, pages 7164–7175. PMLR.

Douglas B Paul and Janet Baker. 1992. The design for the wall street journal-based csr corpus. In *Speech and Natural Language: Proceedings of a Workshop Held at Harriman, New York, February 23-26, 1992*.

Andrei A Rusu, Dushyant Rao, Jakub Sygnowski, Oriol Vinyals, Razvan Pascanu, Simon Osindero, and Raia Hadsell. 2018. Meta-learning with latent embedding optimization. *arXiv preprint arXiv:1807.05960*.

Qianru Sun, Yaoyao Liu, Tat-Seng Chua, and Bernt Schiele. 2019. Meta-transfer learning for few-shot learning. In *Proceedings of the IEEE/CVF Conference on Computer Vision and Pattern Recognition*, pages 403–412.

Sibo Tong, Philip N Garner, and Hervé Bourlard. 2017. An investigation of deep neural networks for multilingual speech recognition training and adaptation. In *Proc. of INTERSPEECH*, CONF.

Efthymios Tzinis, Zhepei Wang, and Paris Smaragdis. 2020. Sudo rm-rf: Efficient networks for universal audio source separation. In *2020 IEEE 30th International Workshop on Machine Learning for Signal Processing (MLSP)*, pages 1–6. IEEE.

Oriol Vinyals, Charles Blundell, Timothy Lillicrap, Koray Kavukcuoglu, and Daan Wierstra. 2016. Matching networks for one shot learning. *arXiv preprint arXiv:1606.04080*.

Steven H. Weinberger. 2014. Speech accent archive.

Genta Indra Winata, Samuel Cahyawijaya, Zhaojiang Lin, Zihan Liu, Peng Xu, and Pascale Fung. 2020. Meta-transfer learning for code-switched speech recognition. *arXiv preprint arXiv:2004.14228*.

Genta Indra Winata, Zhaojiang Lin, and Pascale Fung. 2019. Learning multilingual meta-embeddings for code-switching named entity recognition. In *Proceedings of the 4th Workshop on Representation Learning for NLP (RepL4NLP-2019)*, pages 181–186, Florence, Italy. Association for Computational Linguistics.

Yuan-Kuei Wu, Kuan-Po Huang, Yu Tsao, and Hung-yi Lee. 2020. One shot learning for speech separation. *arXiv preprint arXiv:2011.10233*.

Yubei Xiao, Ke Gong, Pan Zhou, Guolin Zheng, Xiaodan Liang, and Liang Lin. 2020. Adversarial meta sampling for multilingual low-resource speech recognition. *arXiv preprint arXiv:2012.11896*.

Neil Zeghidour and David Grangier. 2020. Wavesplit: End-to-end speech separation by speaker clustering. *arXiv preprint arXiv:2002.08933*.

Barret Zoph, Deniz Yuret, Jonathan May, and Kevin Knight. 2016. Transfer learning for low-resource neural machine translation. *arXiv preprint arXiv:1604.02201*.

Semi-supervised Meta-learning for Cross-domain Few-shot Intent Classification

Judith Yue Li
Salesforce Research / Palo Alto, CA, USA
yuel@alumni.stanford.edu

Jiong Zhang
LinkedIn AI / Sunnyvale, CA, USA
jiozhang@linkedin.com

Abstract

Meta-learning aims to optimize the model's capability to generalize to new tasks and domains. Lacking a data-efficient way to create meta training tasks has prevented the application of meta-learning to the real-world few shot learning scenarios. Recent studies have proposed unsupervised approaches to create meta-training tasks from unlabeled data for free, e.g., the SMLMT method (Bansal et al., 2020a) constructs unsupervised multi-class classification tasks from the unlabeled text by randomly masking words in the sentence and let the meta learner choose which word to fill in the blank. This study proposes a semi-supervised meta-learning approach that incorporates both the representation power of large pre-trained language models and the generalization capability of prototypical networks enhanced by SMLMT. The semi-supervised meta training approach avoids overfitting prototypical networks on a small number of labeled training examples and quickly learns cross-domain task-specific representation only from a few supporting examples. By incorporating SMLMT with prototypical networks, the meta learner generalizes better to unseen domains and gains higher accuracy on out-of-scope examples without the heavy lifting of pre-training. We observe significant improvement in few-shot generalization after training only a few epochs on the intent classification tasks evaluated in a multi-domain setting.

1 Introduction

Recent developments of large scale pre-trained models, such as BERT (Devlin et al., 2019), GPT (Brown et al., 2020) and XLNet (Yang et al., 2020), have significantly advanced the natural language processing (NLP) techniques. However, these models still rely on fine-tuning on a relatively large number of labeled samples (> 1000) to achieve high accuracy even for tasks seen during training (Howard and Ruder, 2018). Recent studies (Brown et al., 2020; Bansal et al., 2019; Dou et al., 2019) have demonstrated that these large language models have the potential to be few shot learners, i.e., capable of adapting to a new task or a new domain by training only on a few examples with the aid of meta-learning. Meta-learning tackles the few-shot learning problem through learning a robust yet flexible representation from a variety of tasks in a so-called meta training stage, so that the model can quickly adapt to new tasks with only a few examples. In addition, random sampling is introduced in the design of meta training tasks to avoid memorization, a phenomenon in which the meta learner memorizes a function that directly associates an input with the label when no real learning occurs (Yin et al., 2019).

Meta-learning approaches such as the optimization-based MAML (Finn et al., 2017), the metric-based Prototypical Networks (ProtoNet) (Snell et al., 2017) and etc., have been successfully applied in NLP domain (Yin, 2020). Dou et al. (2019) successfully applied MAML and its variants to low-resource text classification tasks on the GLUE dataset (Wang et al., 2018). It showed models trained with MAML, first-order MAML and REPTILE (Nichol and Schulman, 2018) outperform strong baseline models such as BERT and MT-DNN (Liu et al., 2015). Bansal et al. (2019) developed a method LEOPARD that generalizes MAML to handle diverse NLP tasks. They used pre-trained BERT (Devlin et al., 2019) as the underlying task-agnostic base model, coupled with a task-dependent softmax classification parameter generator. The meta trained BERT learns better initial parameters, which helped to reach high accuracy across 17 down steam NLP tasks with very few examples per class.

However, successful implementations of meta-learning depend on the availability of a diverse set of tasks with plenty of labeled data during

Proceedings of the 1st Workshop on Meta Learning and Its Applications to Natural Language Processing (MetaNLP 2021), pages 67–75
Bangkok, Thailand (online), August 5, 2021. ©2021 Association for Computational Linguistics

meta training. To create meta-learning tasks in a data-efficient manner, a number of papers have tried to explore the idea of unsupervised meta-learning. These methods explore to learn representations through automatically constructing tasks from unlabeled dataset and utilize learned representation functions for specific task prediction. Hsu et al. (2018) proposed to leverage clustering embeddings to construct tasks from unlabeled data and then apply meta-learning method for explicitly optimizing for adapting to new tasks. Khodadadeh et al. (2020) proposed to sample objects with synthetic labels from the latent space and generate meta-tasks using generative models. In the domain of natural language processing, Bansal et al. (2020b) proposed Subset Masked Language Modeling Tasks (SMLMT), which automatically construct self-supervised tasks by masking out certain tokens from sentences as labels to create few shots classification tasks from unlabeled data. The study showed that meta training with these diverse unsupervised tasks can prevent over-fitting to specific supervision tasks, leading to better generalization than pre-training language-model followed by fine-tuning.

In this study, we focus on cross-domain few shot classification with the goal to investigate whether we can meta train a large pre-trained language model (e.g., BERT) in a semi-supervised fashion without access to a large number of labeled data or meta training tasks. The resulting representation should generalize and adapt well to a new domain, and provide clear separations between in-domain and out-of-scope (OOS) examples (Zhang et al., 2020). Our base meta learner consists of an embedding function (e.g., BERT) and ProtoNet (Snell et al., 2017) as the general supervised classifier, which can be fine-tuned either using the supervised N-way K-shot classification tasks (supervised meta training) or together with the self-supervised SMLMT tasks (semi-supervised meta training). We compares classifiers with supervised meta-training against classifiers trained without the diverse meta training tasks. We then compare the semi-supervised meta-learner with the supervised approach without adding additional labeled data. The resulting text representations will be evaluated in terms of their few-shot generalization accuracy, their capability to detect OOS examples, and their ability to adapt when more training examples are included.

While Bansal et al. (2020b) focuses on the cross-problem transfer capability of SMLMT trained with a general-purpose corpus like Wikipedia, our study further investigates the cross-domain transfer capability of SMLMT within a problem, i.e., whether additional self-supervised training on the unlabeled data from the domain of interest (e.g., dialogues) can help generalize a seen problem to a new unseen domain. Moreover, SMLMT as a classification task combines well with metric-based meta learners like ProtoNet (Snell et al., 2017). Compared to optimization-based meta learners like MAML (Finn et al., 2017), ProtoNet is easier to optimize and scale, has a simpler inductive bias therefore works well for very-few-shot classification problems. These properties are complementary to MAML and can provide good initialization for the latter (Triantafillou et al., 2019).

2 Methods

2.1 Model architecture of ProtoNet with BERT

Prototypical networks (ProtoNet) (Snell et al., 2017) is a metric-based meta-learning approach for the problem of few-shot classification, where an encoder model learns to project samples to an embedding space. In stead of training on batches of training data, meta learners are trained on episodes that contain support set D^{tr} for training and query set D^{ts} for evaluation. The support set will be projected to the embedding space to formulate class prototypes c_n, and then classification of the query example is done by computing the softmax of the negative distances between the embedded query and each class prototype.

$$y^{ts} = g(D^{tr}, x^{ts}) = softmax(-d(f_\theta(x^{ts}), c_n)) \quad (1)$$

Compared to optimization-based MAML, ProtoNet is more memory efficient and easy to optimize. Similar to Nearest Neighbor, ProtoNet is a non-parametric method that can be integrated with any embedding function f_θ, where θ is the learnable meta parameters. This method reflects simpler inductive bias and so far it is limited to classification problems.

The design of the embedding function f_θ can vary depending on the NLP applications. For intent classification, we find the best performance can be achieved by integrating the metric-based meta-learning approach ProtoNet with the popular pre-trained model (e.g., BERT (Devlin et al.,

	N=5, K=5		N=5, K=10	
Dataset	Meta-Test Accuracy	Meta-Test Std	Meta-Test Accuracy	Meta-Test Std
1.unseen examples (banking)	0.935	0.044	0.940	0.042
2.unseen examples	0.914	0.056	0.948	0.040
3.unseen classes	0.883	0.060	0.917	0.049
4.unseen domains	0.870	0.066	0.908	0.055

Table 1: Meta test accuracy and standard deviations for ProtoNet on CLINC150 few shot intent classification dataset.

2019), RoBERTa (Liu et al., 2019)). These large pre-trained language models are quite effective for learning task-agnostic features as well as the task-specific representations with proper fine-tuning. We take advantage of this transfer learning feature of these pre-trained models and use it as the embedding function f_θ. Here the meta parameters θ are the weights of the pre-trained model which will be fine-tuned during meta training to learn a task-agnostic representation that should also generalize well to a new domain during meta testing.

2.2 Subset Masked Language Modeling Tasks

With the hope of further improving classification accuracy, we would like to leverage the unlabeled data set through self-supervision during meta training stage. The key for self-supervised meta-learning is how to construct self-supervised tasks and how it can be combined with the supervised tasks. Following the Subset Masked Language Modeling Tasks (SMLMT) approach (Bansal et al., 2020a), we first construct a vocabulary from tokens in all the sentences except those labeled sentences used as hold-out test set and calculate their frequency. To balance the number of tokens and the number of sentences associated to each token, we select tokens appeared from 30 times to 100 times to be labels and then masked these tokens in associated sentences as training samples for SMLMT, with the token as labels. Since SMLMT is also a classification task, the meta-learner introduced in the last section can be used to solve both the self-supervised and the supervised classification tasks, yielding a new semi-supervised meta training approach to tackle the few shot intent classification problem.

2.3 Out-of-Scope Evaluation

In addition to the standard few shot learning evaluation where the model is only evaluated on samples from in-scope class distribution, a more realistic evaluation setting involves the Out-of-Scope (OOS) class, in which samples come from a different distribution, e.g., random utterances not related to any registered intent class in a dialogue.

We adopt the OOS evaluation strategy (Zhang et al., 2020; Larson et al., 2019) which adds an additional OOS class in the meta testing stage, while the meta training stage remains to be the same. A sample is assigned to the OOS class if the probabilistic prediction for the best class is under a specified threshold T with value between 0 and 1. The threshold values is chosen to maximize J_{in_oos} (Equation 4), the sum of In-Domain-Accuracy (A_{in}, Equation 2) and OOS-Recall (R_{oos}, Equation 3).

$$A_{in} = C_{in}/N_{in} \tag{2}$$

where C_{in} is the number of correctly predicted in-domain intent examples and N_{in} is the total number of in-domain intent examples.

$$R_{oos} = C_{oos}/N_{oos}, P_{oos} = C_{oos}/(N'_{oos}) \tag{3}$$

where C_{oos} is the number of correctly predicted OOS intent examples, N_{oos} is the number of OOS intent examples and N'_{oos} is the number of predicted OOS examples.

$$J_{in\_oos} = A_{in} + R_{oos} \tag{4}$$

We also report the OOS precision P_{oos} and OOS F1 score $F1_{oos}$ for an optimized threshold T.

3 Experiments, Results and Discussion

There have been a number of papers that have explored the idea of unsupervised meta-learning, where tasks are constructed automatically from an unlabeled dataset and a meta-learner is pre-trained on these tasks without using any labeled dataset. Can we extend these ideas to the case where we have a small number of supervised meta-training tasks rather than zero meta-training tasks, to construct a semi-supervised meta-learner? We hope to explore answers to the following questions through experiments: (a) Whether meta training effectively improve domain adaptation? and (b) Will the semi-supervised approach outperform the supervised meta-learning given the same number of labeled data?

3.1 CLINC150 Few Shot Intent Classification

The CLINC150 (Larson et al., 2019) intent classification dataset consists of 150 different intent classes across 10 different domains, i.e., Banking, Credit Cards, Work and Travel. Each domain has 15 tasks, each comes with 150 labeled examples. The data is split in the following ways to evaluate meta-learning for different few shot learning settings:

1. **single domain unseen examples:** Pick only one domain Banking. The training data is sampled from 15 classes from the banking domain, where each class has 100 examples. The validation and testing data is sampled from the same class distributions with 20 and 30 examples per class respectively.

2. **multi-domain unseen examples:** Distribute the 150 classes uniformly among training, validation and testing splits, with a ratio of 100:20:30. The training data is sampled from 150 classes with 100 examples each class from all domains. The validation and testing data consist of 20 and 30 examples per class respectively.

3. **multi-domain unseen classes:** In order to test the model's generalization capability to unseen new classes, the 15 classes under each domain are separated according to 10:2:3 ratio, so that no tasks in testing set or validation set will appear in the training time. The training data, validation set and testing set is sampled from 100, 20, 30 classes among 10 different domains respectively, where each class contains 150 examples.

4. **multi-domain unseen domain:** The problem is made more difficult by creating a data splits in which the training, validation and testing data all come from different domains, which will test whether the model will efficiently adapt to domains unseen. The training data is sampled from 75 classes among 5 different domains (banking, kitchen, home, auto commute and small talk), where each class contains 150 examples. The validation and testing data is sampled from the 2 (utility, credit cards) and 3 (travel, work, meta) domains respectively, where each domain has 15 classes and each class has 150 examples.

We run ProtoNet with BERT on each few shot setting and the results are shown in Table 1. The few shot test accuracy decreases when examples in meta testing time come from a class or a domain that is unseen during meta training time. Increase k or the number of support samples per task improves the test accuracy. For $k = 5$ the best results are achieved by training with learning rate $4e - 6$, 6 ways for 300 episodes during meta training. Note the learning rate is reduced by half for every 50 episodes.

3.2 Cross Domain Intent Classification with Limited Labeled Data

A more challenging but realistic few shot learning setting is that during meta training we don't have enough labeled data available per class, and labeled data in the same domain is not available. Yet we have large amount of unlabeled data from the same domain. How will the result change if we reduce the available labeled examples per class during meta training from 150 to 50 or less for the unseen domain set up?

Following the set up of unseen domains, the problem is made more challenging by sampling training tasks from only 25 classes among 5 different domains (banking, kitchen, home, auto commute and small talk), where each class only contains 50 labeled examples. The validation and testing data is sampled from the 2 (utility, credit cards) and 3 (travel, work, meta) other domains respectively, where each domain has 15 classes and each class has 50 examples. The rest of the examples is aggregated into a pool of unlabeled data for unsupervised training. Details about the data splits is shown in Table 2. To evaluate model performance on OOS examples, we also randomly sample OOS intents from the 1200 Out-of-Scope examples that are not belonged to the 150-intent classes provided

	unlabeled	train	valid	test
# domains	10	5	2	3
# classes	223	25	30	45
# examples	11900	1250	1500	2250

Table 2: The data splits for meta training, meta validation and meta testing

	ProtoNet with meta training	
# labeled data per class	Meta Test Acc	Meta Test Std
20	0.832	0.077
50	0.851	0.068
100	0.846	0.073
150	0.864	0.073

Table 3: Meta test accuracy changes with the number of available labeled data per class

by Larson et al. (2019) during meta testing time.

By varying the number of available labeled examples during meta training, we observe how meta test accuracy and standard deviation changes in respond to more labeled training data. As shown in Table 3, increasing the number of labeled samples per class from 20 to 150 improves the test accuracy from 0.832 to 0.864 for 5-way 5-shot learning.

3.3 CLINC150 with ProtoNet + SMLMT

The next research question is whether we can leverage the unlabeled data to improve the meta test accuracy. Here we create the unsupervised tasks following the SMLMT (Bansal et al., 2020b), where additional meta training tasks are created by masking a randomly picked token (here we use [MASK] from BERT's vocabulary) and let the model classifies which token has been replaced. The token is selected to appear at least 30 times in the examples, but no more than 100 times, which filters out common words and leaves enough examples for the model to learn the representations of important words that differentiate different intents. The most important hyperparameters to tune are learning rate, sampling ratio and number of ways during training. Sampling ratio controls when to train with the SMLMT tasks and when to train with the supervised tasks. The best validation accuracy is reached at learning rate $8e-6$, sampling ratio 0.7 and 9 ways during meta training. Here the training "ways" is typically selected to be larger than the testing "ways" to gain good performance (Snell et al., 2017). The details on the hyper parameters chosen for this experiment can be found in Table 4. After running for 800 episodes, the test accuracy is shown in Table 5. Note the learning rate is reduced by half for every 100 episodes.

	ProtoNet	ProtoNet with SMLMT
learning rate	4e-6	8e-6
N way (meta training)	6	9
K shots (smlmt task)	NA	15
# of episodes per epoch	50	100
# of epoch	6	8
smlmt sample ratio	NA	0.6

Table 4: Hyperparameters used for ProtoNet

As suggested by Table 5 supervised meta training on diverse tasks from different domains (5th and 8th row) improves generalization to tasks in unseen domains. Figure 1 highlights the meta test accuracy and meta test standard deviation of three different approaches for 5 shots and 10 shots scenarios with BERT as the embedding function. ProtoNet with meta training consistently outperforms the baseline results from the nearest neighbor and ProtoNet (meta test only), in which no meta training involved. Even though Nearest Neighbor with the BERT encoder is a strong baseline, which achieves 80% for 5 shots and 85% for 10 shots, the ProtoNet improves the baseline by 5 points through meta training on different tasks in different domains.

The results also suggest that additional self-supervised training through SMLMT further improve few-shot generalization if we compare the ProtoNet results to the ProtoNet + SMLMT results. The blue bar in Figure 1 shows the ProtoNet results, which trained using only supervised task, and the orange bar shows the semi-supervised ProtoNet results using both labeled and unlabeled data. Semi-supervised ProtoNet improves the ProtoNet results further by an additional 5 points, which achieves 90.6% for $K = 5$ and 93.9% for $K = 10$. Note that the the semi-supervised ProtoNet with 50 labeled data outperforms the supervised ProtoNet with 150 labeled data (86.4% in Table 3). These results (details see Table 5) show that meta training on diverse tasks, especially the SMLMT tasks generated from unlabeled data yield better general-

	N=5, K=5		N=5, K=10	
Approach	Meta-Test Accuracy	Meta-Test Std	Meta-Test Accuracy	Meta-Test Std
Nearest Neighbour + BERT	0.795	0.079	0.852	0.066
ProtoNet + BERT (no meta training)	0.795	0.083	0.842	0.073
ProtoNet + BERT (supervised meta training)	0.851	0.068	0.891	0.061
ProtoNet + BERT + SMLMT (semi-supervised meta training)	0.906	0.066	0.939	0.047
ProtoNet + RoBERTa (no meta training)	0.887	0.078	0.924	0.066
ProtoNet + RoBERTa (supervised meta training)	0.975	0.037	0.981	0.033
ProtoNet + RoBERTa + SMLMT (semi-supervised meta training)	0.980	0.038	0.986	0.025

Table 5: Meta test accuracy and standard deviations of applying different meta-learning approaches with K=5 and K=10 respectively for CLINC150 dataset.

Approach	Threshold	OOS F1	OOS Recall	OOS Precision	In-domain Accuracy
ProtoNet + BERT (no meta training)	0.4	0.471	0.772	0.339	0.723
ProtoNet + BERT	0.9	0.494	0.703	0.381	0.796
ProtoNet + BERT + SMLMT	0.9	0.601	0.787	0.487	0.856
ProtoNet + RoBERTa (no meta training)	0.3	0.286	1.000	0.167	0.200
ProtoNet + RoBERTa	0.9	0.632	0.562	0.722	0.958
ProtoNet + RoBERTa + SMLMT	0.9	0.766	0.771	0.761	0.959

Table 6: Evaluation statistics on OOS examples with N=5, K=10 respectively for protoNet with BERT and RoBERTa

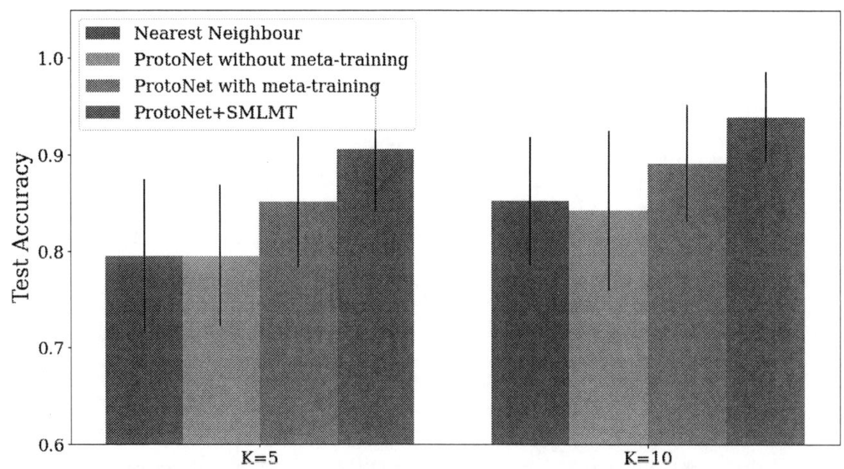

Figure 1: Meta test accuracy of applying four different meta-learning approaches with K=5 and K=10 respectively.

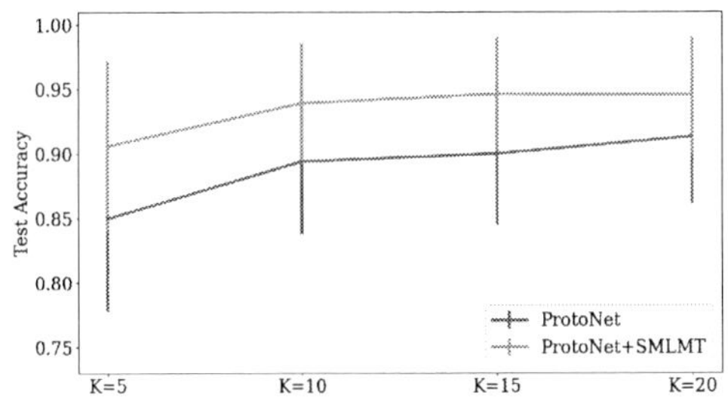

Figure 2: Meta test accuracy of ProtoNet increases with K shots, while performance plateaus around $K = 20$

ization capability.

Varying number of supporting examples K used per task during meta testing also has an effect on the meta testing accuracy. As shown in Figure 2, increase K from 5 to 15 improves test accuracy of ProtoNet with SMLMT from 85% to 94.5%, and ProtoNet from 85.0% to 91.3% while the performance plateaued for $K = 20$ (details see Table 7). Changing embedding function from BERT to RoBERTa ($7^{th}, 8^{th}, 9^{th}$ rows in Table 5) significantly improves the meta test accuracy, suggesting that RoBERTa is a better pre-trained model for intent classification.

3.4 Results on Out-of-Scope Examples

We also evaluate the performance of our meta learners on OOS examples by including an extra OOS class during meta testing. Two embedding functions, i.e., BERT and RoBERTa are evaluated in three settings: no meta training, with supervised meta training and with semi-supervised meta training (with SMLMT). The meta training procedure remains the same as previous setup. During meta testing, we first pick the threshold T (see section 2.3) and then report the F1, precision, recall for OOS and In-domain Accuracy with the selected threshold. While OOS precision and recall usually fluctuates a lot with thresholds, OOS F1 score is a better indicator of OOS accuracy.

As shown in Table 6 meta training improves OOS F1 score significantly and semi-supervised meta training gives the best OOS F1 score, 0.601 with BERT and 0.766 with RoBERTa. RoBERTa as embedding function performs better than BERT after meta training, with a nearly 10-point improvement for in-domain accuracy (0.959 vs 0.856) and OOS F1 score (0.766 vs 0.601). RoBERTa without fine tuning performs worse than BERT when OOS examples are included, probably due to the selecting criterion for the threshold. The inclusion of OOS examples clearly reduce the in-domain accuracy. For example, the in-domain accuracy for ProtoNet + BERT + SMLMT changes from 0.939 without OOS examples (Table 5) to 0.856 with OOS examples (Table 6). However, the accuracy gain compared to no meta training (0.723) and supervised-only meta training (0.796) is quite significant.

3.5 Visualization of Word Importance

To have a better understanding of why meta training on semi-supervised tasks yield better generalization capability, we analyze the token importance by plotting the gradients of the prediction with respect to the token embedding for each token as shown in Figure 3. The token with larger gradient indicates it's more important for the prediction result. Meta training changes the distribution of word importance. For example, for the sentence "I want to schedule a pto request on march 1 - 2". We see that the meta learner shifts its attention from "on march" before training, to the most important word "schedule pto request" after training, which helps it to effectively identify this sentence as a `pto_request` intent. The same observation is true for the sentence "tell me where my flight is scheduled to start boarding", where the top 3 important tokens has changed from "me, where, is" to "my, flight, is" after training, leading to the prediction of intent "flight_status". Therefore, the better generalization is powered by effective representation learning (a pre-trained BERT already yields good representation for intent classification) and also learning to attend to the right words.

4 Conclusion

We proposed a semi-supervised meta-learning approach for cross-domain few-shot intent classification by incorporating the representation power of pre-trained language model with the fast adaptation capability of ProtoNet enhanced through self-supervision. This methodology tackles the realistic few shot learning setting where not enough meta training tasks exist and meta learner trained only on supervised tasks suffers from over-fitting on a small number of labeled data. The experiments have shown that meta learner generalizes better to new domains and predicts more accurately on out-of-scope examples if trained with additional meta training tasks created through self-supervision

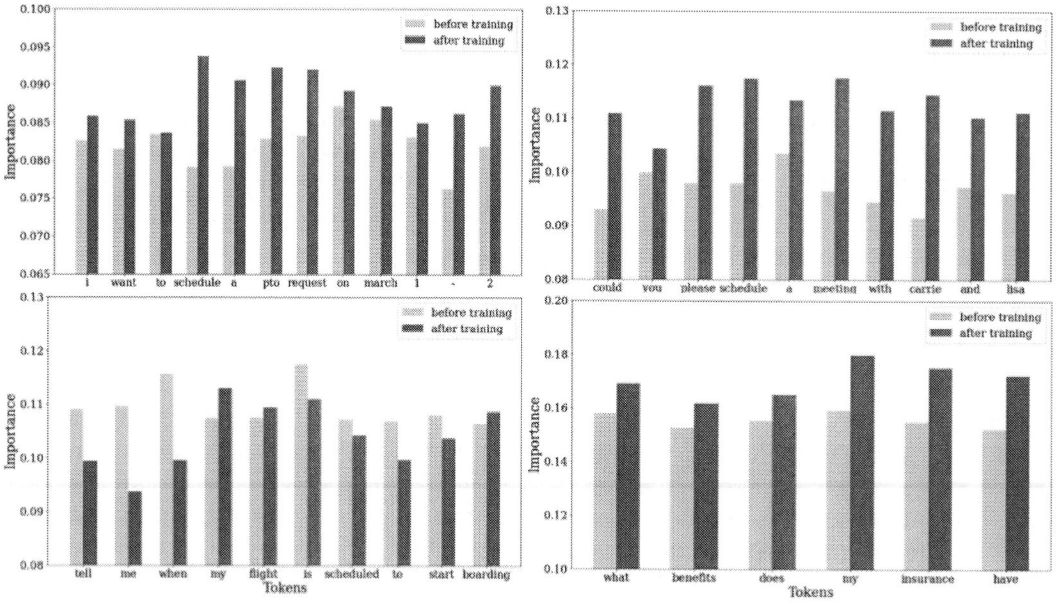

Figure 3: The importance of tokens of each sentence before and after training.

from unlabeled data. Compared to pre-training language models using self-supervision, the volume of unlabeled data required for our semi-supervised meta training is rather small and the optimization is much easier. However, it effectively improve the few-shot generalization and out-of-scope accuracy by learning a better cross-domain representation and learning to quickly attend to the right word in new domains. While ProtoNet has its limitations due to simpler inductive bias, the resulting presentation can be used to initialize more sophisticated meta learner and extend beyond the classification problems. Future directions include exploring different ways to combine various types of meta learners, different designs of self-supervised tasks as well as validating our algorithms on other datasets.

5 Acknowledgement

This work is inspired by our CS330 course project at Stanford. We would like to thank Professor Chelsea Finn for the discussion of research directions and her wonderful lectures on meta-learning.

References

Trapit Bansal, Rishikesh Jha, and Andrew McCallum. 2019. Learning to few-shot learn across diverse natural language classification tasks. *CoRR*, abs/1911.03863.

Trapit Bansal, Rishikesh Jha, Tsendsuren Munkhdalai, and Andrew McCallum. 2020a. Self-Supervised Meta-Learning for Few-Shot Natural Language Classification Tasks. *arXiv*.

Trapit Bansal, Rishikesh Jha, Tsendsuren Munkhdalai, and Andrew McCallum. 2020b. Self-Supervised Meta-Learning for Few-Shot Natural Language Classification Tasks. *arXiv*.

Tom B. Brown, Benjamin Mann, Nick Ryder, Melanie Subbiah, Jared Kaplan, Prafulla Dhariwal, Arvind Neelakantan, Pranav Shyam, Girish Sastry, Amanda Askell, Sandhini Agarwal, Ariel Herbert-Voss, Gretchen Krueger, Tom Henighan, Rewon Child, Aditya Ramesh, Daniel M. Ziegler, Jeffrey Wu, Clemens Winter, Christopher Hesse, Mark Chen, Eric Sigler, Mateusz Litwin, Scott Gray, Benjamin Chess, Jack Clark, Christopher Berner, Sam McCandlish, Alec Radford, Ilya Sutskever, and Dario Amodei. 2020. Language models are few-shot learners.

Jacob Devlin, Ming-Wei Chang, Kenton Lee, and Kristina Toutanova. 2019. Bert: Pre-training of deep bidirectional transformers for language understanding.

Zi-Yi Dou, Keyi Yu, and Antonios Anastasopoulos. 2019. Investigating meta-learning algorithms for low-resource natural language understanding tasks. In *Proceedings of the 2019 Conference on Empirical Methods in Natural Language Processing and the 9th International Joint Conference on Natural Language Processing (EMNLP-IJCNLP)*, pages 1192–1197, Hong Kong, China. Association for Computational Linguistics.

# labeled data per class	N way	K shot	ProtoNet with meta training		ProtoNet with SMLMT	
			Meta Test Acc	Meta Test Std	Meta Test Acc	Meta Test Std
50	5	5	0.850	0.072	0.906	0.066
50	5	10	0.894	0.056	0.939	0.047
50	5	15	0.900	0.055	0.946	0.044
50	5	20	0.913	0.052	0.945	0.045

Table 7: Meta test accuracy of ProtoNet increases with K shots, while performance plateaus around $K = 20$

Chelsea Finn, Pieter Abbeel, and Sergey Levine. 2017. Model-agnostic meta-learning for fast adaptation of deep networks.

Jeremy Howard and Sebastian Ruder. 2018. Universal Language Model Fine-tuning for Text Classification. *arXiv*.

Kyle Hsu, Sergey Levine, and Chelsea Finn. 2018. Unsupervised learning via meta-learning. *CoRR*, abs/1810.02334.

Siavash Khodadadeh, Sharare Zehtabian, Saeed Vahidian, Weijia Wang, Bill Lin, and Ladislau Bölöni. 2020. Unsupervised meta-learning through latent-space interpolation in generative models.

Stefan Larson, Anish Mahendran, Joseph J. Peper, Christopher Clarke, Andrew Lee, Parker Hill, Jonathan K. Kummerfeld, Kevin Leach, Michael A. Laurenzano, Lingjia Tang, and Jason Mars. 2019. An evaluation dataset for intent classification and out-of-scope prediction. In *Proceedings of the 2019 Conference on Empirical Methods in Natural Language Processing and the 9th International Joint Conference on Natural Language Processing (EMNLP-IJCNLP)*, pages 1311–1316, Hong Kong, China. Association for Computational Linguistics.

X. Liu, Jianfeng Gao, X. He, L. Deng, Kevin Duh, and Ye-Yi Wang. 2015. Representation learning using multi-task deep neural networks for semantic classification and information retrieval. In *HLT-NAACL*.

Yinhan Liu, Myle Ott, Naman Goyal, Jingfei Du, Mandar Joshi, Danqi Chen, Omer Levy, Mike Lewis, Luke Zettlemoyer, and Veselin Stoyanov. 2019. RoBERTa: A Robustly Optimized BERT Pretraining Approach.

Alex Nichol and John Schulman. 2018. Reptile: a scalable metalearning algorithm. *arXiv: Learning*.

Jake Snell, Kevin Swersky, and Richard S. Zemel. 2017. Prototypical networks for few-shot learning. *CoRR*, abs/1703.05175.

Eleni Triantafillou, Tyler Zhu, Vincent Dumoulin, Pascal Lamblin, Utku Evci, Kelvin Xu, Ross Goroshin, Carles Gelada, Kevin Swersky, Pierre-Antoine Manzagol, and Hugo Larochelle. 2019. Meta-Dataset: A Dataset of Datasets for Learning to Learn from Few Examples. *arXiv*.

Alex Wang, Amanpreet Singh, Julian Michael, Felix Hill, Omer Levy, and Samuel R. Bowman. 2018. GLUE: A multi-task benchmark and analysis platform for natural language understanding. *CoRR*, abs/1804.07461.

Zhilin Yang, Zihang Dai, Yiming Yang, Jaime Carbonell, Ruslan Salakhutdinov, and Quoc V. Le. 2020. Xlnet: Generalized autoregressive pretraining for language understanding.

Mingzhang Yin, George Tucker, Mingyuan Zhou, Sergey Levine, and Chelsea Finn. 2019. Meta-Learning without Memorization. *arXiv*.

Wenpeng Yin. 2020. Meta-learning for few-shot natural language processing: A survey. *ArXiv*, abs/2007.09604.

Jian-Guo Zhang, Kazuma Hashimoto, Wenhao Liu, Chien-Sheng Wu, Yao Wan, Philip S Yu, Richard Socher, and Caiming Xiong. 2020. Discriminative Nearest Neighbor Few-Shot Intent Detection by Transferring Natural Language Inference. *arXiv*.

Meta-learning for Classifying Previously Unseen Data Source into Previously Unseen Emotional Categories

Gaël Guibon[1,2], Matthieu Labeau[1], Hélène Flamein[2], Luce Lefeuvre[2], and Chloé Clavel[1]

[1]LTCI, Télécom-Paris, Institut Polytechnique de Paris
[2]Direction Innovation & Recherche SNCF
{gael.guibon,matthieu.labeau,chloe.clavel}@telecom-paris.fr
{ext.gael.guibon,helene.flamein,luce.lefeuvre}@sncf.fr

Abstract

In this paper, we place ourselves in a classification scenario in which the target classes and data type are not accessible during training. We use a meta-learning approach to determine whether or not meta-trained information from common social network data with fine-grained emotion labels can achieve competitive performance on messages labeled with different emotion categories. We leverage few-shot learning to match with the classification scenario and consider metric learning based meta-learning by setting up Prototypical Networks with a Transformer encoder, trained in an episodic fashion. This approach proves to be effective for capturing meta-information from a source emotional tag set to predict previously unseen emotional tags. Even though shifting the data type triggers an expected performance drop, our meta-learning approach achieves decent results when compared to the fully supervised one.

1 Introduction

Training a model for a classification task without having access to the target data nor the precise tag set is becoming a common problem in Natural Language Processing (NLP). This is especially true for NLP tasks applied to company data, highly specialized, and which is most of the time raw data. Annotating these data requires to set up a lengthy and costly annotation process, and annotators must have specific skills. It also raises some data privacy issues. Our study is conducted in this context. It deals with private messages, that shall be annotated with emotions as labels. This task is highly difficult because of the subjective and ambiguous nature of the emotions, and because of the nature of the data. We tackle this problem in an emotion classification task from short texts. We assume that meta-learning can serve for emotion classification in different text structures along with a different tag set.

Predicting and classifying emotions in text is a widely spread research topic, going from polarity-based labels (Strapparava and Mihalcea, 2007; Thelwall et al., 2012; Yadollahi et al., 2017) to more complex representations of emotion (Alm et al., 2005; Bollen et al., 2009; Yu et al., 2015; Zhang et al., 2018a; Zhu et al., 2019; Zhong et al., 2019; Park et al., 2019). In this paper, we place ourselves in a situation where we have no access to target data or models of target classes. Therefore, we want to learn information from related data sets to predict labels on our target data, even though label sets differ. Thus, we apply meta-learning using a few-shot learning approach to predict emotions in messages from daily conversations (Li et al., 2017) based on meta-information inferred from social media informal texts, *i.e.* Reddit comments (Demszky et al., 2020a).

With this setup, our goal is to investigate if combining few-shot learning and meta-learning can yield competitive performance on data of a different kind from those on which the model was trained. Indeed, recent work already showed meta-learning is useful when shifting to different topics on a classification task with the Amazon data set (Bao et al., 2020) or different entity relations on the dedicated Few-Rel data set (Han et al., 2018; Gao et al., 2019a). In this paper, we take another step forward by leveraging meta-learning when shifting not only emotional tag sets but also data sources, involving different topics, lexicons and phrasal structures. For instance, the "surprise" emotion is set for "*Wow you found the answer, wish you were on top, will link to you in my post*" in GoEmotions (Demszky et al., 2020a) and for "*Are you from south?*" in DailyDialog (Li et al., 2017), varying both the lexicon used (post related vocabulary for GoEmotions) and the sentence structure (cleaner syntactic structures in DailyDialog).

Our contribution relies on the implementation of a two-level meta-learning distinguishing data

Proceedings of the 1st Workshop on Meta Learning and Its Applications to Natural Language Processing (MetaNLP 2021), pages 76–89
Bangkok, Thailand (online), August 5, 2021.

by their label set and data source at the same time. We also try to quantify the impact of switching data sources in this framework. After summarizing the related work (Section 2), we present the data sets and labels (Section 3) that we consider in our methodology and experiments (Section 4). We then present the results (Section 5) before discussing some key points (Section 6) and conclude (Section 7).

The data preparation code and files, and the implementations are available in a public repository: `https://github.com/gguibon/metalearning-emotion-datasource`.

2 Related Work

Emotion classification approaches (Alm et al., 2005; Strapparava and Mihalcea, 2007; Bollen et al., 2009; Thelwall et al., 2012; Yu et al., 2015; Yadollahi et al., 2017; Zhang et al., 2018a; Zhu et al., 2019; Zhong et al., 2019; Park et al., 2019) usually benefit from using as many examples as possible when training the classifier. However, it is not always possible to obtain large data sets for a specific task: we need to learn from a few examples by applying specific strategies. Few-shot learning (Lake, 2015; Vinyals et al., 2016; Ravi and Larochelle, 2016) is an approach dedicated to learn from a few examples per class and thus to create efficient models on a specific task.

Meta-Learning. While they can be used for different purposes, few-shot learning frameworks are often used for meta-learning (Schmidhuber, 1987), defined as "learning to learn". Like few-shot learning, meta-learning considers tasks for training but with the aim of being effective at a new task in the testing stage (Yin, 2020). To do so, meta-learning can focus on different aspects such as learning a meta-optimizer (various gradient descent schemes, reinforcement learning, *etc.*), a meta-representation (embedding by metric learning, hyper parameters, *etc.*), or a meta-objective (few-shot, multi-task, *etc.*), three aspects respectively represented as "How", "What" and "Why" (Hospedales et al., 2020). Both few-shot learning and meta-learning approaches have mainly been developed in computer vision using different optimization schemes. The main meta-learning approaches use an episodic setting (Ravi and Larochelle, 2016) which consists in training on multiple random tasks with only a few examples per class. Then, each task is an episode made of a number of *shots* (examples per class), a *support set* (set of examples to train from), a *query set* (set of examples to predict and compute a loss), and a number of *ways* (classes).

Optimization-based. Optimization-based meta learning is an approach represented mainly by the Model Agnostic Meta Learning (MAML) (Finn et al., 2017a) which learns parameters meta-initialization and meta-regularization. It possesses multiple variations, such as First-Order MAML (Finn et al., 2017b), which reduces computation; Reptile (Nichol et al., 2018), which considers all training tasks and requires target tasks to be close to training tasks; and Minibatch Proximal Updates (Zhou et al., 2019), which learns a prior hypothesis shared across tasks. Another recent approach focuses on learning a dedicated loss (Bechtle et al., 2021).

Metric learning. Meta-representation and meta-objective aspects of meta-learning are often used together. In this work, regarding the meta-representation aspect, we focus on approaches aiming to learn a distance function, usually named metric-learning. Among these approaches, Siamese Networks (Koch et al., 2015) do not take tasks into account and only focus on learning the overall metric to measure a distance between the examples. Matching Networks (Vinyals et al., 2016) use the support set examples to calculate a cosine distance directly. Prototypical Networks (Snell et al., 2017), for their part, consider class representations from the support set and use an euclidean distance instead of the cosine one. Lastly, Relation Networks (Sung et al., 2018) consider the metric as a deep neural network instead of an euclidean distance, using multiple convolution blocks and the last sigmoid layer to compute relation scores. When applied to image data sets, a recent work showed Prototypical Networks (Snell et al., 2017) possess better efficiency with the lowest amount of training examples (Al-Shedivat et al., 2021) which leads us to use this approach due to our data configuration.

Meta-learning and NLP. Other approaches have recently made use of several optimization schemes (Bernacchia, 2021; Al-Shedivat et al., 2021) and have been adapted to NLP tasks (Bao et al., 2020) especially on Few-Rel dataset, a NLP corpus dedicated to few-shot learning for relation classification (Gao et al., 2019b; Han et al., 2018; Sun et al., 2019). For text classification, meta-learning through few-shot learning has been used on Amazon Review Sentiment (ARSC) dataset (Yu et al., 2018; Geng et al., 2019; Bao et al., 2020; Bansal et al., 2020) by training sentiment classifiers while varying the 23 topics. We draw on their work on Amazon topics to better tackle another type of labels, emotions, while further adapting Prototypical Networks on texts by considering attention in the process.

Meta-learning and Emotions. Recent studies on acoustic set up a generalized mixed model for emotion classification from music data (Lin et al., 2020), or even meta-learning for speech emotion recognition whether it is monolingual (Fujioka et al., 2020) or multilingual (Naman and Mancini, 2021). On the other hand, on textual data one used distribution learning (Zhang et al., 2018b) through sentence embedding decomposition and K-Nearest Neighbors (Zhao and Ma, 2019) while others studied emotion ambiguity by meta-learning a BiLSTM (Huang et al., 2015) with attention in the scope of 4 labels (Fujioka et al., 2019).

Considering both our use-case scenario and the aforementioned recent meta-learning efficiency comparison (Al-Shedivat et al., 2021), we focus on using Prototypical Networks for this work, while varying the encoders to better adapt Prototypical Networks to textual data in a few-shot and meta-learning setting. Thus, we contribute by using metric learning based meta learning while considering emotion classes as tasks for NLP. Moreover, as far as we know, this work is the first one on meta-learning considering a two-level meta-learning by transferring knowledge to new tasks, despite the use of new data sources at the same time.

3 Datasets and Tag Sets

We consider two different English data sets to stay in line with our will to use a source data set on which the meta-model will be trained and a target data set on which we will evaluate the transferring capabilities of our model.

GoEmotions (Demszky et al., 2020a) is the data set we use to train and tune hyper-parameters. It is a corpus made of 58,000 curated Reddit comments labeled with 27 emotion categories. We split it into 3 tag sets (*EmoTagSets*) for meta-training afterwards which detail later on. GoEmotions (Demszky et al., 2020a) also comes with predefined train/val/test splits by ratio, ensuring the presence of all labels in each split. We use them to apply the fully supervised learning.

DailyDialog (Li et al., 2017) corresponds to the target data to be labeled using the meta-trained model. This corpus is initially structured as 13,118 human-written daily conversations, going through multiple topics; but for the purpose of our study, we only use it as individual utterances. We chose this corpus because of its propinquity with our case study: messages from conversational context are usually private and unlabeled. We retrieve utterances from the official test set with their associated emotion label, because studying the conversational context exceeds the scope of this paper. We only focus on utterances, language structure differences, and different emotion tag sets for meta-learning. This leads to a total of 1,419 utterances for 6 emotion labels (*EmoTagSet3*). As for GoEmotions, DailyDialog comes with official train/val/test splits that we use for comparison purposes while using supervised or meta learning approaches.

Tag Sets. To apply meta-learning on emotion labels we consider 3 different tag sets named *EmoTagSets*. As previously said, we made these tag sets considering the different labels from each data set: let Z_G represent the set of GoEmotions' labels and Z_D the set of DailyDialog's labels, we consider the intersection $Z_D \cap Z_G$ as the target labels named *EmoTagSet3*. These target labels are the labels we want to hide from both training and validation phases to only use them during the test phase. The purpose of using the intersection is to enable results comparison on both data sets. The complement of the resulting intersection is then used to create *EmoTagSet1* and *EmoTagSet2*, while taking into account class balance and polarity distribution to ensure each *EmoTagSet1* and *2* possesses a variety of classes. The resulting tag sets and their dedicated usage are visible in Table 1. Table 1 also shows the mapping between the 6 target emotion classes of *EmoTagSet3* and their possible correspondences in regard to other labels. This mapping comes directly from GoEmotions' mapping[1].

[1]https://github.com/google-research/google-research/blob/master/goemotions/data/ekman_mapping.json

EmoTagSet3 *(DailyDialog tags)* *For test and supervised* ↓	**EmoTagSet1** *For training* ↓	**EmoTagSet2** *For validation* ↓
anger →	annoyance	disapproval
disgust →	/	/
fear →	nervousness	/
joy →	amusement, approval, excitement, love, pride, admiration	gratitude, optimism, relief, desire, caring
sadness →	remorse	disappointment, embarrassment, grief
surprise →	realization, confusion	curiosity

Table 1: Tag set mapping to the 6 basic emotions of EmoTagSet3. All these labels are present in GoEmotions while only the EmoTagSet3 is present in DailyDialog. EmoTagSet1 and 2 are mapped to EmoTagSet3 following the GoEmotions' official mapping (Demszky et al., 2020b).

4 Methodology and Experimental Protocol

First, the objective is to retrieve label-level meta-information using Reddit comments (GoEmotions) and the different label sets (*EmoTagSets*). Then, we seek to transfer the meta-information to daily conversation-extracted utterances (DailyDialog), hence varying in data structure and vocabulary.

Meta-training. The first step consists of an emotion-based meta-learning on GoEmotions' training and validation sets in order to learn meta-information that we evaluate on DailyDialog's test set later on. Figure 1 shows this approach. We want to meta-train a classifier from few examples by using few-shot learning with 5 examples per class from GoEmotions' train set, our classes being the different emotion labels. We adopt the Prototypical Networks (Snell et al., 2017) in an episode training strategy to apply few-shot learning to the meta-learning process. For each episode, Prototypical Networks apply metric-learning to few-shot classification by computing a prototype $\mathbf{c}_k$ for each class k (*way*) with a reduced number of examples from the support set S_k (*shots*). Each class prototype being equal to the average of support examples from each class as follows:

$$\mathbf{c}_k \leftarrow \frac{1}{N_C} \sum_{(\mathbf{x}_i, y_i) \in S_k} f_\phi(\mathbf{x}_i)$$

where f_ϕ corresponds to the encoder. We then minimize the euclidean distance between prototypes and elements from the query set Q_k to label them and compare the resulting assignments $d\left(f_\phi(\mathbf{x}), \mathbf{c}_k\right)$ where x represents an element from the query set. This follows the standard Prototypical Networks with the following loss

$$\frac{1}{N_C N_Q}\left[d\left(f_\phi(\mathbf{x}), \mathbf{c}_k\right) + \log \sum_{k'} \exp\left(-d\left(f_\phi(\mathbf{x}), \mathbf{c}_{k'}\right)\right)\right]$$

One key element of the Prototypical Networks is the encoder f_ϕ, which will define the embedding space where the class prototypes are computed. Moreover, it is in fact the encoder which is meta-learned during the training phase. In our experiments, we use various encoders to represent a message as one vector: the average of the word embeddings (AVG), convolutional neural networks for sequence representation (CNN) (Kim, 2014) or a Transformer encoder layer (Vaswani et al., 2017) (Tr.). We define our episodic composition by setting $N_c = 6$, $N_s = 5$ and $N_q = 30$ making it a 5-shot 6-way 30-query learning task where N_c is constrained by the number of test classes: indeed, down the line, the model will be tested on the 6 basic emotions from the DailyDialog tag set. This setting renders obsolete the notion of an unbalanced data set.

Episodic composition for training and validating are the same. We meta-train for a maximum of 1,000 epochs, one epoch being 100 random episodes from training classes (*EmoTagSet1*). We set early stopping to a patience of 20 epochs without best accuracy improvement. Validation is also done using 100 random episodes but from validation classes (*EmoTagSet2*). For testing, however, we test using 1,000 random episodes from test classes (*EmoTagSet3*), in which the query set (N_q) is randomly chosen from the test split in a 6-way 5-query fashion. This means 5 elements to classify in one of the 6 target emotions. Figure 1 shows a global view of our meta-learning strategy, from meta-training to evaluation.

Experimental protocol details are as follows. For each data set, we follow previous studies (Bao et al., 2020) and use pre-trained fastText (Joulin et al., 2017) embeddings as our starter word representation. We also compare the different approaches by using a fine-tuned pre-trained BERT (Devlin et al., 2019) as encoder, provided by Hugging Face Transformers (Wolf et al., 2019) (*bert-base-uncased*), and by using the ridge regressor with attention gen-

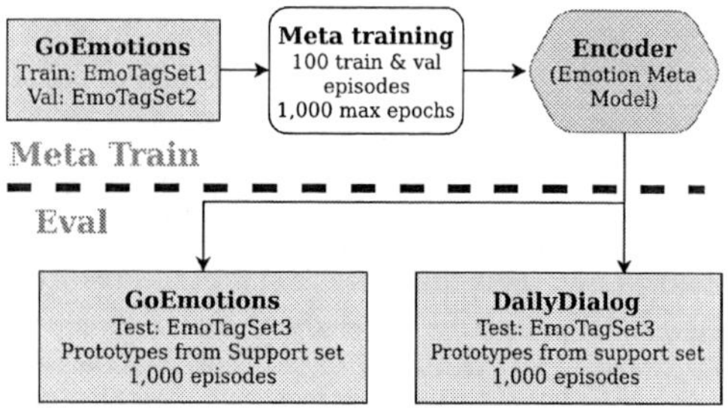

Figure 1: Global view of the meta-learning strategy. While testing on DailyDialog, only utterances from the official test set are considered. EmoTagSet1 ∪ EmoTagSet2 ∪ EmoTagSet3 = ∅.

erator representing distributional signatures (Bao et al., 2020).

Supervised Learning for comparison. We first apply supervised learning by using only DailyDialog's training, validation, and test sets (official splits by ratio) in order to enable later comparison with the meta-learning approach. We use the supervised results as reference scores illustrating what can be achieved in ideal conditions. Ideal conditions also means this does not follow our previously defined scenario. Indeed, a classic supervised learning approach learns using the same labels during training, validation and testing phases, which differ from our scenario. In these supervised results we only used the 6 emotions from *EmoTagSet3* by filtering GoEmotions' elements. Moreover, the encoder and classifier are not distinct as we simply add a linear layer followed by a softmax and use a negative log likelihood loss to compute cross entropy over the different predictions.

The objective here is to enable comparison between our approach and a direct naive supervised one. By naive, we mean that no transfer learning method is used; rather, it only consists in training a fully supervised model on GoEmotions or DailyDialog training and validation sets and applying it on DailyDialog or GoEmotions test sets. Table 2 shows the results of this naive fully supervised approach along with the meta-learning one. However, even with the advantage of using the target labels during training, this fully supervised approach yields lesser scores than our meta-learning approach. This confirms that meta-learning is a viable solution for our use-case scenario which adapts itself to unknown target labels while allowing faster training due to the episodic composition approach (*i.e.* smaller number of batches).

Hyper-parameters tuning. In this paper, we consider the case in which we want to train an emotion classifier while having no access to the target data information. However, to ensure a fair comparison, we use the hyper-parameters obtained through a limited grid-search in our baseline supervised setup. This makes the whole experiment less dependent on specific parameters, leading to a better evaluation process despite not representing a 'real' application case. Hyper parameters are as follows.

The Prototypical Networks' hidden size is set to $[300, 300]$ which is equal to the base embedding size (300 from pre-trained FastText on Wiki News[2]), global dropout is set to 0.1. The CNN encoder consists in three filter sizes of 3, 4 and 5 and is the same architecture as Kim's CNN (Kim, 2014) except for the number of filters which we set to 5000. For the Transformer encoder, we set the learning rate at $1e-4$, the dropout at 0.2, the number of heads at 2 and the positional encoding dropout to 0.1. The embedding and hidden sizes follow the same size as the input embedding with $d = 300$. We considered using multiple Transformer encoder layers but sticking to only 1 layer gave the most optimal results and efficiency.

During supervised learning, we consider an encoder learning rate of $1e-3$ except for the Transformer layer where a learning rate of $1e-4$ gave better results. However, for meta-learning phases we follow optimization methods from recent literature by searching the best learning rate, positive or negative, in a window close to zero and finally set it to $1e-5$ (Bernacchia, 2021). Hence, the learning rate is the only parameter that we do not directly copy from the supervised learning phase's hyper parameters.

Evaluation Metrics. We evaluate the performance of the models by following previous work on few-shot learning (Snell et al., 2017; Sung et al., 2018; Bao et al., 2020) and using few-shot classification accuracy. We go further in the evaluation by adding a weighted F1 score and the Matthews Correlation Coefficient (MCC) (Cramir, 1946; Baldi et al., 2000) as suggested by recent studies in biology (Chicco and Jurman, 2020), but in its multiclass version (Gorodkin, 2004) to better suit our task. Reported scores are the mean values of each

[2]https://dl.fbaipublicfiles.com/fasttext/vectors-english/wiki-news-300d-1M.vec.zip

metrics on all testing episodes with their associated variance ±.

5 Results

Table 2 shows two main different result sets: the ones obtained using supervised learning, and those obtained using meta-learning.

Supervised Learning Results. Results presented in Table 2 come from using the official splits from DailyDialog. As explained in Section 4, we tuned hyper-parameters for each classifier and encoder using this supervised learning phase. Using the Transformer (Vaswani et al., 2017) as classifier requires carefully setting up hyper parameters to converge, especially if the data set size is relatively small. This is the case in this study, and we believe it to be the main reason for the Transformer classifier to perform below the CNN classifier in this fully supervised setting.

Supervised results (top section of Table 2) can be divided into two sub-parts: the supervised learning trained using GoEmotions' training and validation sets then applied on either GoEmotions' test set or DailyDialog's test set, and the results using only DailyDialog's splits. These results serve as a good indication of performance goals for the later meta learning phase. We can see that the naive strategy to use a model trained on GoEmotions to predict DailyDialog's test set yields poor results with up to 34.58% F1-score even though it only considers the same 6 labels (*EmoTagSet3*) during training, validation and test to befit a standard supervised approach.

Meta Learning Quantitative Results. The bottom section of Table 2 shows two sets of results: the meta training phase on GoEmotions (Demszky et al., 2020a) using splits by emotion labels (the *EmoTagSets* from Table 1) and evaluation of these models on the DailyDialog official test set. As expected, meta-learning yields results lesser than the supervised learning when the datasets come from the same source, but highly better ones when the dataset is from a different source. Indeed, the meta-learning process trains on data from different sources, with different tag sets, sentence lengths and conversational contexts. Results show that the more similar the linguistic structure of the train and target data are, the easier the work of meta-learning is, yielding better performance. Indeed, results of meta-learning obtained on GoEmotions are better

Supervised Learning

Supervised Learning trained on GoEmotions tested on GoEmotions (val set – 6 filtered classes)

Enc	Clf	Acc ±	F1 ±	MCC ±
AVG	MLP	72.67 00.8	0.7254 00.8	67.23 00.9
CNN	MLP	76.37 00.7	0.7617 00.7	71.74 00.8
Tr.	MLP	**98.94** 00.7	**98.94** 00.6	**98.73** 00.8

Eval models trained on GoEmotions on DailyDialog (6 classes)

Enc	Clf	Acc ±	F1 ±	MCC ±
AVG	MLP	32.93 13.6	31.07 13.1	19.14 15.7
CNN	MLP	34.71 13.9	32.18 13.4	21.28 15.8
Tr.	MLP	**39.88** 18.5	**34.58** 18.2	**27.42** 23.2

Supervised Learning on DailyDialog Splits (6 classes)

Enc	Clf	Acc ±	F1 ±	MCC ±
AVG	MLP	49.73 18.9	42.06 19.2	42.32 23.7
CNN	MLP	**62.57** 18.7	**54.89** 20.6	**59.12** 22.0
Tr.	MLP	55.35 21.11	48.52 21.4	49.24 26.1

Meta-Learning

Meta-Learning using GoEmotions 6 way 5 shot 30 query

Enc.	Clf	Acc ±	F1 ±	MCC ±
AVG	Proto	25.20 03.5	23.92 03.6	10.61 04.4
CNN	Proto	31.35 04.5	29.82 04.6	17.95 05.5
BERT	Proto	39.82 04.9	39.11 05.1	28.11 05.9
Dist.	RR	31.92 04.9	31.1 05.1	18.81 06.0
Tr.	Proto	**93.02** 04.6	**91.64** 06.1	**92.08** 05.2

Eval Meta-Learned Models on DailyDialog's test set (1,000 episodes)

Enc.	Clf	Acc ±	F1 ±	MCC ±
AVG	Proto	23.95 06.9	22.52 07.0	09.11 08.6
CNN	Proto	17.61 07.5	15.36 07.2	01.23 09.5
BERT	Proto	42.59 09.7	41.50 09.7	31.80 11.9
Dist.	RR	25.78 08.1	24.38 07.8	11.28 10.0
Tr.	Proto	**61.77** 20.8	**58.55** 24.1	**58.82** 22.4

Fine-tuning meta-learned models on GoEmotions test set (1 epoch of 10 episodes) Eval on DailyDialog's test set (1,000 episodes)

Enc.	Clf	Acc ±	F1 ±	MCC ±
AVG	Proto	20.82 06.9	19.23 07.1	05.07 08.5
CNN	Proto	20.34 05.7	18.91 05.4	04.73 07.6
Tr.	Proto	28.59 09.9	21.13 10.6	17.22 13.1

Table 2: Top section: Supervised learning on utterances (official DailyDialog splits). Bottom section: meta learning trained by splitting classes from GoEmotions (train on 11, validate on 10, test on 6). The trained meta model is then applied on DailyDialog's test set. Evaluated using accuracy (Acc), F1-score (F1) and multi-class Matthews Correlation Coefficient (MCC). ± represents the variance over test episodes.

than the ones obtained on Daily Dialog. Contrary to what can be observed in supervised learning results, the Transformer, here associated with Prototypical Networks for meta-training, significantly outperforms other encoders. Even though, using the fine-tuned BERT as encoder yields a slightly better F1-score than recent models such as ridge regressor with distributional signature in our use-case scenario but, more importantly, BERT results show less variance ($\pm$) than our best model. However, our data being not segmented at the sentence level and possessing excessive variable numbers of tokens, BERT cannot be used to its full extent. This confirms prior conclusions from related work (Bao et al., 2020). We believe the poor results yielded by using the CNN (Kim, 2014) as encoder demonstrate the need of attention in the training process to better capture usable meta-information. These results using a Transformer layer (Tr.), BERT or attention generator with ridge regressor (RR) as encoders would confirm previous studies making the same observation (Sun et al., 2019).

If we compare our approaches, using attention based algorithms, to the architecture using distributional signatures with Ridge Regressor presented by Bao *et al.* (Bao et al., 2020), we can see we constantly outperform it on the evaluation metrics used. Moreover, fine-tuning the models trained on GoEmotions using GoEmotions' test set for 10 additional episodes did not improve the final scores. We believe this is due to the fine-tuning starting to change the model's parameters but, by doing so, changing the previously learned meta information.

Meta Learning Qualitative Results. Our best model manages to obtain good results based on quantitative evaluation even if those scores decrease a lot when applied on data from another source and phrasal structure, as shown in Section 1. Table 3 presents one mistake example for each emotion label in the test set. These examples show the most common mistake for each emotion. For instance, the **True** label "joy" is most commonly mistaken with "surprise" (the predicted – **Pred** – label) by the model; "sadness" is most commonly mistaken with "surprise", and so on. These two datasets coming from different platforms, further analysis is needed to dive into the different topics tackled in these messages, which may be one of the main obstacles to obtaining higher performance. We discuss it in the next section (Section 6). The message structure relates to the type of conversations: GoEmotions (*i.e.* Reddit) seems to have a higher number of general comments about a third object/topic/person, while DailyDialog seems to be made of personal discussions between people that are close to each other.

Text	True	Pred
Oh, yes, I would!	joy	surprise
Yelling doesn't do any good.	sadness	surprise
Yes. Then I noticed he was on the sidewalk behind me. He was following me.	anger	disgust
What's wrong with you? You look pale.	fear	surprise
This is all too fast. He's my best friend, and now he's gone.	disgust	surprise
What? What kind of drugs was he using?	surprise	anger

Table 3: Some mistakes made by our best meta-model (Table 2) meta-trained on GoEmotions and applied on DailyDialog. Each line is one example from the most frequent label confusion (*eq.* "joy" mistaken for "surprise" by the model).

6 Discussions

How do meta-trained models manage to perform on previously unseen tags? Prototypical Networks use the support set to compute a prototype for each class (*i.e. way*), hence new prototypes are computed for each episode. This means the trained encoder does not rely on predicting classes, but gathers representative information that will determine the position of the elements in the embedding space. Because it is the *relative* proximity that serves to assign a query element to a specific prototype, having a different tag set that will be embedded "far away" should not hinder how well the model can classify data.

Emotion Label Ambiguity. The 21 emotions from GoEmotions that we use for training and validation are fine-grained but could have overlaps ("annoyance" and "embarrassment" for instance); this is why a mapping to the same 6 emotions as the *EmoTagSet3* is provided with the data set (Table 1). Considering how well the meta-learning works on the emotion label part (see GoEmotions results in Table 2), achieving 91.64% in F1 score, labels' ambiguity and the different granularity seem to be handled well. Moreover, it should be noted that the labels were obtained differently for the two data sets: in isolation for GoEmotions and considering the conversation context for DailyDialog. This makes the task even more difficult.

Meta-learning through Different Data Sources. We want here to investigate whether the difficulty of this meta-learning task comes from varying tag sets or data sources. We fine-tune the models meta-trained on GoEmotions in order to slightly adapt the encoder to the target tag set (*EmoTagSet3*) by leveraging meta-information related to emotion labels. The training tag set is now the same as DailyDialog. The fine-tuning consists of 1 epoch of 10 more episodes instead of a maximum of 1,000 epochs made of 100 episodes during training. Results are reported at the bottom of Table 2. This fine-tuning produced worse results compared to simply meta-training and applying on a different target tag set. This leads to the hypothesis that the different linguistic structures from the two data sources (social network and daily communications) are the main sources of errors in this setup.

To confirm this, we look further in the data sources' specifics of GoEmotions (User Generated Content) and DailyDialog (an idealized version of dyadic daily conversations) by using machine learning based exploration. We study the most frequent nouns that are specific to each corpus. We use SpaCy[3] in order to obtain the Universal Part-of-Speech (UPOS) tags (Nivre and *al.*, 2019) along with the lemmas for both corpora. Then, we retrieve the sets of nouns for each corpus and compute the symmetric difference between both sets in order to see the differences in language level. GoEmotions being User Generated Content (UGC) from Reddit, its top 5 most frequent exclusive nouns are "lol", "f**k" (censored), "op", "reddit", and "omg". On the other hand, the top 5 most frequent exclusive nouns in DailyDialog are "reservation", "madam", "doesn" (tagging error), "taxi", and "courses". It shows a first indication both of language register and lexical field differences[4]. To further confirm the language structure differences, we retrieved the UPOS tags frequencies for both corpora. GoEmotions' top 3 UPOS are "NOUN", "VERB", and "PUNCT" while DailyDialog's top 3 are "PUNCT", "PRON", "VERB". This indicates DailyDialog's language follows a well formed structure with punctuation and pronouns while GoEmotions' language structure is more direct with mainly nouns and verbs[5]. All these data sources' specifics can provide explanation for the lower performance of our system on DailyDialog. The data sources' differences lead to prototypes differences during the two testing phases. Table 4 shows that the average euclidean distance between query elements $\mathbf{x}$ and class prototypes $\mathbf{c}_{k'}$ from the same class $-d\left(f_\phi(\mathbf{x}), \mathbf{c}_{k'}\right)$ is greater when tested on GoEmotions than on DailyDialog.

happiness	sadness	anger	fear	disgust	surprise
-9.30	-9.65	-8.80	-9.23	-9.32	-8.71
-7.91	-8.12	-8.15	-8.18	-8.09	-8.11

Table 4: Average euclidean (l2) distance from queries to predicted emotions using our best model (Tr.+Proto), on GoEmotions (go) and DialyDialog (dd).

Varying Pre-Trained Language Models. To confirm our preliminary results on pre-trained language models on this task, we further explore fine-tuning several of them. Results are visible in Table 5. In addition to BERT, we fine-tune XLNet (Yang et al., 2019) (*xlnet-base-cased*) and RoBERTa (Liu et al., 2019) (*roberta-base*) from the Transformers library (Wolf et al., 2019) along with their distilled variants. Results show fine-tuning BERT is better than other pre-trained language models on this task. This confirms our initial results on Table 2 of our model being better at retaining meta-information while only considering static pre-trained embeddings from FastText (Joulin et al., 2017).

Enc.	Acc	±	F1	±	MCC	±
DistilBERT	23.24	±04.0	22.98	±04.1	08.11	±04.8
XLNET	25.80	±04.2	25.85	±04.1	11.06	±04.8
roBERTa	25.58	±04.1	25.17	±04.0	10.76	±05.0
distilroBERTa	27.38	±04.5	26.83	±04.4	12.86	±05.3
BERT	**42.59**	09.7	**41.50**	09.7	**31.80**	11.9

Table 5: Results on DailyDialog's test set using multiple pre-trained language models for meta learning following the same scenario as Table 2's bottom section: meta trained on GoEmotions and meta test on DailyDialog. These language models are fine-tuned during meta-training.

Using Empathetic Dialogues as Training Source. We consider the same meta learning scenario using a different data set to train the meta-models. We choose utterances from the Empathetic Dialogues (Rashkin et al., 2019) full

[3]https://spacy.io/

[4]For more details, see the tables 8 and 9 in appendix.

[5]For more details, see figures 3 and 4 in the appendix.

data set while considering the dialogues label (i.e. the "context" column) as the label for each utterance. To apply meta learning on emotion labels, we select labels based on balancing polarity and numbers of occurrences, leading us to consider the following sets: 13 labels for training (*caring, confident, content, excited, faithful, embarrassed, annoyed, devastated, furious, lonely, terrified, sentimental, prepared*), 13 different labels for validation (*grateful, hopeful, impressed, trusting, proud, embarrassed, annoyed, devastated, furious, lonely, terrified, sentimental, prepared*) and 6 test emotions, keeping the set from DailyDialog (*joyful, sad, angry, afraid, disgusted, surprised*). Results for this meta learning experiment using Empathetic Dialogues are shown in Table 6.

Meta-Learning using ED
6 way 5 shot 30 query

Enc.	Clf.	Acc ±	F1 ±	MCC ±
AVG	Proto	27.43 ±04.2	25.95 ±04.3	13.16 ±05.2
Dist.	RR	31.73 ±04.7	31.11 ±05.1	18.51 ±05.8
Tr.	Proto	97.80 ±03.4	97.54 ±04.1	97.49 ±03.8
		Eval Meta-Learned Models on DailyDialog's test set (1,000 episodes)		
AVG	Proto	18.07 ±03.0	16.58 ±03.1	02.21 ±03.8
Dist.	RR	26.29 ±08.1	24.90 ±08.1	11.86 ±10.0
Tr.	Proto	**66.24** ±18.2	**66.09** ±18.0	**60.43** ±21.9

Table 6: Meta learning trained on Empathetic Dialogues (ED) before applying the model on DailyDialog's test set.

Empathetic Dialogues is a merge of multiple data sets, with DailyDialog among them. Hence, evaluating the meta model learnt using Empathetic Dialogues on DailyDialog's test set does not allow for fair comparison with our previous model. Indeed, we obtain here significantly better results on DailyDialog's test set. However, results show similar trends between evaluation sets and types of models as our main meta learning scenario (Table 2), which confirms our overall conclusions on this task.

7 Conclusion

In this paper, we are interested in a classification scenario where we only possess a certain kind of training data, with no guarantee that the testing data will be of the same type nor use the same labels. We choose our training data from common social media sources (Reddit) with fine-grained emotion labels. We address this problem using meta-learning and few-shot learning, to evaluate our model on conversation utterances with a simpler emotion tag set.

We consider metric learning based meta-learning by setting up Prototypical Networks with a Transformer encoder, trained in an episodic fashion. We obtained encouraging results when comparing our meta-model with a supervised baseline. In this use-case scenario with a two-level meta-learning, our best meta-model outperforms both other encoder strategies and the baseline in terms of meta-learning for NLP. Moreover, our approach works well for learning emotion-related meta-information but still struggles while varying data types.

For future work, we wish to investigate if this meta-learning approach could integrate the conversational context for classifying the utterances of the target dialog data. We also plan on applying this approach to another language than English.

Acknowledgements

We want to thank the anonymous reviewers for their insights and useful suggestions. This allowed us to better put forward our contributions by specifying additional comparisons.

References

Maruan Al-Shedivat, Liam Li, Eric Xing, and Ameet Talwalkar. 2021. On data efficiency of meta-learning. In *Proceedings of The 24th International Conference on Artificial Intelligence and Statistics*, volume 130 of *Proceedings of Machine Learning Research*, pages 1369–1377. PMLR.

Cecilia Ovesdotter Alm, Dan Roth, and Richard Sproat. 2005. Emotions from text: machine learning for text-based emotion prediction. In *Proceedings of the conference on Human Language Technology and Empirical Methods in Natural Language Processing - HLT '05*, pages 579–586, Vancouver, British Columbia, Canada. Association for Computational Linguistics.

P. Baldi, Søren Brunak, Y. Chauvin, and Henrik Nielsen. 2000. Assessing the accuracy of prediction algorithms for classification: An overview. *Bioinformatics*, 16(5):412–424.

Trapit Bansal, Rishikesh Jha, Tsendsuren Munkhdalai, and Andrew McCallum. 2020. Self-supervised meta-learning for few-shot natural language classification tasks. In *Proceedings of the 2020 Conference on Empirical Methods in Natural Language Processing (EMNLP)*, pages 522–534, Online. Association for Computational Linguistics.

Yujia Bao, Menghua Wu, Shiyu Chang, and Regina Barzilay. 2020. Few-shot text classification with distributional signatures. In *International Conference on Learning Representations*.

Sarah Bechtle, Artem Molchanov, Yevgen Chebotar, Edward Grefenstette, Ludovic Righetti, Gaurav Sukhatme, and Franziska Meier. 2021. Meta-learning via learned loss.

Alberto Bernacchia. 2021. Meta-learning with negative learning rates.

Johan Bollen, Alberto Pepe, and Huina Mao. 2009. Modeling public mood and emotion: Twitter sentiment and socio-economic phenomena. *arXiv:0911.1583 [cs]*. ArXiv: 0911.1583.

Davide Chicco and Giuseppe Jurman. 2020. The advantages of the matthews correlation coefficient (mcc) over f1 score and accuracy in binary classification evaluation. *BMC genomics*, 21(1):6.

Harald Cramir. 1946. Mathematical methods of statistics. *Princeton U. Press, Princeton*, 500.

Dorottya Demszky, Dana Movshovitz-Attias, Jeongwoo Ko, Alan Cowen, Gaurav Nemade, and Sujith Ravi. 2020a. GoEmotions: A dataset of fine-grained emotions. In *Proceedings of the 58th Annual Meeting of the Association for Computational Linguistics*, pages 4040–4054, Online. Association for Computational Linguistics.

Dorottya Demszky, Dana Movshovitz-Attias, Jeongwoo Ko, Alan Cowen, Gaurav Nemade, and Sujith Ravi. 2020b. GoEmotions: A dataset of fine-grained emotions. In *Proceedings of the 58th Annual Meeting of the Association for Computational Linguistics*, pages 4040–4054, Online. Association for Computational Linguistics.

Jacob Devlin, Ming-Wei Chang, Kenton Lee, and Kristina Toutanova. 2019. BERT: Pre-training of deep bidirectional transformers for language understanding. In *Proceedings of the 2019 Conference of the North American Chapter of the Association for Computational Linguistics: Human Language Technologies, Volume 1 (Long and Short Papers)*, pages 4171–4186, Minneapolis, Minnesota. Association for Computational Linguistics.

Chelsea Finn, Pieter Abbeel, and Sergey Levine. 2017a. Model-agnostic meta-learning for fast adaptation of deep networks. In *Proceedings of the 34th International Conference on Machine Learning*, volume 70 of *Proceedings of Machine Learning Research*, pages 1126–1135, International Convention Centre, Sydney, Australia. PMLR.

Chelsea Finn, Pieter Abbeel, and Sergey Levine. 2017b. Model-agnostic meta-learning for fast adaptation of deep networks. In *International Conference on Machine Learning*, pages 1126–1135. PMLR.

Takuya Fujioka, Dario Bertero, Takeshi Homma, and Kenji Nagamatsu. 2019. Addressing ambiguity of emotion labels through meta-learning. *CoRR*, abs/1911.02216.

Takuya Fujioka, Takeshi Homma, and Kenji Nagamatsu. 2020. Meta-learning for speech emotion recognition considering ambiguity of emotion labels. *Proc. Interspeech 2020*, pages 2332–2336.

Tianyu Gao, Xu Han, Zhiyuan Liu, and Maosong Sun. 2019a. Hybrid Attention-Based Prototypical Networks for Noisy Few-Shot Relation Classification. *Proceedings of the AAAI Conference on Artificial Intelligence*, 33:6407–6414.

Tianyu Gao, Xu Han, Hao Zhu, Zhiyuan Liu, Peng Li, Maosong Sun, and Jie Zhou. 2019b. FewRel 2.0: Towards More Challenging Few-Shot Relation Classification. *arXiv:1910.07124 [cs]*. ArXiv: 1910.07124.

Ruiying Geng, Binhua Li, Yongbin Li, Xiaodan Zhu, Ping Jian, and Jian Sun. 2019. Induction Networks for Few-Shot Text Classification. *arXiv:1902.10482 [cs]*. ArXiv: 1902.10482.

Jan Gorodkin. 2004. Comparing two k-category assignments by a k-category correlation coefficient. *Computational biology and chemistry*, 28(5-6):367–374.

Xu Han, Hao Zhu, Pengfei Yu, Ziyun Wang, Yuan Yao, Zhiyuan Liu, and Maosong Sun. 2018. FewRel: A Large-Scale Supervised Few-Shot Relation Classification Dataset with State-of-the-Art Evaluation. *arXiv:1810.10147 [cs, stat]*. ArXiv: 1810.10147.

Timothy Hospedales, Antreas Antoniou, Paul Micaelli, and Amos Storkey. 2020. Meta-Learning in Neural Networks: A Survey. *arXiv:2004.05439 [cs, stat]*. ArXiv: 2004.05439.

Zhiheng Huang, Wei Xu, and Kai Yu. 2015. Bidirectional lstm-crf models for sequence tagging.

Armand Joulin, Edouard Grave, Piotr Bojanowski, and Tomas Mikolov. 2017. Bag of tricks for efficient text classification. In *Proceedings of the 15th Conference of the European Chapter of the Association for Computational Linguistics: Volume 2, Short Papers*, pages 427–431, Valencia, Spain. Association for Computational Linguistics.

Yoon Kim. 2014. Convolutional neural networks for sentence classification. *arXiv preprint arXiv:1408.5882*.

Gregory Koch, Richard Zemel, and Ruslan Salakhutdinov. 2015. Siamese Neural Networks for One-shot Image Recognition. *ICML*, page 8.

Brenden Lake. 2015. LakeEtAl2015Science-startOfFewShot.pdf. *Sciences Mag*.

Yanran Li, Hui Su, Xiaoyu Shen, Wenjie Li, Ziqiang Cao, and Shuzi Niu. 2017. Dailydialog: A manually labelled multi-turn dialogue dataset. In *Proceedings of The 8th International Joint Conference on Natural Language Processing (IJCNLP 2017)*.

Sung-Chiang Lin, Chih-Jou Chen, and Tsung-Ju Lee. 2020. A multi-label classification with hybrid label-based meta-learning method in internet of things. *IEEE Access*, 8:42261–42269.

Yinhan Liu, Myle Ott, Naman Goyal, Jingfei Du, Mandar Joshi, Danqi Chen, Omer Levy, Mike Lewis, Luke Zettlemoyer, and Veselin Stoyanov. 2019. Roberta: A robustly optimized bert pretraining approach.

Anugunj Naman and Liliana Mancini. 2021. Fixed-maml for few shot classification in multilingual speech emotion recognition.

Alex Nichol, Joshua Achiam, and John Schulman. 2018. On first-order meta-learning algorithms. *arXiv preprint arXiv:1803.02999*.

Joakim Nivre and *al.* 2019. Universal dependencies 2.4. LINDAT/CLARIN digital library at the Institute of Formal and Applied Linguistics (ÚFAL), Faculty of Mathematics and Physics, Charles University.

Sungjoon Park, Jiseon Kim, Jaeyeol Jeon, Heeyoung Park, and Alice Oh. 2019. Toward dimensional emotion detection from categorical emotion annotations. *arXiv preprint arXiv:1911.02499*.

Hannah Rashkin, Eric Michael Smith, Margaret Li, and Y-Lan Boureau. 2019. Towards empathetic open-domain conversation models: A new benchmark and dataset. In *Proceedings of the 57th Annual Meeting of the Association for Computational Linguistics*, pages 5370–5381, Florence, Italy. Association for Computational Linguistics.

Sachin Ravi and Hugo Larochelle. 2016. Optimization as a model for few-shot learning.

Jürgen Schmidhuber. 1987. *Evolutionary principles in self-referential learning, or on learning how to learn: the meta-meta-... hook*. Ph.D. thesis, Technische Universität München.

Jake Snell, Kevin Swersky, and Richard Zemel. 2017. Prototypical networks for few-shot learning. In *Advances in neural information processing systems*, pages 4077–4087.

Carlo Strapparava and Rada Mihalcea. 2007. Semeval-2007 task 14: Affective text. In *Proceedings of the Fourth International Workshop on Semantic Evaluations (SemEval-2007)*, pages 70–74.

Shengli Sun, Qingfeng Sun, Kevin Zhou, and Tengchao Lv. 2019. Hierarchical Attention Prototypical Networks for Few-Shot Text Classification. In *Proceedings of the 2019 Conference on Empirical Methods in Natural Language Processing and the 9th International Joint Conference on Natural Language Processing (EMNLP-IJCNLP)*, pages 476–485, Hong Kong, China. Association for Computational Linguistics.

Flood Sung, Yongxin Yang, Li Zhang, Tao Xiang, Philip HS Torr, and Timothy M Hospedales. 2018. Learning to compare: Relation network for few-shot learning. In *Proceedings of the IEEE Conference on Computer Vision and Pattern Recognition*, pages 1199–1208.

Mike Thelwall, Kevan Buckley, and Georgios Paltoglou. 2012. Sentiment strength detection for the social web. *Journal of the American Society for Information Science and Technology*, 63(1):163–173.

Ashish Vaswani, Noam Shazeer, Niki Parmar, Jakob Uszkoreit, Llion Jones, Aidan N Gomez, Łukasz Kaiser, and Illia Polosukhin. 2017. Attention is all you need. In *Advances in neural information processing systems*, pages 5998–6008.

Oriol Vinyals, Charles Blundell, Timothy Lillicrap, Daan Wierstra, et al. 2016. Matching networks for one shot learning. In *Advances in neural information processing systems*, pages 3630–3638.

Thomas Wolf, Lysandre Debut, Victor Sanh, Julien Chaumond, Clement Delangue, Anthony Moi, Pierric Cistac, Tim Rault, Rémi Louf, Morgan Funtowicz, Joe Davison, Sam Shleifer, Patrick von Platen, Clara Ma, Yacine Jernite, Julien Plu, Canwen Xu, Teven Le Scao, Sylvain Gugger, Mariama Drame, Quentin Lhoest, and Alexander M. Rush. 2019. Huggingface's transformers: State-of-the-art natural language processing. *ArXiv*, abs/1910.03771.

Ali Yadollahi, Ameneh Gholipour Shahraki, and Osmar R Zaiane. 2017. Current state of text sentiment analysis from opinion to emotion mining. *ACM Computing Surveys (CSUR)*, 50(2):1–33.

Zhilin Yang, Zihang Dai, Yiming Yang, Jaime G. Carbonell, Ruslan Salakhutdinov, and Quoc V. Le. 2019. Xlnet: Generalized autoregressive pretraining for language understanding. *CoRR*, abs/1906.08237.

Wenpeng Yin. 2020. Meta-learning for Few-shot Natural Language Processing: A Survey. *arXiv:2007.09604 [cs]*. ArXiv: 2007.09604.

Liang-Chih Yu, Jin Wang, K. Robert Lai, and Xue-jie Zhang. 2015. Predicting Valence-Arousal Ratings of Words Using a Weighted Graph Method. In *Proceedings of the 53rd Annual Meeting of the Association for Computational Linguistics and the 7th International Joint Conference on Natural Language Processing (Volume 2: Short Papers)*, pages 788–793, Beijing, China. Association for Computational Linguistics.

Mo Yu, Xiaoxiao Guo, Jinfeng Yi, Shiyu Chang, Saloni Potdar, Yu Cheng, Gerald Tesauro, Haoyu Wang, and Bowen Zhou. 2018. Diverse Few-Shot Text Classification with Multiple Metrics. In *Proceedings of the 2018 Conference of the North American Chapter of the Association for Computational Linguistics: Human Language Technologies, Volume 1 (Long Papers)*, pages 1206–1215, New Orleans,

Louisiana. Association for Computational Linguistics.

Yuxiang Zhang, Jiamei Fu, Dongyu She, Ying Zhang, Senzhang Wang, and Jufeng Yang. 2018a. Text Emotion Distribution Learning via Multi-Task Convolutional Neural Network. In *Proceedings of the Twenty-Seventh International Joint Conference on Artificial Intelligence*, pages 4595–4601, Stockholm, Sweden. International Joint Conferences on Artificial Intelligence Organization.

Yuxiang Zhang, Jiamei Fu, Dongyu She, Ying Zhang, Senzhang Wang, and Jufeng Yang. 2018b. Text emotion distribution learning via multi-task convolutional neural network. In *IJCAI*, pages 4595–4601.

Zhenjie Zhao and Xiaojuan Ma. 2019. Text emotion distribution learning from small sample: A meta-learning approach. In *Proceedings of the 2019 Conference on Empirical Methods in Natural Language Processing and the 9th International Joint Conference on Natural Language Processing (EMNLP-IJCNLP)*, pages 3957–3967, Hong Kong, China. Association for Computational Linguistics.

Peixiang Zhong, Di Wang, and Chunyan Miao. 2019. Knowledge-Enriched Transformer for Emotion Detection in Textual Conversations. *arXiv:1909.10681 [cs]*. ArXiv: 1909.10681.

Pan Zhou, Xiaotong Yuan, Huan Xu, Shuicheng Yan, and Jiashi Feng. 2019. Efficient meta learning via minibatch proximal update. *Advances in Neural Information Processing Systems*, 32:1534–1544.

Suyang Zhu, Shoushan Li, and Guodong Zhou. 2019. Adversarial Attention Modeling for Multi-dimensional Emotion Regression. In *Proceedings of the 57th Annual Meeting of the Association for Computational Linguistics*, pages 471–480, Florence, Italy. Association for Computational Linguistics.

A Open Source Code

The anonymous code is available to reviewers in supplementary materials. A link to the Public Github repository containing the code to run experiments along with data will be added to the article. The code base has been implemented in Python using, among others, PyTorch and Hugging Face Transformers (Wolf et al., 2019) for BERT. All training runs were made using an Nvidia V100 Tensor Core GPU[6].

B Hyper Parameters

Prototypical networks hidden size is set to $[300, 300]$ which is equal to the base embedding size (300 from pre-trained FastText on Wiki News[7]), global dropout is set to 0.1.
CNN hyper parameters:

- cnn filter sizes: 3, 4, 5
- number of filters: 5000
- learning rate: 0.001

Transformer hyper parameters:

- learning rate: 0.0001
- transformer dropout: 0.2
- embedding size: 300 (from FastText)
- attention heads: 2
- hidden size: 300
- transformer encoder layers: 1
- position encoding dropout: 0.1

Please note that these hyper parameters are the one inferred from the supervised learning. During meta-learning we only change the learning rate and set it to $1e-5$ as explained in Section 4 of the paper.

[6]https://www.nvidia.com/en-us/data-center/v100/

[7]https://dl.fbaipublicfiles.com/fasttext/vectors-english/wiki-news-300d-1M.vec.zip

C Training Additional Information

Models trained for 72 epochs using average embeddings as encoder, 42 epochs using Transformer encoder, and 35 epochs using CNN as encoder. Depending on the run, our best meta-model (Transformers with Prototypical Networks using a learning rate of 1e-5) converges between the 87th epoch and the 165th epoch. The total training time does not exceed one hour.

D Additional Results Information

Figure 2 shows the confusion matrix for our best meta-model trained on GoEmotions and applied on DailyDialog (the row obtaining 58.55% F1 score in Table 2).

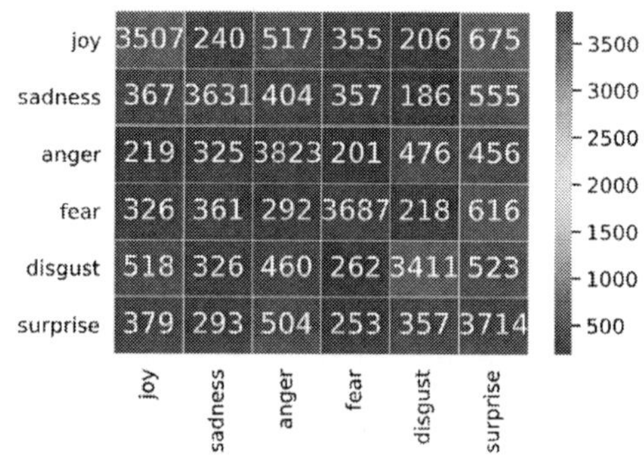

Figure 2: Confusion matrix for our Tr.+Proto meta-learning trained on GoEmotions and tested on DailyDialog. This is the 1,000 test episodes' outputs merged together. Rows represent reference labels while columns represent predicted labels.

To ensure the relative stability of our best model, we did 3 meta-learning runs using our Transformer encoder in Prototypical Networks using a learning rate a 1e-5. The results of these runs (including the one reported in Table 2) are visible in Table 7.

E Data Comparison & Information

In Section 6 we discussed data sources differences. Here you can see more in-depth information. On the other hand, Tables 8 and 9 shows side by side the top ten most frequent tokens for the predicted NOUN UPOS. Figures 3 and 4 show the predicted part-of-speech distribution for each corpus.

Runs (trained and applied on GoEmotions)				
Encoder	Classifier	Accuracy	F1-score	MCC
Transformer	Proto	0.9302 ±0.0463	0.9164 ±0.0607	0.9208 ±0.0515
Transformer	Proto	0.9183 ±0.0423	0.9016 ±0.0572	0.9075 ±0.0468
Transformer	Proto	0.9301 ±0.0464	0.9163 ±0.0608	0.9207 ±0.0516
Runs (same model applied on DailyDialog)				
Encoder	Classifier	Accuracy	F1-score	MCC
Transformer	Proto	0.6177 ±0.2078	0.5855 ±0.2408	0.5882 ±0.2241
Transformer	Proto	0.6573 ±0.2016	0.6256 ±0.2354	0.6248 ±0.2179
Transformer	Proto	0.6253 ±0.2093	0.5929 ±0.2442	0.5937 ±0.2258

Table 7: Additional runs of our best model to ensure results' stability.

token	count
lol	576
f**k	248
op	204
reddit	147
omg	145
lmao	143
' '	133
congrats	115
*	110
meme	106

Table 8: Top 10 frequent nouns (SpaCy) exclusive to GoEmotions

token	count
reservation	267
madam	143
doesn	142
taxi	127
courses	102
shipment	79
noon	50
aren	49
aisle	47
exhibition	45

Table 9: Top 10 frequent nouns (SpaCy) exclusive to DailyDialog

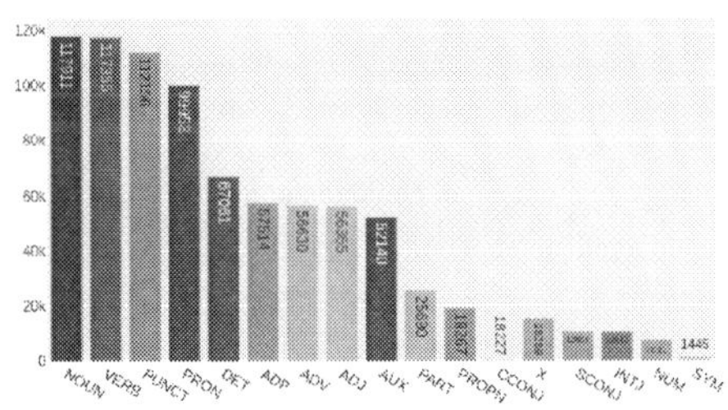

Figure 3: GoEmotions POS distribution (POS tagged using SpaCy)

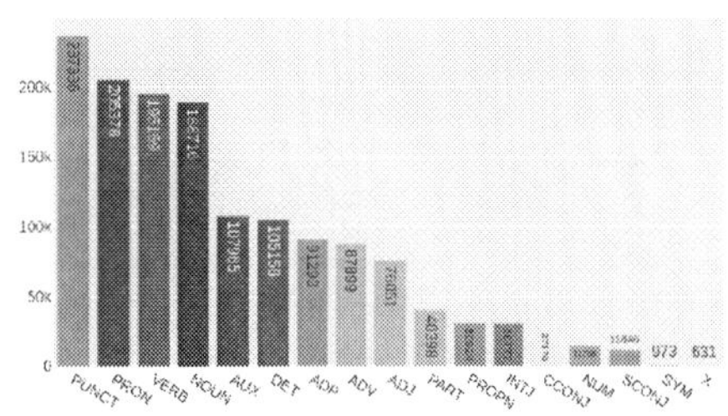

Figure 4: DailyDialog POS distribution (POS tagged using Spacy)

Author Index

Association for Computational Linguistics
209 N. Eighth Street
Stroudsburg, Pennsylvania 18360

CURRAN ASSOCIATES INC.
proceedings.com

ISBN 978-1-7138-3380-2